BLACK
FOUNDERS

CASSANDRA PYBUS is one of Australia's most admired writers and is currently a Professorial Fellow at the University of Sydney. She is the author of *Community of Thieves* (1991), *Gross Moral Turpitude* (1993), *White Rajah* (1996) and *The Devil and James McAuley* (2000) and *Epic Journeys of Freedom* (2006). She has also written two volumes of auto-biography, *Till Apples Grow on an Orange Tree* (1998) and *Raven Road* (2001). She was formerly editor of the literary magazine *Island* and founding editor of the electronic forum, *Australian Humanities Review*.

BLACK FOUNDERS

The unknown story of
Australia's first black settlers

Cassandra Pybus

UNSW
PRESS

For Ian Duffield, who showed me the way

A UNSW Press book

Published by
University of New South Wales Press Ltd
University of New South Wales
Sydney NSW 2052
AUSTRALIA
www.unswpress.com.au

National Library of Australia
Cataloguing-in-Publication entry

Pybus, Cassandra Jane.
Black founders: The unknown story of Australia's first
  black settlers
Bibliography.
Includes index.
ISBN 0 86840 849 2.
1. Africans - Australia - History.
2. Australia - History - 1788–1900. I. Title.

994.00496

Design Di Quick
Front cover gettyimages.com
Back cover *Billy Blue, 1834* by JB East, oil portrait,
reproduced courtesy of the Mitchell Library, State Library of
New South Wales (ML 560)
Print Everbest, China

CONTENTS

Acknowledgments   vii

Abbreviations   viii

Note on sources   ix

Prologue   1

1   Liberty or death   11

2   Fleeing the founding fathers   26

3   Starving in the streets of London   40

4   Back to Africa   56

5   Bound for the fatal shore   74

6   Recalcitrant convicts at Sydney Cove   87

7   The dread of perishing by famine   106

8   An incorrigibly stubborn black   120

9   Sportsman to General Grose   136

10 Tugging at the oars; playing in the band   148

11 The Old Commodore   164

Afterword   179

Appendix: Biographies of the black founders   183

Notes   188

Bibliography   201

Index   211

✱

ACKNOWLEDGMENTS

Foremost I must acknowledge the path-breaking research of two historians to whom I am greatly indebted: Mollie Gillen and Ellen Gibson Wilson. Many individuals have contributed valuable insights to this project and I especially thank Alan Atkinson, Emma Christopher, Deirdre Coleman, Ian Duffield, Michael Flynn, Lucy Frost, Rhys Isaac, Jim Kohen, Iain McCalman, Christopher Brown, Marcus Rediker, Hamish Maxwell-Stewart, Georgina Pinkas, Ray Fairall and Fiona Pollack. I reserve special appreciation for James Bradley's superb assistance with archival research in Australia. I am grateful for the assistance of archivists at the National Archives of the United Kingdom, the manuscripts section of the Library of Congress, the Greater London Record Office, the Clements Library at the University of Michigan, the Thomas Jefferson Library, the Rockefeller Library at Colonial Williamsburg, the Huntington Library, the archives of the University of Illinois at Chicago, the New York Historical Society, the Public Archives of Nova Scotia, the Archives of New South Wales and the Mitchell Library.

The complicated research for this book was made possible by two Discovery Grants and a Professorial Fellowship from the Australian Research Council, for which I am profoundly grateful. I was also greatly assisted by a Fulbright Senior Scholar's Award to Washington DC in 2002, a Coca Cola International Fellowship at the International Center for Jefferson Studies in Virginia in 2003, and a Visiting Fellowship at the Rockefeller Library in Williamsburg, Virginia, in 2004. There are no words to express my appreciation for the support of my husband and some-time research assistant, Michael Lynch.

✳

ABBREVIATIONS

ADM	Records of British Admiralty
AO	Records of the British Auditor
ASSI	Records of the Justices of Assizes in United Kingdom
BDM	Births', Deaths', and Marriages' Registers, NSW
BL	British Library, London
CJ	*House of Commons Journal*
CL	Clements Library, University of Michigan
CO	Records of British Colonial Office
CRBP	Committee for Relief of the Black Poor
CS	Colonial Secretary's Correspondence
CWM	College of William and Mary
FO	Records of British Foreign Office
GLRO	Greater London Record Office
HCSP	*House of Commons Sessional Papers*
HL	Huntington Library
HO	Records of British Home Office
HRA	*Historical Records of Australia*
HRNSW	*Historical Records of New South Wales*
KCA	Kent County Archives
LOC	Library of Congress
ML	Mitchell Library, State Library of New South Wales
NA	National Archives, United Kingdom
NYHS	New York Historical Society
OBSP	Old Bailey Session Papers
PANS	The Public Archives of Nova Scotia
PRO	Domestic Papers of the National Archives, United Kingdom
SRNSW	State Records of New South Wales
T	Records of British Treasury
UIC	University of Illinois at Chicago
VSL	Virginia State Library
WO	Records of British War Office

✳

NOTE ON SOURCES

In consulting a huge range of eighteenth-century sources I found no consistency whatsoever in the use of capital letters and ampersands, so I made a decision to standardise the quotes to modern usage in the matter of capitalization and ampersands, but to keep the idiosyncratic spelling. Anyone who wants to read the quote exactly as written should consult the original document or a definitive edited version, as cited in the notes.

*

The 'convict' who comes down to us in the pages of his oppressors is a social and political construction: he exists as a reflection of a body of rules, as a personification of transgression, a figure of speech necessary to the ruling class's self-justification and the perpetuation of its power. To let the convicts speak for themselves would have been to entertain the unthinkable: mutiny, another history.

Paul Carter, *The Road to Botany Bay*

*

PROLOGUE

Liberty Plains, New South Wales

On 14 February 1796, John Winbow and his unnamed convict companion were footslogging through virgin bush about five miles west of Sydney Cove in search of a fugitive known as Black Caesar. They moved with deliberate caution; an unwary footfall could bring them down on a snake with venom strong enough to kill a man in hours. If snakes were not enough to make them apprehensive, they knew the native blacks had turned murderous and begun to attack white intruders with vengeful fury. All about, concealed in bush, there might be silent and watchful Aborigines, with their long, barbed spears.

Late afternoon they reached a ridge of sandstone where a narrow opening in the rock face was almost entirely obscured by gnarled she-oaks sprouting needles like a witch's broom. The dense carpet of these dead needles absorbed the crunch and thud of their clumsy convict-issue boots. Having located the hideout of his quarry, Winbow resisted making any rash assault, choosing to wait in the stifling summer heat until the fugitive showed himself. February was the most oppressive time in the colony, when the heat intensified to such a swelter that settlers and convicts alike were prostrate with exhaustion. After days of torrid temperatures, a tremendous rainstorm would sweep in from the ocean, simultaneously drenching the land and igniting fires with lightning strikes. Birds instinctively understood this volatile weather. A sure sign of an approaching storm were flocks of funereal black cockatoos whose hoarse plee-erk, plee-erk shattered the suffocating stillness.

Hunkered down among the she-oaks, the sweat stinging the myriad of tiny cuts to his forearms, Winbow needed to remind himself of the lavish reward his quarry would bring. It went against the grain for one who had once made his living as a highwayman to be hunting a fellow outlaw, but 5 gallons of rum represented a small fortune in Sydney.

*

A convicted felon had little capacity to pay the exorbitant prices charged by the army officers who controlled the trade in spirits. A few years earlier Winbow had been unloaded from the stinking hold of a convict transport like an ox carcass and slung over the side into a waiting long-boat, where horrified marines held rags to their faces in a vain attempt to ward off the stench. Scurvy-racked after six months of lying shackled and starved in the ship's hold, he was dragged onto the shore like a dead man, stupefied from the first intake of fresh air. Many of his fellow convicts were dead, but Winbow was one of the lucky ones. The native currants that grew around the settlement helped repair his body, but it was the rum brought to Sydney Cove by the American ship *Hope* that obliterated his memory. Now he needed all he could get; the man for whom he waited was his ticket to oblivion.

At dusk his quarry made an appearance: a well-muscled man in his late twenties, a good head taller than most in the colony, holding a musket at the ready. The musket had been stolen from the commissary in Sydney Cove a few months earlier and was certainly loaded with shot, since, despite the governor's prohibition, there were ex-convicts in the outlying districts prepared to share ammunition with the outlaw. He was alone; there was no sign of the other convict runaways who had formed a band with him. Caesar was a match for any in the colony and had sworn he'd never be taken alive. The two bounty hunters were taking no chances as he eased backwards through the opening into his rock shelter. In the morning he would have to reappear and then it would be Winbow whose musket was loaded and cocked.

Perhaps it was the screech of the startled cockatoos rising from the twisted branches that alerted Caesar that his fate was waiting for him beyond the concealed entrance of the cave. Emerging into the sharp morning light he blindly swung his musket around to where Winbow stood ready. Too late. One close shot brought him down. A case of self-defence, Winbow would later insist, with a witness to back him up. Though grievously wounded, Caesar was not yet dead; his hunters had to drag him down to the flat, where a wheelbarrow was fetched from the farm of Thomas Rose, a free settler nearby. As Rose's hut lay close to the carriage road from Parramatta, word of the capture was speedily got to the authorities at Sydney Cove.

The first official to receive the news from Liberty Plains was the judge advocate of the colony, David Collins, who was hearing a case of burglary, assisted by half a dozen military officers who constituted the criminal court in New South Wales. A meticulous chronicler of life in the infant colony, Collins transcribed the events of his court in considerable detail. With relish he recorded how on 15 February a sitting was interrupted by the news that the outlaw known as Black Caesar had died at Thomas Rose's hut. 'Thus ended a man who certainly during life, could never have been estimated at one remove above the brute', he wrote.

What was there about this particular individual that could merit such an obituary in a penal colony that was constituted almost entirely by the brutalised and the brutalising? In his seventeen years at Sydney Cove, Collins presided over numerous incidents of murder and child rape, yet nothing so wicked could be attributed to the dead man, whose only crime was to take to the bush and steal food. And what did it mean that he was called Black Caesar?[1]

*

Australia's first bushranger was as black as pitch. He was not Aboriginal, as one might suppose. Collins described him being 'of darker hue' than the indigenous people, though as 'full as far removed from civilization'. He was a man of the African diaspora who arrived in New South Wales as a convict aboard the First Fleet transport ship *Alexander*. Nor was Caesar the only African who fetched up in this impossibly remote outpost of the British Empire in 1788. There were eleven black men on the First Fleet who have been identified by the superb detective work of Gillen in *Founders of Australia*. All of these convicts were sentenced in England: Caesar at the Kent Assizes for stealing money; John Randall at the Manchester Quarter Sessions for stealing a watch-chain; John Martin at the Old Bailey for stealing a bundle of clothing; Janel Gordon at Winchester for the theft of clothing; James Williams at the Old Bailey for the theft of clothing and shoes; John Coffin at Guildhall for stealing plates and some other things; John Williams at the Kent Assizes for stealing a wooden cask of liquor, silver, clothes, etc.; Thomas Orford at the Old Bailey for stealing items of clothing; Samuel Chinery at Exeter in Devon for the theft of a linen shirt; George Francisco at the Old Bailey for stealing clothes from a man who allowed him to sleep in his shop; John Moseley at the Old Bailey for impersonating a seaman in order to

*

receive his wages. These convicts were illiterate. What they said in their own defence during the trial was rarely recorded. The sparse, one-line entries in the hulk lists and transportation indents provide few clues to their history. There is no account of where they were from or how they came to be in England. Nevertheless, the bare fact of these black founders was enough to intrigue me. I felt that it must be possible to recover the story of these illiterate black men from the callous indifference of history.

The only one of the black convicts to merit attention from the early colony's many diarists was serial absconder and outlaw, Caesar. Naval Lieutenant William Bradley had no direct contact with him, but he remarked in passing that Caesar was 'a native of Madagascar', though he did not say why he thought so. No other diarist even cared to hazard a guess about the man. His mock heroic name, bereft of a surname, strongly indicated that he was once a slave, and may have been enslaved at the time of his arrest. I was sure he could not be from Madagascar, because slave-traders were expressly forbidden to operate in Madagascar throughout the eighteenth century and slaves from that source were rare indeed. However Bradley's guesswork did point to something significant: people from Madagascar looked quite different from Africans. Enslaved people with the distinctive features of the Malagasy could be found in the American colonies in the eighteenth century because several slave-traders managed to circumvent the prohibition and import five shipments from Madagascar into Virginia between 1719 and 1721. These Malagasy slaves were remarkably successful in reproducing themselves as a distinct people, as evidenced by runaway notices generations later that identified American-born slaves as 'a Madagascar', or as having the 'the Countenance of a Madagascar'. On the basis of this evidence, I thought it highly likely that Caesar came from America.[2]

I found shards of evidence about other black convicts in nineteenth-century archival documents at the Mitchell Library and the New South Wales Archives. In 1800, John Randall was accepted into the New South Wales Corps as a private. I discovered several things about Randall's entry into the corps that were significant: first, only emancipated convicts who were veterans of the British army were permitted to enlist; second, the man who facilitated Randall's entry into the corps observed that 'the black played on the flute and tambour'; and third, personal details recorded in 1808 stated that he was a native of New Haven, Connecticut, and he was then aged 44. Taken together, these small items of information strongly suggested that Randall was one of many black youths recruited as drummers into British regiments at the time of the American Revolution.[3]

John Moseley provided the explanation for his past life more than a quarter of a century after his transportation when he reapplied for his conditional pardon and explained to the muster master that his previous occupation was 'a tobacco planter in America'. In eighteenth-century America tobacco was grown intensively in the Tidewater region of Virginia and Maryland. While there were some small-scale tobacco growers and a tiny few of these were free blacks, overwhelmingly, tobacco cultivation was carried out on large plantations owned by white grandees and worked by slave labour. At the time of Moseley's trial in 1784 he was in his early twenties; it would have been next to impossible for such a young black man to have his own tobacco plantation. Almost certainly, he was a tobacco planter in the sense of being part of the huge enslaved labour force of the Tidewater.

The most detailed evidence to the origins of our black founders was discovered in the petitions of the ferryman William Blue, after whom Blues Point in Sydney is named. Blue was a contemporary of those on the First Fleet, although he arrived on the *Minorca* in 1801, after being sentenced in 1796 for stealing sugar from a West India ship. A misreading of his indictment caused him to be listed incorrectly on the indent of the *Minorca* as a sailor from Jamaica. By Blue's own admission, as well as the evidence of his trial, he was not from Jamaica. Blue said that he came from New York and in a petition to Governor Brisbane in 1823, he indicated that he had spent much of his adult life in the British military in America during both the Seven Years' War and the American Revolution. In the petition transcribed for him by someone else, Blue made what at first sight appear to be extravagant and implausible claims about his service record. The petition states:

> That Petitioner is now 89 years of Age was in the service of his Majesty King George the third at the time he was crowned And went as a Marreen on the first expedition after his Crownation to Germany, Pet[r] was at Queabeck with General Wolf when he was killed, also with Major Andrews when he was taken, And with Lord Cornwallace at

Little York in Virginea as a Spie or Guide for his Army, and was also for a considerable time, a Serj^t of Pineneers on the continent, Pet^r was his whole Lifetime in his Majestys Service untill Pet^r came to this colony.

William Blue was an old scallywag and his statement gilded the lily somewhat. His claim to a lifetime of service before his transportation to New South Wales obliterated five years spent in the prison hulks, but the omissions and inconsistencies in the petition may be the fault of his amanuensis rather than Blue himself, who was unable to read what had been written on his behalf. In another version of the petition he claimed to have been twice wounded, while on another occasion he explained to the Magistrate's Court in his own words that he had served with both General Wolfe and General Howe. Blue's claims are not the fantasy that his biographer has suggested. My detailed interrogation of his claims has convinced me that Blue was telling the truth; that this unlettered black man was indeed involved in some of the most significant military engagements of the eighteenth century.[4]

During the Seven Years' War, many provincial regiments and independent companies were raised in the American colonies, especially New York, which sent over 9000 men to the war effort. As the war dragged on recruitment became much harder, even though the colony was paying handsome bounties for enlistment. Inevitably blacks found their way into these companies; some as free men who willingly signed up for the bounty and yet others as slaves substituting for reluctant white men or who signed up as boatmen, wagoners, artificers and labourers. Even more black New Yorkers were recruited as sailors. At the battle of Quebec there were seven independent Ranger companies that might have included William Blue, aged about 24. More likely he was a sailor on a Royal Navy ship having been recruited or impressed in New York. Seamen off the Royal Navy ships were used as part of the fighting force on land during the battle to take Quebec where General Wolfe was killed in 1759. After that episode, Blue must have left America when the majority of the British forces returned to England in the autumn of 1760, not long before the death of George II on 25 October.[5]

In England, Blue must have been recruited as a marine by the British forces desperate for reinforcements, having lost many men to desertion. About a week before the monarch's demise, 8000 men, including a division of marines, many of them freshly impressed, were embarked for a secret expedition to Germany, but were returned to shore when they heard the news of the defeat of the French forces at Kloster Kampen on 16 October. Three months later, by which time George III had ascended the throne, these same regiments were again embarked for Europe under the command of Commodore Keppel. On 29 March 1761 they sailed from Spithead, under convoy of ten ships, for an unknown destination. As was later revealed, the troops invaded the French island of Belle Isle, but for someone like Blue, to whom Europe was totally unfamiliar, they might just as well have been in Germany. The casualties among the marines were high and a number of marines were returned wounded to England where they were subsequently discharged. Blue may well have been one of those wounded marines. After Belle Isle was secured for the British in 1761, the remnant of the force was consolidated into several regiments for service in Portugal against the Spanish. At the request of the Portugese commander a company of pioneers was also raised in Britain to be attached to the Portuguese army. This non-combat corps probably accompanied the two British regiments in Portugal posted to Minorca in 1763 after the conclusion of peace with Spain.[6]

Given this service record, it makes perfect sense that after the outbreak of war Blue was included in the pioneers corps that accompanied Brigadier Generals William Howe, John Burgoyne and Henry Clinton and a large army to Boston in 1775. Howe had been with Wolfe at Quebec and he was involved in the invasion of Belle Isle, as was Burgoyne, who went on to garner more glory in Portugal. The pioneers followed the army into retreat to Nova Scotia, returning with Howe to invade New York in July 1776. When Howe consolidated the British forces in New York, a corps of pioneers was attached to every regiment, so it would have been very feasible for Blue to have been at the garrison at Stony Point on the Hudson River in New York in September 1780. Just a few miles below Stony Point was where Major John André (later mythologised in folklore as Major Andrews) secretly met with the traitor Benedict Arnold on 21 September and it was very near Stony Point that André was subsequently captured and executed as a spy.[7]

In searching for confirmation of Blue's military service at the National Archives in England, I began to understand that the explanation for our black founders was to be found in the internecine turmoil of the American

Revolution. With this in mind, weeks were spent rummaging through War Office muster lists, ships' logs and musters, evacuation reports in the Admiralty records, the correspondence of the judge advocate for North America, the personal papers of Lord Cornwallis and Sir Guy Carleton, as well as the memorials to the Loyalist Claims Commission. It was a hugely ambitious undertaking, completely out of my area of expertise, although I was greatly assisted by the multi-volume survey, *Documents of the American Revolution*. When the archives in Kew were closed, I searched London newspapers in the British Library and poured over hundreds of pages of raw data on adult black baptisms extracted from parish records by the London Metropolitan Records Office.

One of the most remarkable archival documents I found was a compilation of the names of nearly 3000 black men, women and children, who were evacuated from New York between April and November 1783, all but a few carrying certificates of freedom signed by a British general. This document, known as the *Book of Negroes*, provided a brief description of each person, along with the name of their former owner. I have since established that this list accounted for about one-third of the blacks who left America during the British withdrawal and it is the most substantial piece of evidence of alliance between fugitive slaves and the British military during the Revolution.[8]

Surfing the web, I found the Institute for Advanced Loyalist Studies, with all kinds of scattered archival documents on the black allies of the Loyalist cause, which encouraged me to go to Nova Scotia. In Halifax, I trawled through the archives for records of the thousands of black refugees who were resettled in that province in 1783. A momentous breakthrough came when a researcher at the Nova Scotia Museum informed me that the *Book of Negroes*, which I had previously seen handwritten in the Carleton Papers in London, was now transcribed and could be downloaded onto my laptop. I was then able to search by name, place and date to locate several of the people I was seeking, although I was puzzled that they were listed as evacuated to Nova Scotia, when their trial records placed them in England. I was able to resolve this conundrum with the help of a very able research assistant who diligently searched through all the Nova Scotia military and civilian musters, tax lists, land grant approvals, as well as court and prison records from 1783 till 1792, to establish that these men had either failed to arrive in Nova

Scotia, or, having arrived, were so dismayed by the place they caught the first available ship to England.[9]

With the help of another research assistant, I was able to perform a demographic analysis of the *Book of Negroes*, as well as cross-reference the names with musters from Nova Scotia, the data on black adult baptisms from parish records in London, the names of applicants to the Loyalist Claims Commission, and the lists of recipients compiled by the Committee for the Relief of the Black Poor. It then remained for me to track particular individuals back into the American colonies, which meant tackling the daunting archive of revolutionary sources in the United States.

A Fulbright Senior Fellowship in 2002, followed by two more research fellowships in 2003 and 2004, allowed me to work my way through the major documents of the revolutionary period, many of them, thankfully, reproduced in excellent scholarly editions. At the Clements Library, University of Michigan, the sprawling, uncatalogued papers of Sir Henry Clinton yielded fragmentary evidence, as did several smaller collections of papers from British officers. Other tantalising fragments were extracted from runaway slave notices, petitions from slave owners and reportage in colonial newspapers. Luckily, my diligent excavation in these vast archives did unearth traces of several key individuals I could then follow to England and then Australia.

Back in Australia, I scoured all the extant records of criminal and civil proceedings, the Colonial Secretary's Papers and the *Sydney Gazette* and even then I gained only fleeting glimpses of how these people lived and died. Like all Australian colonial historians, I was deeply grateful to the inveterate scribblers aboard the First Fleet, yet persistently annoyed that these self-important young officers rarely bothered to supply the names of the convicts with whom they lived so intimately. David Collins's meticulous journal was the outstanding exception. Here individuals with particular characteristics and experiences were identified, instead of being rendered as nameless and faceless bodies, such as 'the black man who carried the tents'. From attentive diarists such as Collins, as well as the accumulation of tattered bits of administrative flotsam discovered in the archives in the United States, Canada, England and Australia, I was able to discern the lineaments of the lives of Australia's black founders.

✳

In attempting to reconstruct their biographies, I have not strayed into speculation that the evidence cannot support. Still, it remains possible that I have formed the wrong conclusion in some of the fine detail. A boy located in a runaway slave notice in Virginia in 1775 might not be the exact same person transported in 1788 who died in Sydney in 1833, but if it was not that particular fugitive slave, then it was someone like him; of that I am certain. In defence of my approach I can do no better than quote Edward Thompson, who said of his own work:

> The structure of historical explanation which I have offered depends in part upon logic, and only in part upon fact. A few identifications may be wrong, although I doubt very much whether the general identification of social composition and conflict is wrong. More identifications might be made, and much could be discovered as to the fortunes of [these historical subjects] by the patient work of local historians … somewhere – among some unsearched gentry or public papers – important information may come to light. This will undoubtedly upset some of my conclusions, although the work of upsetting should be made easier by what I have done.[10]

LIBERTY OR DEATH

It was early spring, 1775, at the 7000-acre estate of Colonel George Washington at Mount Vernon in Fairfax County, Virginia. Vestiges of snow lingered on the lawn that swept down to the Potomac River, while along the lovingly tended cherry walk, plump buds showed the first hint of bloom. Despite the beguiling promise of incipient cherry blossom, these were uncertain, turbulent times. The threat of war with Britain loomed, a prospect Washington dreaded. He knew there had already been fatal skirmishes with British troops near Boston and he anticipated British retaliation. As a seasoned army officer and the elected commander of a number of independent militias across the northern part of Virginia, Washington understood that he would be the one to lead the American forces into a conflict more bloody than he had ever before witnessed. On the morning of 15 March, he was leaving his handsome estate to attend the Second Virginia Convention, which chose to meet in the small town of Richmond, rather than the colonial capital of Williamsburg, in order to avoid the wrath of the royal governor, John Murray, Earl of Dunmore.

For the townsfolk of Richmond to have the colonial elite debating matters of great urgency in their village was cause for much excitement. Word would have spread like wildfire about Patrick Henry's electrifying performance on 23 March, when he laid out the choice Virginians faced between freedom and enslavement. 'Is life so dear, or peace so sweet, as to be purchased at the price of chains and slavery?', he demanded, his voice rising to a crescendo. 'Forbid it, Almighty God! I know not what course others may take; but as for me' – he allowed an exaggerated pause while he held an ivory letter-opener poised above his heart – 'give me liberty or give me death!' With this emotive appeal, Henry was inviting the Virginian gentry to transform their provincial lives into a theatre of heroic resistance and republican virtue, and he succeeded in persuading his fellow delegates to resist any attempt by the British to impose their authority on Virginia. Washington shared Henry's assessment of the stark

✳

choices facing the colonists, having said much the same thing six months earlier, when he wrote to his friend Bryan Fairfax, 'the crisis is arrived when we must assert our rights, or submit to every imposition that can be heap'd upon us; till custom and use, will make us as tame, and abject slaves, as the blacks we rule over with such arbitrary sway'. By the time Washington returned home, a fortnight later, a black frost had burnt the blossom from his cherry trees and the prospect of his continuing peacefully amid the rustic pleasures of Mount Vernon was equally blighted. With a heavy heart he wrote to his brother that he had resolved 'to devote my life and fortune to the cause we are engaged in, if need be'.[1]

Patrick Henry's rhetorical flourish gave an heroic gloss to sentiments that had been reverberating for months through the colony of Virginia. The cries of 'liberty' heard at the rowdy gathering at the county courthouse, and in the ardent talk swirling about the streets of every town, were discreetly absorbed by enslaved people who mingled unobtrusively in the excitable crowd. Passionate chatter about liberty and despotism, which animated the dining tables and drawing rooms of Virginian plantations, was not lost on the footmen and cooks, the valets and maids, who were as much a fixture of the plantation house as the furniture. Even if Virginia planters had been canny enough to send their slaves out of earshot, it would not have been possible to quarantine the ideas they discussed with friends and neighbours. Snatches of talk overheard were almost instantaneously channelled from plantation to plantation, through the complex networks of the enslaved community. In the Tidewater region, dominated by long established plantations with a large slave workforce, the slave quarters would house twenty or more people who were related, and they were likely to have other siblings, spouses, uncles, aunts and cousins living within the neighbourhood. These people had intricate means of communication, barely understood by their masters. Under the cover of darkness, they would congregate together for songs and story-telling, and the word would spread. On Sunday, they would come together from all over the county to sell the produce raised in their family plots and to trade information. 'The Negroes have a wonderfull art of communicating intelligence among themselves', two southern planters explained to leading Patriot, John Adams. 'It will run severall hundreds of miles in a week or a fortnight.'[2]

The young James Madison intuitively understood there was a potential for danger emanating from the slave quarters. A few months earlier,

Madison had warned a friend that if hostilities did break out the British would promote a slave revolt. Trouble of this sort had already been instigated, he confided. 'In one of our counties lately a few of those unhappy wretches met together and chose a leader who was to conduct them when the English troops should arrive – which they foolishly thought would be very soon and that by revolting to them they should be rewarded with their freedom.' He was pleased to report that the plot had been discovered and 'proper precautions taken to prevent the infection'. Madison, who regarded slave-holding with distaste, chose not to elaborate about the 'proper precautions' taken in this instance. Very likely the 'unhappy wretches' were savagely flogged and mutilated, although some may have been dispatched to the West Indies, a common practice for dealing with refractory slaves. As a final caution, Madison advised, it would be 'prudent such attempts should be concealed as well as suppressed'. By the summer of 1775, he must have realised what a Herculean and grisly task it would be to arrest the contagion of liberty, since the air was thick with infection issuing from the mouths of impassioned slave-owners. A great deal more in the way of 'proper precautions' would be required.[3]

In May, as a mantle of soft pink dogwood blossom settled across Virginia, George Washington again set out from Mount Vernon, this time for the Second Continental Congress in Philadelphia; he was not to return for eight years. As his convoy of Virginian delegates approached Philadelphia, 500 horsemen rode out to meet him. Further on a martial band and several companies of soldiers formed a massive parade to usher him into the city. When he strode into the Congress wearing his militia uniform the die was cast. As he anticipated, Washington was elected commander-in-chief of the American Continental Army on the first ballot. Almost immediately he left for Massachusetts, although he did not arrive before the first real battle of the war had been fought and lost.

By that time a large number of British troops with three brigadier-generals had arrived in Massachusetts. William Blue must have been attached in this force as part of the non-combat corps of pioneers who brought up the rear as the army took up its offensive position on the Heights of Charlestown across the harbour from Boston. On 17 June, the entire British force stormed the defensive earthworks that Patriot militia had constructed on a hilly promontory close by. Hours of bloody carnage ensued as the British infantry in strict formation marched remorselessly up Breeds Hill toward the Patriot redoubts, 'stepping over the bodies of their dead comrades as if they were logs'. When the ammunition of the Patriot militia was exhausted, the British soldiers continued their relentless advance, firing all the while. Scrambling over their own dead, the defenceless militia broke into a disorderly retreat. Watching the awful spectacle of mass slaughter were hundreds of anxious spectators crowded onto the surrounding hills. No one was more anxious than the General John Burgoyne, who was nervously observing proceedings from a British command battery while engaging in the dreadful reflection 'that a defeat was perhaps the loss of the British Empire in America'. Such grim thoughts made the scene before him 'a complication of horror and importance beyond any it ever came to [my] lot to witness'. At the end of the engagement (known as the Battle of Bunker Hill), 223 British soldiers were killed with four times that number wounded.[4]

When the news from Boston reached Virginia, the royal governor had taken refuge on a warship in the James River. Lord Dunmore was forced to flee his mansion in Williamsburg having unduly inflamed the passions of the white population by announcing any rebellion against his office would cause him to 'arm my own Negroes and receive all others that will come to me, who I shall declare free'. To even utter the slightest hint of such a thing was to terrify white Virginians, greatly outnumbered by their 180 000 slaves, for whom 'even the whispering of the wind was sufficient to rouze their fears'. From the relative safety of a British warship on the James River, Dunmore began to assemble a squadron to strike back at the rebellious Virginians, welcoming any fugitives that were able to make their way across to his fleet. Throughout the summer, tenders from the ships cruised up and down the river openly inciting slaves to come on board, spreading indignation and alarm throughout the Tidewater. The stark evidence that the British intended fully to use enslaved people against white Virginians 'raised our country into perfect phrensy', so Thomas Jefferson reported.[5]

In August 1775, Edward Hack Moseley, a prominent planter of Princess Anne County, near Portsmouth, placed a notice for three runaways between the ages of 16 and 18 that he named Jack, Daniel and Peter. Since Moseley was a friend of Lord Dunmore, his runaways probably did not head for the nearby British ships but did as Moseley supposed; they took refuge in one of the port towns of Portsmouth, Hampton or Norfolk. Planters were consistently angered by the willingness of white artisans and tradesmen in the towns to shelter runaways rather than return them. Jack appears to have found work with Captain John Cunningham, an Irish master whose ship was refitting in Portsmouth after a mast had been damaged on his voyage from Ireland carrying supplies to the British army in Boston.[6]

Even if Moseley's runaways were not making a beeline for Dunmore's ships, plenty of fugitives were. About 100 had reached his fleet by November 1775. This was exactly the 'tampering with the slaves' that James Madison had most feared. 'To say the truth', he confided to his friend, 'that is the only part in which this Colony is vulnerable ... we shall fall like Achilles by the hand of one that knows that secret'. Lord Dunmore knew well that secret. Made bold by the idea of what might be accomplished should the trickle of runaways become a flood, Dunmore declared martial law on 14 November 1775 and published a proclamation that freed 'all indented Servants, Negroes, or others ... that are able and willing to bear Arms'. He made no distinction between Patriot and Loyalist property.[7]

Here was every white Virginian's worst nightmare. Dunmore must be crushed, George Washington warned, or the momentum of slave defections would be 'like a snow ball in rolling'. When the *Virginia Gazette* published the proclamation it was accompanied by grim warnings to slaves, and the Fourth Virginia Convention emphasised the necessity of inflicting on apprehended runaways the punishment either of instant death by hanging or the slow death of intolerable labour in the lead mines. With the other hand they offered a pardon to any who voluntarily returned 'to their duty'. This combination of punitive threat and compassionate promise failed. 'Letters mention that slaves flock to him in abundance', the President of the Convention, confided, glumly.[8]

Any stampede to the British was against huge odds. The danger of recapture and savage punishment was terribly real, and also militating against irrevocable flight were the bonds of family from which the enslaved community drew its fortitude. By 1775 most of those enslaved in the Tidewater dwelt in families: children with their mothers and young siblings, and sometimes with their fathers, grandparents, aunts, uncles and cousins. While the close-knit kinship networks facilitated the short-term protection of runaways by providing hospitality and shelter, the familial bond was a powerful force against making a decisive break from which there was no return. Unless whole families absconded together – almost unheard of – a lifetime of separation from close kin was the consequence.[9]

Added to the psychological pressures of abandoning family, there was the fundamental difficulty of reaching Dunmore's small fleet in the mouth of the James River. Enslaved people could only move about the country with signed passes, and plantation owners kept a close watch on their watercraft. Slave patrols were doubled throughout the region and armed militia were stationed along the Chesapeake shores. Notwithstanding the surveillance and intimidation, hundreds made a determined attempt. At the end of November, Dunmore could report 'between two to three hundred [runaways] already come in and these I form into a Corps as fast as they come'. They came mostly from Hampton, Norfolk and Portsmouth and were often maritime workers, especially pilots. Others ran off with the British forces when they cruised along the James River, while still more absconded from plantations close to navigable waterways. They mostly arrived on small craft, though some, propelled by sheer willpower, were on foot and swam out to Dunmore's ships. Recruits for Lord Dunmore's Ethiopian Regiment, as the governor styled his new corps, were provided with weapons and taught how to use them.[10]

Virginian newspapers encouraged white Virginians to subsume their fears about slave insurrection by ridiculing the idea that the British could create an effective regiment from black recruits. Regardless of the contempt the Virginia elite showered upon the Ethiopian Regiment, their property continued to flee to Dunmore's floating base camp, even when it moved into Chesapeake Bay. Lund Washington, who was managing Mount Vernon for his illustrious cousin, might sneer at Dunmore, but he was unable to sidestep the realisation that slaves were motivated to join Dunmore by the selfsame passion for freedom that animated the Patriots to oppose the governor. In his evaluation of the loyalty of Mount Vernon's bonded workforce, both indentured and enslaved, Lund was of the view 'there is not a man of them, but woud leave us, if they believe'd they could make there escape … yet they have no fault to find. Liberty is sweet.'[11]

As the slave exodus increased, so the backlash against Virginia Loyalists intensified. In the absence of an executive head of the colony, the Virginia Convention in August 1775 set up a Committee of Safety, to act as the legal arm of the de facto government. In December 1775 the Committee of Safety ordered that Edward Hack Moseley and his son be detained. Captain John Cunningham too came under suspicion. His ship *Fanny*, loaded with British army provisions, was seized as a prize. Cunningham managed to persuade the Committee of Safety that he had been coerced into transporting supplies for the British, and he was compensated for his loss of wages, even though his cargo was auctioned off. Soon after, he applied to leave Virginia. This may have been the time that Moseley's young runaway Jack decided to throw in his lot with the King's men and join Dunmore. Eight years later, John Moseley, aged 25, was working for the Wagon Master General's Department in New York. In giving an account of himself, he said he had left the employ of John Cunningham in Portsmouth and joined the British in 1776.[12]

In due course Edward Hack Moseley and son persuaded the authorities that they were not acting against the interests of Virginians and they were granted parole, even though suspicions lingered about their connections with Dunmore. Consequently, they were required to move at least 30 miles inland. To enforce submission, the Committee of Safety ordered their slaves to be taken by the militia, providing a motivation and an opportunity for the remainder of Moseley's slaves to bolt to Dunmore. Whether or not they were encouraged by the actions of young Jack, they would certainly have been in terror either of being sold or banished to the lead mines. The new government of Virginia's finances were extremely fragile, and the sale of seized slaves was one way to ameliorate the situation. It auctioned off eleven enslaved people left by Lord Dunmore during his flight from the governor's mansion in Williamsburg. Another eight seized slaves belonging to Loyalist defectors were transported to the lead mines. Worse still seized slaves might be sold to the West Indies – the fate of one of Moseley's runaways captured before reaching Dunmore's floating sanctuary. In May 1776 he was put aboard a ship bound for Antigua, and there, together with several others, was sold.[13]

The Moseley runaways were part of a very large group of fugitives from Princess Anne and Norfolk counties, including 87 people from the plantation of a fellow Loyalist suspect John Willoughby. A woman in her mid-fifties from Moseley's plantation took with her several children aged between 3 and 11, while simultaneously her husband and son absconded from another plantation. The list of 'Negroes gone to Dunmore' that Willoughby compiled gave the names of sixteen men with ages ranging between 16 and 60, as well as twenty-one women with ages ranging from 18 to 55, who were accompanied by fifty children. This pattern of slave flight was typical of the defections to Dunmore between January and June 1776, though quite unlike what had happened before the Revolution, when it was almost always the young men who bolted. The majority of the runaways in 1776 were husbands and wives, or mothers with children or even grandparents; all of them taken aboard Dunmore's fleet.[14]

Blatant recruitment of their slaves by the deposed governor provided the Patriots with the perfect argument as to why they were no longer able to give allegiance to the Crown. Patrick Henry protested at the Fifth Virginia Convention, held in Williamsburg throughout May and June 1776, that for a representative of the Crown to be 'encouraging insurrection among our slaves, many of whom are now actually in arms against us' revealed the King to be a 'tyrant instead of the protector of his people'. The only honourable response, Henry argued, was 'an immediate, clear, and full Declaration of Independency'. A resolution to that effect was carried unanimously on 29 June 1776, a week before the Congress made its own declaration on 4 July 1776. Henry was elected the first governor of the independent Commonwealth of Virginia. In his new role, he proved ineffectual in stemming the tide of slave defections to the enemy. Sometime during his stay in Williamsburg, one of his own enslaved servants, a man in his early twenties named Ralph, slipped away to join Dunmore, one more who took the fiery Virginian orator at his word.[15]

Along the length of Chesapeake Bay alarmed plantation owners and managers did their best to staunch the defections by promoting benevolent paternalism over the precarious dangers of freedom. At Mount Vernon, Lund Washington was confident that the enslaved community understood that General Washington's care and protection was best for them. He had 'not the least dread' that the slaves might make a bolt for Dunmore's fleet. Several counties away, on the Rappahannock River,

Washington's irascible friend, Landon Carter, was surprised, and profoundly wounded, to discover on 26 June 1776 that eight of his enslaved workforce 'ran away – to be sure, to Lord Dunmore', after stealing guns, shot and powder. The flight was clearly premeditated as two slaves from an upriver plantation had gone with them in Landon's large canoe. After weeks of hearing contradictory stories about his runaways, Landon sent his manager on a circuit to get information from both sides of the Rappahannock. When the man returned with no information, Landon turned eagerly to local gossip about the fate of his people. In July he recorded with sardonic glee a story that Dunmore had re-enslaved the runaways and sent them off to be sold in the West Indies. Even as he slept he visited misery upon his absconded chattel. In his dreams these poor, deluded souls, now reduced to the condition of wild animals, longed for the intervention of their indulgent master, pleading that Carter 'would endeavour to get them pardoned, should they come in'. During the waking hours it must have been galling that no such plea was made. As if to heap coals upon his head, even more slaves, with ingratitude in their heart, fled to Lord Dunmore. What Carter's gossip mill had failed to convey was that if his chattel had succeeded in reaching Dunmore, they may have died, not from ill-use or starvation, as he fervently desired, but from disease.[16]

Along with war, smallpox had invaded North America in 1775. The British were largely immune, but the native-born population, white and black, were mostly defenceless: few had been inoculated against the disease, fewer still had had contact with the virus, and most were highly susceptible to its ravages. Of all epidemic diseases, this one held a particular horror. From the moment the distinctive rash appeared, it rapidly covered the entire body, sometimes haemorrhaging under the skin, causing bleeding from the gums, eyes, nose, and other orifices. Most cases broke out with ugly pustules on the palms of the hands, the face, forearms, neck and back. After two weeks of acute suffering, scabs started to form and flesh came away in evil-smelling clumps with the victims emitting such a pungent smell healthy people were unable to tolerate the stench. Sixty per cent of cases died, usually after ten to sixteen days of suffering, although patients remained contagious until the final scab fell off. Survivors carried numerous scars, some were blinded and lame, but they were immune for life. Inoculation, in which live *variola* were implanted under the skin, caused a milder version of the disease, with much less scarring, yet the same level of subsequent immunity. Before the use of cow-pox vaccine, it was a risky business, as the inoculation process potentially caused debilitating sickness, which left the inoculated vulnerable to typhus.[17]

The explosive combination of the *variola* microbes and massed humans in close proximity was, to Washington's horror, already wreaking havoc in the ranks of the Continental army. In British-controlled Boston, which had been besieged by Patriot forces since June, the situation was equally dire. There the disease was cutting swathes through the population. It was no respecter of sides; Loyalist supporters and the hapless Patriots trapped in the city were equally susceptible. Everyone without immunity to the disease was inoculated under threat of severe sanction if they refused, and then were isolated in a separate section of the city. One Bostonian who escaped reported a prohibition on the tolling of the church bells, because there were up to thirty funerals a day. For those besieged within the city, the depredations of smallpox were compounded by epidemics of scurvy and dysentery. By the spring of 1776 the city was facing a devastating famine. A sudden, silent evacuation was organised between 13 and 16 March 1776. William Blue, in the pioneers corps, would have been among the very last to be embarked. On 17 March, 8000 soldiers and another 1000 Loyalist refugees, both black and white, with as many stores, essential equipment and horses as could be crammed onto the ships, sailed for Nova Scotia.[18]

About this time the *variola* virus reached Virginia, where it devastated the black recruits in Dunmore's overcrowded flotilla. With relish, the *Virginia Gazette* noted that their bodies were 'tumbled into the deep, to regale the sharks'. On advice from the naval surgeons, Dunmore moved his forces to a small neck of land near Portsmouth, where he created 'pretty good barracks' for his 'Ethiopian Corps'. It was at this fateful time that the Moseley runaways joined Dunmore. They were part of a steady influx of new recruits who kept the contagion alive, wreaking havoc on Dunmore's military ambitions and killing off 'a great many fine fellows'. In order to isolate the sick after the surgeons had inoculated new recruits, in late May Dunmore moved his base to Gwynn Island. He left behind him the graves of almost 300 people.[19]

Still they died. Dunmore reported to his superiors that 'there was not a ship in the fleet that did not throw one, two or three or more dead overboard every night'. Virginians found diseased corpses drifting ashore on the tide the next day, as many as a dozen at a time. Those who recovered from the inoculation succumbed to an outbreak of 'fever' which 'carried off an incredible number of our people, especially the blacks', Dunmore lamented. In this dreadfully weakened condition, Dunmore's force was easily driven from the island in early July 1776, and they took refuge on the fleet once again. Among those able to leave the island were at least ten people from Moseley's plantation, including young Jack.

When the dispirited Dunmore sailed out of the Chesapeake, he joined General Henry Clinton in a much larger British fleet, reinforced with additional troops from England under Lord Cornwallis, which was sailing toward New York. Clinton's plan had been to reclaim the southern colonies for the Crown. However, his ill-judged assault on South Carolina turned to a complete rout. As the damaged British fleet limped northward to New York, it must have seemed to the black runaways that they had made an unwise choice in throwing their lot in with the British now that they were repulsed from the southern colonies and forced to evacuate Boston.

Two weeks later, when the fleet reached Staten Island, they must have been heartened to find that an army of 9000 troops had arrived with General William Howe from Nova Scotia, along with several dozen black men and women who had escaped enslavement in Boston and now provided support services in the pioneer corps attached to each regiment, or serving as wagoners, labourers and cooks. Additional forces from Europe, including 13 000 Hessian mercenaries, brought the strength of the combined British force to 30 000 men. Among the new reinforcements disembarking at Staten Island in August were numerous battle-hardened veterans of the Seven Years' War. The black New Yorker William Blue was no doubt struck by the strangeness of returning to his homeland as a member of an invasion force.[20]

The campaign opened with a mass landing on Long Island on 22 August and by the end of the month Washington's army was in retreat beyond White Plains, leaving the British with a Loyalist stronghold that included Long Island, Staten Island, Sandy Neck and Lower Manhattan. It was to this enclave of royal authority that the dispirited Lord Dunmore brought the remnant of his shattered dream. With him were about 300 of his original recruits, including Jack and other runaways from Moseley. Also arriving in New York with Dunmore was General Washington's enslaved ostler, Harry, and Patrick Henry's absconded valet, Ralph.

On the heels of the withdrawal of the Continental army, disgruntled Patriots started a fire that swept through the western side of Lower Manhattan, reducing about a quarter of the buildings to smouldering rubble. The fire created opportunities at the same time as it brought disaster. Enslaved people who had stayed behind after the white population fled the city, as well as those who arrived with the British army, were in high demand. Washington's withdrawal gave the British control of territory that was almost contiguous with the Patriot-controlled colonies of New Jersey and Connecticut, separated from them by relatively short stretches of water. At one point it was possible to wade across the Hudson River to New Jersey. The permeable borders allowed runaways from adjoining colonies to slip into the throng of foreign soldiers and Loyalist refugees in New York without attracting scrutiny. They found an enthusiastic welcome in the civil departments of the army, which needed all the labour they could find just to provide the logistical support necessary for the maintenance of a very large army. Most of the black recruits from Lord Dunmore's disbanded Ethiopian Regiment found work within the pioneer corps attached to the Royal Artillery Department, the Quartermaster General's Department, the Forage and Provision Departments, or the Commissary, while Moseley's runaway Jack went to work for the Wagon Master General.

One of the most significant actions undertaken by black people in the British zone of New York was choosing a name. Taking one's own name was far more than a symbolic act; it was a potent gesture of self-emancipation. In a society where enslaved people were universally known only by a single mocking or infantilising name, it marked them as chattel as clearly as a brand. Runaway notices commonly observed that the fugitives they sought would probably change their names, or that they already had more dignified names by which they wished to be known. The mock regal names commonly bestowed on slaves were dignified by becoming a surname, and first names were commonly formalised from their infantilising diminutive form. More often than not, the new surname was an inheritance from the past life, the usage reflecting the British practice of adding the owner's surname when they entered a runaway's name on a muster. So Patrick Henry's runaway became known as Ralph Henry, George Washington's ostler took the name Harry Washington and Edward Moseley's runaway Jack transformed himself into John Moseley.

Runaways who flocked into the city found employment simply by asserting that they were free, their labour quickly absorbed by the voracious British war effort. Many more claimed to be free than had papers to prove it, but inside the British lines few cared to make a distinction. After June 1779, any pretence was no longer necessary. The Commandant of New York declared that 'all Negroes that fly from the enemy's country are free – No person whatever can claim a right to them – Whoever sells them shall be prosecuted with the utmost severity.' While some company commanders feared being overwhelmed with black indigents, especially women and children, the British accommodated everyone, regardless of age or gender. Only occasionally did they remonstrate with 'idle' black men, threatening expulsion if they did not work. Because of the shortage of white workers, there was plenty of employment.[21]

Black artisans worked on rebuilding projects and in the naval yards; black teamsters hauled provisions and collected firewood; black nurses and orderlies staffed the hospitals; black laundresses and needlewomen did the washing and sewing; black pilots guided the ships safely in and out of the port; black fiddlers and banjo players provided entertainment at balls and in taverns; black jockeys rode horses at the races; black cooks, servants and valets ensured the comfort of the elite. A whole world of opportunity, hitherto denied, was opened to black people. In almost all cases they were paid for their services, and they could be paid well if they possessed sought-after skills, such as carpentry and pilotage. They were also provisioned, for the most part, and they were not required to pay taxes. For these reasons alone, the British zone was a magnet to runaways. During the period of British occupation, the number of absconding slaves from New York and its neighbouring colonies exploded.[22]

Persistent British incursions into the seaports of eastern Connecticut further stimulated black recruitment to the British military. John Randall was most probably scooped up in one of these raids. Randall left no explicit testimony to his past. Nevertheless, many years later, in the later

Australian phase of his life, he signed on as a soldier with the New South
Wales Corps, when it was noted that originally he came from New Haven
and was born about 1764. Since Randall was not a recorded surname in
New Haven at that time, he may actually have been from New London
where the name was common. It is possible he was from the enslaved
workforce of a prominent Patriot, Captain John Randall, of Stonington,
near New London, and one of several enslaved people from Stonington
who fled to the British. His age, plus the fact that he was noted for
playing the flute and tambour, point to Randall being a drummer.[23]

With the British army concentrated in New York, along with the tens
of thousands of Loyalist refugees, conditions of life in the British zone
were basic. Every necessity was in short supply, especially shelter.
Between Broadway and the Hudson River the burnt-out neighbourhood
was not rebuilt and the charred ruins were used to support rough
dwellings created from canvas and found materials. For the most part,
the black recruits were crammed into these unsanitary, makeshift shel-
ters. Those formally on the payroll, such as people employed in civil
branches of the army and the pioneers, were lucky enough to be
provided with housing. John Moseley, who was employed by the Wagon
Master General's Department, lived in 'Negro barracks' across the East
River near the wagon yard in Brooklyn.

The Black Pioneers working for the Royal Artillery Department had
similar barracks, created out of four row-houses in lower Manhattan
where they were provided with weekly rations, as well as a lamp and a
pint of oil for each room. That runaway slaves should occupy even these
meagre lodgings infuriated some white Loyalists. Complaint to that effect
was registered by one, who recorded his disgust that available houses
were not rented to deserving whites and were instead 'occupied by dirty,
idle, thieving, Negroes invited into the lines'. Worse still, he bemoaned,
these 'wretches' were supplied with 'rations of all kinds, equally with the
Kings troops'. In fact this level of accommodation was better than the
King's troops who were sleeping four to six men to a tent.[24]

Whether they lived in barracks or in the canvas town of the burnt-
out district, the black recruits formed communities. Although they came
from several colonies and had diverse life experiences, they were bound
by a struggle to survive and collective memories that reached back to an
African past. Music was the rhythmic centre of traditional African life

＊

and in the multi-ethnic slave communities of America traditional musical forms were reinvented to express a common experience of enslavement. To the accompaniment of the fiddle, banjo, gourds, bells and the insistent drumming of feet and hands, improvised song and dance found resonance with people from disparate places, allowing them to share the experience of work, exile and yearning, as well as their hopes for the future.

Story-telling held a central place in a community of displaced and entirely illiterate people. In the repertoire of stories were many variations on the exploits of the trickster, transposed from older African tales, as well as new stories thrown up by the turmoil of revolution. Tales of black heroes, like the New Jersey runaway known as 'Colonel Tye', who led daring guerrilla raids into New Jersey as the commander of the Black Brigade, made thrilling listening for the thousands toiling at menial tasks behind the British lines. Music and dancing; stories and prayers; these were the elements that mitigated the separation from kin and softened the challenging business of staying alive in New York.[25]

2

FLEEING THE FOUNDING FATHERS

By June 1779 the British commander-in-chief, General Henry Clinton, was prepared to mount a full-scale campaign in the south. Before he left New York, he published a proclamation calculated to stimulate a new wave of slave defections. He warned that any slave taken in the service of the rebel army would be considered a prize of war and purchased for the public service. But anyone who voluntarily came over to the British would enjoy 'full security to follow within these lines, any occupation which he shall think proper'. The effect of Clinton's proclamation was as dramatic as Dunmore's had been, but stretched across a far wider canvas. Clinton's bold policy was master-minded by his charismatic aide-de-camp, John André, who wryly observed, '[t]heir property we need not seek, it flies to us and famine follows'.[1]

When the British forces landed in South Carolina, they had no difficulty in recruiting runaways to work as labourers, wagoners, boatmen, foragers and nurses. Defecting slaves found an enthusiastic welcome if they knew the terrain and were willing to act as spies and guides. After Charleston fell, runaways poured into the British lines drawn by the lure of paid work. Enslaved people abandoned in the city had an advantage in that they could claim to be free. Jack Gordon, a tailor in his late thirties, who had once been enslaved to Benjamin Gordon, insisted that he had been given his freedom on the fall of the city. Tailors were in demand to attend to regimental uniforms, so the British authorities were only too happy to take him at his word, as long as he was prepared to work on their behalf. When General Clinton returned to New York in May 1780, he took with him 500 of his black workforce and their families in a large company of Black Pioneers, while British and Hessian officers returning to New York also took runaways as servants. One way or another, Jack Gordon was part of the force that returned to New York.

Some months after his triumphant return, Clinton began clandestine negotiations with Benedict Arnold, the most impressive of Washington's

*

6

generals, who was now commander of the American fortress at West Point, about 40 miles up the Hudson River. Arnold, who had agreed to defect, was to arrange for the British to take this strategic garrison in return for £20 000. Clinton's dashing young aide, John André, was appointed the go-between with Arnold.

The arrival of another large British fleet in September 1781 gave Clinton the opportunity to distract Washington's attention from New York by embarking an invasion force supposedly bound for Virginia. André simultaneously sailed up the Hudson in the warship *Vulture*. On the night of 21 September, he was rowed ashore by a boatman for a conference with Arnold on the banks of the river, just within the American lines near Stony Point. While the two men were discussing details, the *Vulture* came under fire and was forced to drop downriver. André and Arnold spent the night with a local Loyalist sympathiser and the next day, when Arnold returned to West Point, André crossed the river in disguise into the British zone but was captured by a group of renegade militiamen he mistook for Loyalists. Beneath his disguise, André was found to be wearing his British uniform, while carrying incriminating letters from the turncoat Arnold. Half a century later William Blue claimed to have been present at the highly charged incident 'when Major Andrews was taken'. That could not possibly have been the case. But it is feasible that Blue was part of the British garrison on duty at Stony Point and thus was in close proximity to the events.

The morning after André's capture, the commander of West Point was at breakfast when he received the news. Without waiting to complete his dress, Arnold hastily kissed his young wife goodbye and ran to his official barge, telling the startled crew to row him to the waiting British warship. The American turncoat general was welcomed aboard and his hapless boatmen made prisoner. Arnold informed the captain that André was taken so there was no point in waiting for him any longer and to sail immediately for the British garrison. Arnold's treachery and his lack of gallantry ensured that he was detested by just about everyone within the British camp, even though they were obliged to pay him and give him a commission as a Brigadier General. As for André, he was hanged as a spy on 2 October 1781, sending a shockwave through the entire British army. General Clinton was overcome by grief and he never recovered fully from his bitter sorrow. This young officer's charisma, as well as his gallantry in the face of ignoble death, even won the admiration of his captors. Popular songs celebrating the bravery of 'Major Andrews' were sung on both sides of the ideological divide.

Whether William Blue was on duty up the Hudson, or in the garrison at New York, the emotional impact of André's capture and execution was so profound that fifty years later he could have believed that he was part of these dramatic events. It was certainly possible that Blue took part in Benedict Arnold's first campaign for the British at the beginning of 1781, when the defector was despatched to Virginia with a force of 1600 men to establish a naval base at Portsmouth. For this operation in enemy territory Arnold wanted to have black recruits who would blend unobtrusively into the local population to operate as spies and took several with him from New York. At his first point of call, the huge Byrd plantation at Westover on the James River, he set about obtaining more black recruits. The mistress of Westover was cousin to his wife, which ensured a civil welcome for Arnold, even though the traitorous general was viewed with almost universal distaste.

Arnold's duplicity in switching sides was of no consequence to the enslaved workers he sought to recruit; for them he represented the promise of an independent life. Mary Byrd loaned her favourite serving man, Wat, to Arnold to act as a guide, fully expecting her property to be returned. Wat saw the relationship quite differently. He never went back to Westover, preferring precarious freedom with Arnold, and later Cornwallis, to indulgent enslavement with Mrs Byrd, even though he left there a wife and children. At the end of the war, settled as a free man in New York with the name Walter Harris, he showed himself indifferent to Mary Byrd's handsome inducements to return.[2]

After leaving Westover, Arnold's aggressive push up the James River brought him huge numbers of defecting slaves, some of them from very illustrious estates. The governor of Virginia, Thomas Jefferson, made his escape from Richmond by a hair's breadth, galloping away from the town on his horse, having already sent Mrs Jefferson and his daughters to safety with several of his most trusted slaves. According to Isaac Jefferson, one of the seven domestic slaves Jefferson left behind, 'within ten minutes not a white man was to be seen in Richmond'. Isaac was only five years old at the time but he could already play the drum. His skill must have caught the attention of Arnold's officers, who were actively recruiting black drummers. When they left, they took with them Isaac and the rest of Jefferson's domestics. At the plantation of Benjamin Harrison, soon to be the next governor, they confiscated 'all his valuable Negroes'. A resident of Richmond reported that nearby plantations had lost 'a considerable part of their slaves'. An adolescent boy known as Caesar was among those hundreds who were reported to have absconded, no doubt one of the many youths recruited into Arnold's line regiments as a trumpeter or drummer. By the time Arnold moved to secure Portsmouth as a naval base, his force had been augmented by Jefferson's seven slaves and hundreds more belonging to other Patriots.[3]

In May the county of New Kent was hard hit by slave defections to Arnold's army, including yet another youth named Caesar, who subsequently disappeared from the list of taxable slaves on General Washington's New Kent estate. Soldiers from Cornwallis's army also raided the plantation Washington had established in the Great Dismal Swamp, taking the steers, 50 head of cattle, 200 barrels of corn, all the work implements and 21 men, 1 woman and 5 children, who were over half of the enslaved workforce. On 12 April, the British warship HMS *Savage* cruised up the Potomac River, dropping anchor near Mount Vernon, where the log recorded taking on board 13 'black refugees'. Another 5 were taken from the shore a little north of Mount Vernon on 15 April. These 18 'black refugees' seem to have comprised 16 enslaved workers of General Washington and another 2 people enslaved to his cousin Lund.[4]

Washington was disquieted by the loss of chattel. But of far greater concern was the possibility that Lund had supplied the British ship with refreshments in an attempt to prevent the house being burned. In a fury-filled letter to Lund, Washington implied that the British had stolen his property, even though his friend, the Marquis de Lafayette, had told him quite bluntly, 'when the enemy came to your house many Negroes deserted to them'. Even as Washington spoke of plantations along the Potomac being 'stripped of their Negroes and moveable property', he knew his slaves had left of their own volition, just as his white indentured servants had done. In his response to the young Frenchman, Washington also chose to apply the verb 'deserted' rather than saying they were taken. Perhaps he remembered what Lund had written at the time of Dunmore's proclamation: 'there is not a man of them, but woud leave us, if they believe'd they could make there escape … Liberty is sweet.'[5]

✳

At the end of spring 1781, the army of Lord Cornwallis marched north from North Carolina to join forces with Arnold in Virginia, with at least 1000 runaway slaves in train. By the time the two armies merged, health problems had taken a toll on the army at Portsmouth, where many of the black recruits had been affected by a deadly outbreak of typhus. Cornwallis added smallpox to the noxious cauldron of contagion. Yet even these well-publicised epidemics did nothing to halt the slave exodus. Word was out that the British fed their labourers good rations and paid them wages – treatment never before experienced by these enslaved people. Little wonder they continued to take their chances in the disease-ridden British camps.

Despite the sorry state of his soldiers – many reduced to wearing makeshift shoes of cowhide bound to their feet – Cornwallis immediately determined to attack the Continental army of the Marquis de Lafayette encamped near Richmond. Having dislodged Lafayette's forces, Cornwallis continued to pursue them up the James River valley, without managing to engage. In early June, Cornwallis set up his headquarters at Elk Hill, one of Thomas Jefferson's plantations on the James River in Goochland County. When he left ten days later, 23 people enslaved to Jefferson, including an old woman and 16 young children, departed with him. These defections had the hallmarks of a well-planned and premeditated action. People ran from three different plantations: Elk Hill in Goochland County, Willis Creek in Cumberland County and Monticello, 50 miles to the west in Albemarle County. Soon after, Jefferson ruefully recorded the names of the 23 in his farm book, noting how they had 'fled to the enemy' or 'joined the enemy' or simply 'run away'.[6]

Like Arnold, Cornwallis found black recruits indispensable, and he used them as spies and guides in this unfamiliar and hostile territory. He had a dozen or so working in that capacity, including William Blue and Mrs Byrd's serving man Wat, who now called himself Walter Harris. These men had been transferred to Cornwallis when Arnold returned to New York. In addition Cornwallis had collected thousands of black 'followers of the flag', who supported the army in numerous capacities. A senior Hessian officer with the army was appalled at the size of Cornwallis's motley entourage, which resembled 'a wandering Arabian or Tartar horde'. Every place this variegated horde passed 'was eaten clean, like an acre invaded by a swarm of locusts'. This ravaging caravanserai was essential to

Cornwallis for the supply of his army, foraging food for the hungry forces, driving off livestock, and stripping the fields and storage cellars. They also procured much-needed horses, which they rode bareback in the army's train. In the James River valley alone they took some 800 horses, much to the despair of General Lafayette. 'Nothing but a treaty of alliance with the Negroes can find us dragoon horses', he bemoaned to Washington, 'and it is by this means the enemy have so formidable a cavalry.'[7]

By August 1781, Cornwallis was employing several thousand black runaways to assist in fortifying the town of Little York (later known as Yorktown), which he had chosen as a naval base in preference to Portsmouth. All able-bodied men, white and black, were required to construct a series of redoubts around the garrison. Soon all the troops had become weakened by the hard labour of building fortifications and an inadequate diet of 'putrid ships meat and wormy biscuits'. In early September, venesection by the surgeons revealed everyone's blood to be pink, a sure sign of anæmia. A short time later, almost a quarter of the troops were stricken with typhus. There was no possibility of getting any supplies of fresh food. To compound these health problems, in October a smallpox epidemic erupted among the white Loyalist refugees and black recruits, by which time the British were hemmed in by a combined army of nearly 16000, and blockaded by the French fleet, with a mere 3500 men fit for duty.[8]

Once the forty-one American siege cannons opened fire on 9 October, the night sky above Yorktown became a brilliant spectacle, with dozens of fiery tails of comet-like cannonballs streaking through the darkness. Behind the battered defences terrified civilians huddled under the cliff face at the edge of the river, seeking shelter from the hard rain of bombardment, while Cornwallis was forced to move his headquarters into a cave. The besieged town was hell as a charnel house: ships sunk in the river, houses on fire, piles of mutilated bodies and scattered body parts everywhere. Hundreds were dead. There was no food – a forage party had been able to locate only burnt corn. Even a partial retreat was unlikely to succeed. An officer in the Franco-American camp reported that a British journal had washed ashore which read 'our provisions are now almost exhausted and our ammunition totally'.[9]

On 14 October 1781 Cornwallis ordered the horses to be slaughtered and dragged into the river, where their bloated carcasses drifted back with the tide, bumping against the shattered hulks of British ships. Having already sent out of Yorktown those sick with smallpox, he now expelled a large group of runaways from the hospital on the opposite shore at Gloucester Point to fend for themselves with what pitiful rations could be found. When a desperate attempt to retreat across the river to Gloucester Point on the night of 16 October was ruined by a freak storm, Cornwallis could no longer delay the inevitable capitulation.[10]

The booming of cannon, the roar of fire, the screams of pain, the stench of death and the sight of terrified runaways disfigured by small-pox must have made an indelible impression on those like William Blue and Walter Harris, who managed to survive the horror. At dawn on 17 October a frightful bombardment blasted Yorktown. There was no answering fire; the British ammunition was exhausted. At ten o'clock that morning, a drummer boy appeared on the ramparts of Yorktown, beating a tattoo that could barely be heard over the pounding cannon, and accompanied by an officer holding aloft a white handkerchief. The officer was blindfolded and escorted to the Patriot headquarters to present Cornwallis's request for a 24-hour cessation of hostilities, so the commanders might agree upon terms of surrender. Washington saw no need to be indulgent. He gave Cornwallis two hours to capitulate. That night an uncanny silence fell on Yorktown as the siege cannons shut down. The only reminder of the horror of the siege was a trail of fire from two meteors that streaked across the clear, starlit sky. At dawn, pipers from the British camp signalled the surrender. After a few eerie minutes the band of a French regiment struck up the reply from Washington's camp. When the sun rose and the cannon smoke cleared, the besieging army could see for the first time the full disaster of Yorktown. 'How vain the hope of such a place', a shocked officer wrote in his journal.[11]

No one will ever know just how many runaways fled from Yorktown before the fateful day of 19 October, when the humiliated British army marched out to a solemn drumbeat, dressed in smart new uniforms, but with their colours furled and the drums covered with black handker-chiefs. In asking for time to discuss terms, Cornwallis fully expected to negotiate with Washington to take his army back to England. Confronted by Washington's stern intransigence, all he hoped for was 'good treat-ment during their captivity', a courtesy, he knew, that definitely would not be extended to the thousands of fugitive slaves who had joined him; they would have to look out for themselves as best they could. Reports from the Franco-American camp spoke of 'herds of Negroes' in the woods, and on entering Yorktown the victors found the place littered with the 'sick and dying in every stage of small pox'. After such a long and brutal war, Cornwallis's hope of decent treatment was in vain. The post-surrender environment was savage, with no compassion on offer. Within the battered garrison the wounded and sick 'died like flies' because they were left without medicine or food. The amputated limbs that lay on the blood-soaked ground were gorged by the dogs. 'All hearts had turned to stone', Ewald sorrowfully reported. 'There was neither consolation nor money to be found and everyone was left to his own fate.'[12]

The Articles of Capitulation stipulated that Americans could recover their property from Yorktown. To facilitate this, Washington gave orders that all captured runaways were to be given over to a designated officer, with whom they would remain until claimed. Washington himself was able to recover two of the young women who had absconded from Mount Vernon, although the rest of his runaways eluded him. Washington, unlike Thomas Jefferson, had prudently inoculated his slaves at both Mount Vernon and the New Kent plantation. Those that fled from Washington's property had a fair chance of surviving Yorktown, while almost all of Jefferson's runaways died of the disease. Most of those that survived avoided capture and escaped northward to Philadelphia, while others were taken to New York.

The Yorktown Articles of Capitulation also stipulated that nearly 9000 soldiers and sailors be detained in Virginia as prisoners of war, but permitted the Royal Navy to take paroled British and Hessian officers to New York. The warship *Bonetta* was allowed immediately to sail for New York with Cornwallis's dispatches and any officers he chose to send. From the moment the surrender was finalised, guards were placed along the shore to prevent runaways escaping to the ship, although it was feared that many were already hidden on board. The governor of Virginia wrote to Cornwallis that 'Negroes are attempting to make their escape by getting aboard the *Bonetta* ... [where] they will endeavour to lie concealed from your Lordship till the vessel sails.' Washington too was deeply suspicious about the *Bonetta*, but he had given his word that the

*

ship could sail without examination, so he had grimly to accept that runaways concealed aboard would evade capture, even though there was every possibility that his own property was thus stowed away.[13]

Whatever answer Cornwallis gave the governor, he himself was perfectly aware of the runaways secreted away upon the *Bonetta,* for they were there at his own bidding. During the transfer of paroled officers that followed, many more runaways were taken to New York. According to eyewitness accounts of their arrival there, all the ships were densely crowded, 'packed together with two servants for each officer'. Ewald reported that the ship that carried the German officers also bore '143 officers' servants and camp followers among whom twenty-four had their wives and children'. To these were added another fifty people of both sexes whose faces were hidden. These, he surmised correctly, were American deserters and black runaways who were being spirited away to avoid retribution. Walter Harris was one of them; William Blue must have been another.[14]

The shock news from Yorktown that Cornwallis had lost the campaign for the South came as a terrible blow to runaways sheltering behind the British lines in New York. Worse was to come when the British government granted independence to the American colonies and sued for peace. The day the treaty was signed, 29 November 1782, a hastily written amendment was scribbled in the margin of Article Seven, to prohibit 'carrying away any Negroes or other property of the American Inhabitants'. One of the fugitive slaves behind the lines later recalled that the news of the peace 'diffused universal joy among all parties; except us, who had escaped from slavery and taken refuge in the English army'. Promises of freedom made by successive British commanders had been contingent on the British winning the war and retaining control of the colonies. Now that the British government had conceded the American colonies and signed a treaty that prohibited them from taking runaways out of America, those promises could not be considered binding. Unless the black allies behind the British lines had papers of emancipation, as very few did, they might expect to be returned to enslavement in perpetuity, for themselves, their children and their children's children.[15]

Patriot slave-owners came into the city freely, mingling with Loyalists in the streets of Manhattan. According to a Hessian officer, 'almost five thousand persons have come into this city to take possession again of their former property'. His figure may have been exaggerated, but there can be no doubt that a great many slave-owners gained entry into the British zone to recover their property. Without warning, runaways could find themselves knocked on the head, bound hand and foot, kidnapped and taken back to the place from whence they had fled.[16]

Few runaways behind the British lines were prepared passively to submit to re-enslavement. Having experienced years of freedom, they were horrified at the prospect of being turned over to their former masters. They vehemently refused 'to be delivered in so unwarrantable a manner', a Hessian officer noted in his diary. 'They insist on their rights under the proclamation.' Day and night they pressed their case with the British authorities to make good the promises of freedom and remove them from the clutches of their vengeful owners. Fortunately the British commander-in-chief lent a willing ear to their pleas. Sir Guy Carleton, who arrived in New York in May 1782, found the handover of the American colonies a repugnant duty that he undertook with as much dignity as he could muster; steadfastly he refused to renege on a debt of honour with regard to the proclamations of his predecessors. Quite simply, he was not prepared to meet the terms of the peace treaty when they became known in late March 1783. Indeed, he preferred his own interpretation of the words 'Negroes and other property of the American inhabitants'.[17]

As soon as the spring thaw began, Carleton sent a fleet to Nova Scotia carrying some 5000 refugees, including an unknown number of runaways. By the time the fleet had sailed, he was assailed by a cacophony of protest from state governors, delegates in Congress, and slave-owning individuals. 'They mean to make a clamour about the evacuation of New York', he told the judge advocate in England. Carleton instructed his officers that any black allies that had been within the British lines for a year or more were to be issued with a certificate of freedom. He then appointed commissioners from both the British and American forces to supervise the embarkation to ensure that no one without evidence of free status was allowed to depart.[18]

Outraged Virginians petitioned Congress to stop the embarkation of runaways, while the governor of Virginia, Benjamin Harrison, went one better. He complained directly to George Washington. 'I have but little expectation that many will be recovered', Washington replied. '[S]everal of my own are with the enemy, but I scarce ever bestow a thought on them; they have so many doors through which they can escape from New York.' Washington bestowed more thought on his own runaways than his letter to Harrison implied. He was anxious for their return and engaged the army contractor, Daniel Parker, to keep an eye out for his lost property. He forwarded a list of Harrison's runaways to Parker, together with the names of the slaves who had absconded from his cousin Lund. As for his own runaways he was 'unable to give you there descriptions; their names being so easily changed, will be fruitless to give you', he told Parker. 'If by chance you should come at the knowledge of any of them, I will be much obliged by your securing them so I may obtain them again.' In his capacity as Washington's slave catcher, Parker proved impotent. Three sailed away to Nova Scotia under his very nose carrying certificates of freedom signed by Brigadier General Samuel Birch, Commandant of the New York Garrison.[19]

The certificates of freedom typically stated that the bearer had 'reported to the British lines in consequence of the proclamations of Sir William Howe and Sir Henry Clinton' and therefore had permission to 'go to Nova Scotia or any where else he may think proper'. Even with the best intentions, the process of issuing certificates to thousands of runaways, who had first to be interrogated about their personal history, was chaotic and time-consuming. Terror and apprehension drove many to take their chances in embarking for Nova Scotia before they received certificates, travelling under the protection of departing Loyalists. When questioned they offered a variety of explanations as to their status. The story given by Jack Gordon, who was embarked on the *Polly*, was that his master had given him freedom at the siege of Charleston, though he had no papers to prove it.[20]

In early May, after two fleets had departed for Nova Scotia, Carleton and his entourage sailed up the Hudson River to Orangetown for a conference with General Washington. As the victorious commander, Washington opened the meeting by reiterating the resolution of Congress regarding 'the delivery of all Negroes and other property'. In response, the defeated Carleton indicated that in his desire for a speedy evacuation he had already sent off some 6000 refugees, including 'a number of Negroes'. Washington was almost certainly aware of this fact. Daniel Parker, his informal slave catcher, would have informed him that the fleet that had sailed in late April had carried hundreds of runaways, including Washington's own property. Nevertheless, if Washington knew, he was at pains to conceal this intelligence. Observers from both sides noted his consternation as he remonstrated with Carleton that the action was against the expressed provisions of the treaty. Calmly, Carleton offered the unapologetic explanation that the British government would never have agreed 'to reduce themselves to the necessity of violating their faith to the Negroes'. Warming to his subject, he further insisted that 'delivering up Negroes to their former masters ... would be a dishonourable violation of the public faith'. In the unlikely event that the British government placed a different construction on the treaty, he promised compensation would be paid to the owners, and to this end he had directed 'a register be kept of all the Negroes who were sent off'. Protesting, as he was bound to do, Washington understood the depth of feeling behind the words 'dishonourable violation of the public faith'. By the time the meeting came to its inconclusive end, he had privately conceded defeat. That night, Washington sat at his desk and wrote to Governor Harrison that he was now convinced 'the slaves who have absconded from their masters will never be restored to them'.[21]

The American commissioners appointed to supervise the British embarkations, including Daniel Parker, were frustrated nearly every time they attempted to retrieve known slaves. In a series of letters addressed to General Washington they indicated that while thousands had been sent off, they had been able to retrieve a mere seven. The transports they were permitted to inspect contained only a fraction of those departing, they complained, because they were prohibited from inspecting naval and military transports, as well as the many merchant vessels leaving the port. Black seamen, who made up about 10 per cent of the Royal Navy and its accompanying fleet of privateers, simply sailed away. There were plenty of military officers who took with them their black servants, suffering no scrutiny from the commissioners. Runaways were still on the musters of regiments when they departed. Nevertheless, the American commissioners continued until the end of October the fruitless task of supervising embarkations, when the inspections were finally abandoned. Subsequently, Washington was to characterise the whole exercise as 'little more than a farce'.[22]

It was not a farce for the few people the American commissioners did manage to remove from the ships. There was inevitable heartbreak when cases were disputed, usually the wives and children of runaways who had not come into the British lines within the prescribed twelve months and so were deemed to remain the 'the property of American subjects'. Dramas of grief and forced separation were played out every Wednesday when the board established to adjudicate disputed cases met at a Manhattan tavern. A ruling that children were not capable of responding to a proclamation meant that many orphans among the runaways in New York were likely to be reclaimed as property, unless they had been born within the British lines. Consequently, unaccompanied children and youths under the age of 15 were usually identified as the property of departing Loyalists on outgoing transports, even though there were no papers to prove it. In some cases, the relationship between adult and child was more equivocal. Caesar, a 'stout fellow', with an estimated age of 14, was embarked on the *Minerva* for Spithead, England, in August 1783 in the company of a Yorkshireman named John Watson, who claimed that 'he had brought him up'; an ambiguous explanation offered to deflect suspicion that the youth was a runaway.[23]

A war-weary George Washington finally laid claim to all of the United States of America on 25 November 1783. His satisfaction at victory was somewhat diminished by the magnitude of the Loyalist defection, which saw up to 60000 Americans take their leave. Just how many fugitive slaves had also gone, he had no way of knowing, but he was correct to assume that it was greater than the 3000 listed in the documentation the British commissioners later sent to Congress. Taking into account the people who had left from the southern ports, as well as from Boston and other northern ports, plus those in the army and navy, the number of runaways who had departed the American shore as free people must have been close to 9000.

With the city finally in his hands, General Washington led his army on a victory march through Manhattan streets packed with jubilant Patriots, who had flooded back into the city, their hats and bonnets adorned with ribbon cockades or sprigs of laurel. A week later, a spectacular display of fireworks was staged to celebrate victory. Roars of approval from the boisterous crowds wafted out to Staten Island, where the final British fleet lay waiting for a fair wind to take them to Nova Scotia. On board the *Danger* was Patrick Henry's runaway Ralph Henry, who would have seen Washington's triumphal fireworks light up the clear night sky. Also watching from the *Concord* on that still, cold night was Daniel, who had been enslaved on Washington's Mount Vernon plantation only three years before. That he had survived the war and was now leaving America as a free man was his own particular triumph.[24]

STARVING IN THE STREETS OF LONDON

London was the greatest city in the world in 1783, home to over 750 000 souls. The crush of humanity in its congested streets, with the cacophony of hawkers' cries, church bells, horses' hooves, wagon wheels, organ grinders, animal calls and a general hubbub of voices, presented bewildered newcomers with a violent assault on the senses. The greatest city in the world was also the most odiferous, its air polluted with coal dust and reeking with the stench from untreated human waste, rotting rubbish, slaughterhouses and tanneries. There were days when the city was completely enveloped in a dark suffocating miasma of fog mixed with coal ash. Animals left to decompose in the streets leached into the puddles of urine and stagnant water, and even a discarded human corpse might be found among the decaying detritus. Through this stinking, noisy wen threaded the city's *raison d'etre* and life-blood, the River Thames, carrying along 'all the drugs, minerals, and poisons, used in mechanics and manufacture, enriched with the putrefying carcasses of beasts and men; and mixed with the scourings of all the wash-tubs, kennels, and common sewers, within the bills of mortality', so Squire Matt Bramble observed in Smollett's *Humphrey Clinker*.[1]

The city was divided along an axis of east to west: brutal poverty and ostentatious wealth, bare subsistence and conspicuous consumption; The West End was a rapidly developing Mecca of theatrically designed shops that dazzled even the most sophisticated of visitors, as well as spectacularly grand houses. At the East End, the city disintegrated into an evil-smelling concentration of decrepit tenements in places such as the Minories, Wapping, St Katherine's-by-the-Tower, Whitechapel, Spitalfields, Shadwell, Limehouse, Ratcliffe Highway, Stepney, and Mile End New Town, all within spitting distance of the Pool of London, as the port was then known.

John Moseley arrived in this teeming and torrid metropolis in November 1783, having been discharged as crew from HMS *Loyalist*. He

*

was listed in the *Book of Negroes* as bound for Nova Scotia on the *Elijah* in October 1783, but he never took the voyage. Subsequent musters in the various settlements in Nova Scotia include no record of him. He had worked for some time in or near New York City's dockyards where he would invariably have come into contact with crews from British ships. Moseley appears to have befriended one of the black seamen, Amos Anderson, on the *Loyalist*, which regularly ran between New York and Charleston. With his connections, nothing could have been easier than jumping ship from the *Elijah* to sign on for the *Loyalist* before the latter left New York to return to England.[2]

John Moseley and Amos Anderson fetched up in the East End, where they competed with poor Londoners for space in the lodging-houses of Wapping. For sixpence a night, they could sleep head-to-toe with light-fingered strangers on vermin-infested straw pallets, or, if they had less than sixpence, they might take turn about with the prostitutes and their tricks, or else make do with a nest of loose straw beside the stinking privy. During the day, they and others like them jostled with the multitude in a labyrinth of narrow streets and laneways, dodging the wagons and hackney coaches, carrying slops, running errands, cajoling, begging or picking pockets. There was plenty of entertainment to be found. The noisy, serpentine streets were a theatre of curiosity where every form of human oddity was on display, along with a menagerie of performing animals. The theatre of cruelty was also very evident, with public executions on Tower Hill and at the regular Tyburn Fairs, located near present-day Marble Arch. The year Moseley arrived the first hangings took place outside the gates of Newgate Gaol. Gallows were prominently situated at sites along the Thames, especially Execution Dock at Wapping, where the bodies swaying from the gibbets were certain to arrest the attention of people arriving in the city. Lesser felons would be confined in stocks or flogged through the streets. Oblivion was never hard to find; one could get blind drunk on gin or rough cider for just tuppence.[3]

Danger was everywhere, particularly for stray black men. If the press-gangs were no longer active around the taverns and lanes, man-stealing was an ever-present threat for the black refugees. Within weeks of his discharge in London, Amos Anderson was shanghaied, hustled aboard a ship and taken to the West Indies to be sold. For Moseley, the fate of his shipmate must have been a cruel reminder that despite the ruling of Lord Mansfield in the Somerset decision, freedom for black men in London was a tenuous business. His distress must have been all the greater knowing that wages still due to Anderson remained unclaimed, while he had desperate need of the money. Apparently he had not heard of the Loyalist Claims Commission.

In an area known as Goodman's Fields, close by the Pool of London between the Tower and Whitechapel, a large group of black refugees rented space in the lodging-house of John Williams and Thomas Watkins. It was almost certainly these white landlords who alerted the black lodgers that Parliament had established a commission to inquire into the payment of compensation for losses incurred during the war and for property that had been confiscated. Five of the black lodgers submitted a joint petition to the Loyalist Claims Commission asking for relief from destitution, which plaintively declared that the cessation of war had brought 'hope of ease and plenty to most' but had rendered them 'unemployed, unprotected and homeless objects of poverty, want and wretchedness'. The petition was written by a prominent white Loyalist, Colonel Edward Fanning. Couched in the appropriate language of submission, it nonetheless expressed indignation that these black veterans had 'not had any reward, recompense or emolument whatever for such services ... loss and sufferings'.[4]

For their part, the commissioners were not impressed with these ragged black men and were inclined to regard them either as dupes or opportunists. The commissioners quickly perceived the claims to be a scam operated by the landlords Williams and Watkins on behalf of the refugees who lodged with them. Almost every petition that was submitted by a black claimant in September 1783 came with identical documentation to validate the loss of property, written and signed by the two landlords. 'The case of many of these black men is an absolute imposition', the commissioners stated in response to one such application; 'many of them pretend to have the same quantity of land which is written and valued and certified by John Williams and Thomas Watkins who have an interest in representing a falsity to us'. It was the opinion of the commissioners that if any money were awarded to the black claimants, 'probably these men are to have a considerable charge of it'. Nevertheless, they believed Colonel Fanning's recommendation to be genuine, and on the strength of his word alone they agreed to grant some financial compensation.[5]

Blank refusal was a more common response from the commissioners, who looked upon the black claimants as largely undeserving of compensation because they believed nearly all of them were slaves who had had the good fortune to be emancipated by the British. Typical was the man who applied to the commission in his own hand in November 1783. He had lost land and a small house in America 'and dare not return again to that country'. In a strange new environment, with a wife to maintain, he was unable to get a position and found himself 'reduced to great poverty'. Even though the petitioner said he had recently been baptised and understood the nature of the oath he had taken, the commissioners refused to believe him. They decided he had been a slave emancipated by the war and that was reward enough. The choleric response of the commissioners to the application of another barely literate applicant gave the flavour of their general view of many claims. 'Instead of suffering by the war, he gained by it for he is in a much better country where he may with industry get his bread', the commissioners declared, 'where he can never more be a slave, for notwithstanding he pretends to have been born free we cannot easily give credit to it being the common tale of them'.[6]

That black claimants were given short shrift by the Loyalist Claims Commission was not entirely due to the class and racial biases of the commissioners. The documentation the commission required, such as written proof of property losses and certificates of status, was rarely provided by the black claimants; when it was, the commissioners had reason to be suspicious. Anyone without supporting testimonials from illustrious British officials had poor prospects before the commission, even when they did not lodge with Messrs Williams and Watkins. One-third of the black claimants were left empty-handed. Somewhat grudgingly, the commissioners allowed twenty-six of the black claimants temporary relief payments of between £5 and £20. Four claimants were awarded lifetime pensions, the largest pension of which, £18 per annum, went to Shadrack Furman, who recounted to the commissioners an astonishing tale of woe. His troubles had begun in 1781, when Benedict Arnold invaded Virginia. Furman had provided the army with accommodation and supplies and, as a consequence, enraged Patriots burned his house and crops. His petition detailed how he was tortured for information, then tied to a post and given 500 lashes, finally being left for dead, blinded in both eyes, with one leg nearly severed by an axe and 'so much impaired from the wounds in his head received from them, that he is sometimes bereft of reason'. Blind, crippled, friendless and impoverished, Furman was reduced to playing the fiddle in London's streets, 'entirely depending on the charity of the public' to provide for himself and his wife. Another successful petitioner pleaded that 'I endeavoured to get work but cannot'. 'I am really starvin about the streets, having nobody to give me a morsel of bread and dare not go home to my own country again.' This man's account of his hair-raising escape to join the British forces was dismissed by the commissioners as 'a very incredible story ... the sort of thing which would have pretty strong proof to support but he not only gives no proof but admits he cannot therefore we pay no credit to the story'. When he returned with a letter from Lord Dunmore to vouch for his 'incredible story', he was awarded £10.[7]

Whatever the circumstances that deposited black refugees in England, within a year or so of arrival almost all were out of work and living by their wits on the crowded London streets. The distant world to which they had been carried, with or without their consent, proved to be an alien and uncongenial environment. It was a desperate predicament to be unemployed in England at a time when the labour force was swamped with demobilised soldiers and sailors. The black refugees from America who flooded into the city had no support networks on which they could draw, and their situation was worsened because they did not fit easily into the existing framework of the Poor Laws. A pauper was required to return to his 'parish of settlement' before being entitled to receive relief. The Scots and Irish were sent back to their country of birth, yet it was neither practical nor desirable to return refugees to America. Instead, poor blacks were 'unfeelingly driven from place to place by parish officers', according to one observer.[8]

The problem was that there was no work by which the black refugees could earn their bread in the London of 1783. Of the forty-five black claimants, only a few indicated that they had paid employment. Those who had come to England as servants to officers and then lost their positions when the officers resigned their commissions were in dire straits. Massive demobilisation of hundreds of thousands of veterans had created fierce competition for unskilled employment, and black refugees from America, with work experience confined to plantation slavery and support services for the war effort, had few saleable skills. The story told of 'starvin about the streets' was the experience of the great majority of black claimants. Like Shadrack Furman with his fiddle, many black refugees found themselves 'depending on the charity of the public' to survive. Those without musical skills were thrown back on their light fingers and resources of guile.[9]

Contemporary estimates of the number of people in this marginal, impoverished community were wildly unreliable. In 1772, Edward Long gave an estimate of 3000 for the black community in England, which he quickly revised upward to 15000 to correspond with the figure cited during the Somerset case. This landmark legal case focused on the rights of the slave James Somerset, who had escaped from his master in London during 1771, but was recaptured and forced aboard a ship to be taken to Jamaica. With help from the prominent humanitarian and anti-slavery campaigner, Granville Sharp, Somerset obtained a writ of *habeas corpus* to prevent his forcible removal to Jamaica. In what became a high-profile case, the Lord Chief Justice, Lord Mansfield, ruled that no master could ever take a slave out of the country to be sold abroad. This decision effectively meant that slavery in England, while still technically legal, had become impractical. The lobby for the West India slave trade, of whom Long was the chief spokesperson, inflated the number of slaves in England because it wanted to frighten the English into believing they could be swamped by idle and indigent blacks freed from slavery. In 1788 this figure was further inflated to 40000 by another West India lobbyist.[10]

Greater London was undoubtedly the site of the densest concentration of the black diaspora in the 1780s, with a black population of around 10000. London parish records indicate that apart from a large number of servants living in Westminster, most were living by or near the river, particularly in the East End, but also south of the river in Deptford. Most of the parishes in these areas registered between 1 per cent and 3 per cent of baptisms as being of people identified as black, predominantly adults, while in a small parish like the Minories, fast by the Tower, the proportion jumped to 16 per cent. Black baptisms were also a feature in Marylebone, a huge parish in the west of London, where black servants were employed and where there was also a large workhouse founded in 1751. The parish of St Giles in Soho also had a workhouse, an indication of the growing impoverishment of both these once fashionable areas.[11]

Some members of the black community of London were enslaved. In the late eighteenth century slaves in England were almost always domestic servants brought from the Caribbean and America, or imported direct from Africa by wealthy English families. A decade after the Somerset judgment, people who had once been slave-servants could be found living independently in the poorest parishes of London. Between 1775 and 1782, the number of black servants baptised in Marylebone declined, while at the same time baptisms of black adults became a feature of parishes such as Wapping and Stepney, probably because the population was gravitating towards the river where greater opportunities existed for obtaining casual work. Many of these had escaped from domestic slavery, or been manumitted, or simply turned out of doors by owners who realised their property had lost saleable value. Those who remained in service may have been technically slaves, working for no wages, since Mansfield had ruled only that slaves could not be shipped out of England, not that they were entitled to be paid for their service.[12]

No one knew just how many slave-servants there were in the 1780s, as the line between employment and enslavement was blurred. Famous black servants, such as Francis Barber who worked for Samuel Johnson, were certainly free, while others were just as certainly enslaved. Evidence of black servants can be found in criminal indictments of the period. The man identified as the 'bell wether' of the mob that forced its way into Newgate Gaol and liberated the prisoners during the Gordon Riots in June 1780 was a black servant who was brought to England from America in 1774. Another prominent rioter was a black servant to a lawyer in Westminster. Whether these two were enslaved or free was never established.[13]

The ambiguous status of servant or slave was also an issue in the case of the young man known only as Caesar, who was convicted at the Kent Assizes in March 1786 of stealing 4s 4d. His slave name and the absence of a surname strongly implied that he was household chattel. In one of the court records he was described as a servant, although this may have been an error, since at his indictment Caesar was designated a labourer, the usual label for a male with no specific employment. The most plausible interpretation is that he had recently been a slave-servant and was now unemployed. Caesar's trial record provided no indication of his origin. His was the most ubiquitous male name for chattel in English slave societies. But while the name indicates that he was one among the millions of African victims of the slave trade, it provides no clues to his origins. Most probably he was either an enslaved person brought to England by a refugee Loyalist, or else a runaway who came as part of the final British evacuation, maybe as a servant.[14]

There were more than a dozen men called Caesar listed in the *Book of Negroes* during the evacuation from New York in 1783. Only one was evacuated to England, a 'stout fellow' embarked for Spithead, in the service of a John Watson who, as mentioned above, was said to have 'brought him up', an ambiguous claim no doubt offered to deflect the suspicion that the youth was a runaway. The age given for Caesar at embarkation in New York was said to be 14, which was probably the guesswork of the commissioners. The estimated ages in the *Book of Negroes* were wildly unreliable, so the 'stout fellow' said to be 14 years old in August 1783 could have been older and might well have been the same person who was sentenced at the Kent Assizes three years later, when his age was estimated to be 22.[15]

At the time of his trial, Caesar lived in the parish of St Paul, Deptford, an impoverished maritime district of London with a rapidly expanding black population that was in some ways very different to the poor East End parishes where most factories, workshops, finishing, and dirty trades were to be found. Deptford, on the other hand, was geared towards its agricultural hinterland of market gardens, as well as servicing the needs of the Royal Navy. It was home to the huge Naval Dockyard, where warships were built, refitted and supplied. It was also in close proximity to Greenwich. Many merchant ships moored off Deptford, even though the cargo had to be unloaded up-river on the north side of the river where the customs houses were. Those inhabitants of Deptford engaged in river-side work, if they were not employed by the navy, needed to travel across the river. But for sailors, Deptford was a logical place of residence and the evidence suggests that most of the black Deptfordians were seamen.

Even before the American Revolution Deptford was developing a noticeable black presence, consisting largely of seamen. In the years following the Somerset decision in 1772, London became a magnet for slave runaways because of the increased anonymity and chances for employment provided by this huge centre of trade and industry, far away from their former masters. Word was carried from port to port in the Atlantic that slaves who reached England could not be returned against their will. Ironically, the vehicle for freedom was often a slave ship. African-American and African-Caribbean men, often runaways, joined ships heading for England, taking the place of the large number of European seamen who had deserted. African seamen, whose maritime expertise saved them from being sold into the American and Caribbean markets, were employed as sailors, interpreters, cooks, sentinels and stewards on slaving vessels, especially the Kru from Sierra Leone and the Fante sailors from the Gold Coast. These African seamen may have crossed the Atlantic many times, were well adapted to European ways and usually spoke a hybrid form of a European language. Like the runaway slaves from the Americas these African sailors were also to be found eking out a precarious existence in Deptford.[16]

Among the motley crew at Deptford were black mariners from the Royal Navy. Brutal and coercive though service in His Majesty's Navy could be, it had appeal for men of the African diaspora. As well as the lure of prize money and pensions, the navy provided a measure of protection against man-stealers and slave-owners as the British authorities generally refused to surrender slaves working aboard their ships. During the Seven Years' War the British recruited black men as cooks, musicians and sailors. The most famous black man of the age, anti-slavery campaigner Gustavus Vassa (known to us by the name Olaudah Equiano), served on board a British warship as an officer's slave-servant, and took part in engagements as a powder monkey. In the same war, the New Yorker, William Blue, was serving on board warships as a marine and had probably also served as an able seaman. Indeed, both men were involved in the invasion of Belle Isle. Equiano's best-selling autobiography tells a very similar story to Blue's, although it is more articulate. He described how his ship *Ætna* went into Spithead to join a 'large fleet that was thought to be intended against the *Havannah*, but about that time the king died: [which] caused our ship to be stationed at Cowes in the Isle of Wight till the beginning of the year sixty-one'. In March, he explained, his ship again received orders to fit out for another expedition. 'When we got ready, we joined a very large fleet at Spithead, commanded by Commodore Keppel, which was destined for Belle-Isle, and with a number of transport ships with troops on board to make a descent on the place.' Both Blue and Equiano saw action in this campaign.[17]

During the American Revolution, the Royal Navy and the accompanying fleet of privateers vigorously recruited seaman all along the American seaboard, with ships' masters and press-gangs actively recruiting black runaways because they were less likely to desert than white seamen. The port towns along the coast of Massachusetts and Connecticut were persistently raided for skilled slave seaman and there was a ready pool of skilled maritime workers in Virginia and South Carolina who willingly fled enslavement to join the Royal Navy. Nearly every ship in the British fleet in America carried at least a handful of black crew and some had as many as 20 per cent, while on privateers the percentage could be even higher. Numerous black men serving in the British fleet began to appear in the London baptism registers during the American Revolution. In the period immediately after the war, as thousands of African-American seamen were discharged, the two Deptford parishes registered a tenfold increase in the number of black adult baptisms.[18]

John Williams had recently been baptised in Deptford when he came before the Kent Assizes in August 1784 charged with stealing a cask of wine, two silver spoons, a greatcoat and 20 shillings. He was hardly more than a boy and this was his second offence. The previous December he had been charged with stealing clothes, which he had given to another boy who was two years older. In his defence Williams had said 'this lad was a ship mate of mine, we came up together from Plymouth on Saturday night'. Williams had secured a job as a servant in a house in Deptford but his mate had not, so he persuaded Williams to steal clothes from the house with the intention of pawning them. For this crime Williams had been sentenced to a public whipping and then imprisoned for a week in Newgate, while his companion had been punished with fourteen years transportation. At his second trial a year later, when he was fifteen, Williams was treated more severely. The sentence was death, later commuted to transportation.[19]

He was by no means the only black seaman to fall foul of the law; many were indicted and tried for remarkably similar crimes. In May 1782, the black sailor John Martin was caught red-handed just as he was about to exit a London house with a bundle of clothes. Thomas Orford was indicted for stealing items of clothing from the clothes-line of the house of a Strand tailor in July 1784. When challenged by the watchman, Orford 'spoke in broken English' protesting that he was only taking the clothes into the country to iron them. In court he said that he came from on board ship and that a man gave him a pint of beer to carry the clothes to a house in the country. George Francisco was a homeless seaman of 19, who was tried at the Old Bailey in December 1784 for stealing clothing and money from a shop where he had been allowed to shelter from the bitter cold. In his account of himself, Francisco claimed to have spent three years in a French prison (1781–83), before being repatriated to England, where he was able to claim prize money, which indicates that he had been captured by the French allies of the Americans aboard a British ship. When 16-year-old James Williams was tried at the Old Bailey for the theft of clothing and shoes in May 1785, he said he was on an errand to deliver letters from the captain of a West India ship.[20]

Many in the black maritime community were like these convicted felons, homeless and in desperate straits, still waiting on their wages and prize money. Whatever their loyalties, they had not always freely chosen England as their destination. As one discharged seaman lamented to the Loyalist Claims Commission, he had little say in the dramatic life changes that had uprooted him from America and deposited him in England where 'I got nothing to help me and my wife after leaving what little I had behind me'. Yet another runaway from Boston, recently discharged from the navy, told the commission that he had not been paid for his previous service because 'when he went to Broad Street to receive [his wages] they told him it had been paid to some persons who had forged his name'. The commissioners dismissed this claim as 'incredible', yet this was the very same story Amos Anderson recounted to a judge at the Old Bailey in April 1784.[21]

By a stroke of luck, Anderson had escaped from his re-enslavement and got a berth on a ship from Rhode Island to arrive in England in March 1784. He immediately went to the Naval Office to claim his wages, only to find that someone had defrauded him. He was able to identify the impostor, a man who was arrested in Wapping under the name of John Shore. At his trial the captain of the *Loyalist* gave evidence that he knew the accused man well, saying 'he came on board as John

Moseley'. The captain further testified that Anderson and Moseley had applied together for the certificates to claim their wages after the ship arrived in England at the end of November 1783 and that Moseley returned to the *Loyalist* in late December to get a certificate for Anderson's wages for an earlier voyage between Charleston and New York in 1780. Explaining that Anderson was sick in Wapping, Moseley induced the captain to sign the certificate to say that Anderson had not deserted. He was then able to claim Anderson's wage. Even though Moseley had changed his name, he had not moved away from Wapping, which was where Anderson tracked him down. Moseley, who called no one in his own defence, was found guilty and sentenced to death.[22]

A common complaint of those who applied to the Loyalist Claims Commission was that they had been forced to leave their wives and families behind and they lacked the wherewithal to be reunited with them. Since the black refugees came to England as seamen or officers' servants or soldiers, the cohort was almost exclusively male, in contrast to those who went to Nova Scotia, nearly half of whom were women. The addition of thousands of male refugees from America made for a dramatic gender imbalance within the black community in London that was already dominated by seamen from Africa and the West Indies. In parishes such as Stepney and Wapping there were four black men for every woman. In Deptford, the ratio was 16 to 1. About a quarter of the black claimants to the Loyalist Claims Commission indicated that they had married in England, and the implication was that their wives were white Englishwomen. Parish records and other sources reveal no stigma attached to black men in the late eighteenth century, at least among the poor, as evidenced by the high level of interracial marriage. It took a rabid apologist for slavery, such as Edward Long, to see the prevalence of mixed racial marriages as objectionable. It was the fault of degraded lower class women, he said, who were 'remarkably fond of the blacks, for reasons too brutal to mention'.

Long feared that within a few generations miscegenation would 'spread so extensively, as even to reach the middle, and then the higher orders of the people, till ... every family catches infection from it'. His racist invective pinpointed a key issue for people of the African diaspora in late eighteenth-century England: they were unlikely to perpetuate themselves as a distinct community. Whereas Long saw the influx of black men contaminating English blood so that eventually everyone would be the same corrupted type, others understood black people would be completely assimilated into the dominant racial group. As a friend of Dr Johnson observed, all this racial mixing was 'preparing us for the moment when we shall all be made one fold under one shepherd'.[23]

Not everyone was as sanguine as Dr Johnson and his circle about the large numbers of indigent black men making their appearance on the streets of London. The West India interests were quick to draw attention to the hopeless plight of those who had escaped the paternalistic benefits of slavery, issuing dire warnings of the threat to the property of white Londoners, despite the fact that the war's end had reduced many times more white men and women to crime or beggary. The very harsh winter of 1784–85 was particularly cruel for an indigent black community struggling to survive on whatever could be begged, borrowed or stolen. Poor Law restrictions were relaxed in some parishes, such as Marylebone and Wapping, to allow starving black people access to food and shelter. It was too little, too late. In December 1784 three young black men died in a workhouse in Wapping.[24]

The plight of indigent black people in London became a matter of public concern on 5 January 1786, when the *Public Advertiser* reported that a gentleman had authorised a baker in the city to give out quarter loaves of bread to 'every black in distress'. That same gentleman was taking subscriptions to assist this purpose. Five days later he met at a coffee house with several other gentlemen – all prominent individuals and known philanthropists, including the chairman and a director of the Bank of England – to form the Committee for the Relief of the Black Poor. The driving force was Jonas Hanway, a man already famous for his concern for the poor. Hanway first thought that the subjects for charity were Lascar seamen from the East India ships, but after surveying the people who had applied, the committee discovered that the overwhelming majority were refugees from America, at least half of them sailors. This understanding of the problem gave an additional impetus to their philanthropic concern. As one correspondent to the *Public Advertiser* pointed out on 19 January 1786, these black refugees had a special claim on British justice. Not only had they 'served Britain', by fighting 'under her colours', they had done so at considerable risk to themselves: 'having quitted the service of their American masters, ... [they depended] on the promise of protection held out to them by British governors and commanders'. Such loyal allies could not be left to 'perish by famine and cold, in the sight of that people for whom they have hazarded their lives, and even (many of them) spilt their blood', the writer continued, 'because they are unfriended and unknown'. Another correspondent went so far as to suggest that Lord Cornwallis should 'exert himself to make relief permanent to the poor remains of his sacrifice in Virginia'.[25]

The direct appeal to Cornwallis was not so very far-fetched. In facilitating the flight of enslaved African-Americans, British generals such as Cornwallis and Carleton understood their actions might serve as moral redemption from the ignominy of defeat. They had nothing to gain in protecting and evacuating their black allies; by not repatriating runaways to their former owners they opened themselves to charges of duplicity and dishonour. On the other side of the ledger they accumulated moral capital just when national self-regard was at a particularly low ebb. So it was that a decade later, Prime Minister William Pitt instructed the United States' emissary, John Adams, that the evacuation of runaway slaves was a moral decision, taken according to the dictates of the laws of humanity, which constituted a higher authority than the dictates of a treaty that his government had signed. In its steadfast refusal to abide by the conditions of the Treaty of Paris, the British government provided the Americans with a rationale for resisting the repayment of pre-war debts amounting to a staggering £5 million.[26]

That material benefit might be sacrificed for moral satisfaction indicated a significant shift in British thinking, which had been taking place ever since Lord Mansfield had made his ambiguous judgment in the Somerset case that slaves in England might possess the rights of Englishmen. His decision led intellectuals in Britain to an intensified self-scrutiny about the imperial enterprise, in which complicity in slavery was seen to have sullied the moral character of the nation. As tension with the American colonies mounted, they began to articulate views about slavery that would distinguish the British from the slave-owning American colonists. It was during the war with America that Granville Sharp, the champion of Somerset, put forward the view that the slave trade was a national disgrace and the emblem of imperial tyranny, which undermined the nation's claim to integrity. The notion that slavery was an institution inconsistent with British law and repugnant to British sensibility was increasingly voiced as an index of national virtue, especially in the face of ignominious defeat. Sharp went so far as to suggest the disastrous war was a form of divine punishment for Britain's complicity in the slave trade. In the wake of an unpopular and ultimately disastrous war, benevolence towards runaway slaves had a critical role to play in maintaining national pride and integrity. Since the impoverished blacks of London were the closest many people might come to victims of the abhorrent trade in slaves, the ready response to their plight should be understood as an aspect of incipient abolitionism in English society.[27]

By April 1786, the Committee for the Relief of the Black Poor had raised close to £900. Donors included the Duchess of Devonshire, the Countess of Salisbury, the Countess of Essex, the Marchioness of Buckingham, and the leader of the Government, William Pitt. William Wilberforce and Granville Sharp, who were to achieve prominence the following year as leaders of the London Abolition Society, were among the subscribers to the appeal, while the largest single donation came from the most vocal source of anti-slavery opinion, the Society of Friends. The committee hired a room in the White Raven in Mile End and another at the Yorkshire Stingo on Lisson Green in Marylebone, which they kept open for several hours each day to distribute relief. Through newspapers and word of mouth, impoverished blacks were directed to apply at these places to get broth, a piece of meat, and a twopenny loaf. In the first few months they served over 200 people each day, many of them very ill.

To extend their philanthropy, the committee also established a hospital in Warren Street. This was a curious choice of location, as it bordered Fitzrovia and Marylebone, far removed from the centre of the black population in the East End where most of the suffering was occurring. Perhaps one of the patrons of the committee, like the Duchess of Devonshire, owned property there. The hospital took in some fifty people suffering from various fevers, venereal disease, rheumatism, consumption, inflammation of the breast and terrible ulcerations. It was apparent that illness was often a consequence of poor black people having to pawn their shoes, shirts and jackets and being exposed to the elements without warmth or shelter. Individuals were given straw and blankets, and sometimes they were provided with lodgings. A few sailors were outfitted and sent to sea, while three people were given passage back to the West Indies. One woman was returned to America.[28]

As news of the Committee for the Relief of the Black Poor spread, the number of needy attending the White Raven and the Yorkshire Stingo rose dramatically. It soon became apparent that short-term relief was no answer to the entrenched problem of poverty among London's black community; the fundamental cause was chronic unemployment. Finding jobs for a few black seamen had no impact on the thousands of black refugees who arrived after 1783, when unemployment had already reduced many whites to beggary. The committee sought help from George Rose and Thomas Steele, secretaries of the Board of Treasury, both incipient abolitionists whose sympathy for the committee's work was known.[29]

From the time the Treasury became involved, food relief was replaced by a direct payment of sixpence a day, paid weekly out of Treasury coffers. Although this handout was scarcely enough for subsistence, the provision of financial relief without any work requirement was very rare. It was a measure of the particular humanitarian concern that Rose and Steele felt for the black refugees that this system was implemented, as they demonstrated no inclination to provide relief payments to London's white poor. When it became apparent that many of the black refugees were unhappy at finding themselves in a destination they had not chosen, the idea took root that the most appropriate response to their plight was to relocate them to 'such a place as may put them in a condition of getting their bread in freedom and comfort'.[30]

4

BACK TO AFRICA

Among the many disagreeable aspects of the revolt of the American colonies was that it put an abrupt end to the traffic in convicts whereby some 50 000 people were transported to the American colonies as indentured labourers. It had been a lucrative business for tobacco merchants like Duncan Campbell who contracted to transport the convicts on his outbound ships and sell them into indenture for seven years in the colonies of Maryland and Virginia, returning to England with a cargo of tobacco. For Campbell, the war had been an economic disaster. It also had disastrous consequences for Britain's inadequate gaols since the courts continued to dole out sentences of transportation to America as if nothing had changed.

Under the draconian sentencing regime of the day, death was the penalty for some 200 crimes, most against property, and public hangings were a common feature of life in London. As the numbers of men and women facing execution spiralled upward, the legal fraternity became increasingly squeamish about their city festooned with gibbeted corpses. The Transportation Act of 1719 had authorised a sentence of transportation beyond the seas for those pardoned of capital offences, and this was liberally applied to reprieve about half the number of felons sentenced to the gallows. In addition, transportation was given as the initial sentence, instead of being reserved for a conditional pardon.[1]

When the black sailor John Martin appeared at the Old Bailey on 3 July 1782, justice was perfunctory. The owner of the house told the judge and jury how he had apprehended Martin with four overcoats, several waistcoats and a pair of breeches all of which he valued at 68 shillings. No statement was recorded in Martin's defence. For Justice Buller and the Middlesex jury this ought to have been a clear-cut matter: larceny over the value of 40 shillings was a capital offence. For whatever reason the jury, however, saw fit to exercise discretion and found Martin part guilty, thus placing the value of stolen goods below the 40 shilling

*

threshold for the death penalty. Consequently, he was sentenced to seven years' transportation rather than the gallows. Transportation to where, exactly, no one could hazard a guess.[2]

Every kind of carceral institution was overflowing with felons sentenced to transportation with nowhere to go and an ever-increasing number of debtors. As the prison reformer John Howard discovered in 1777, it was because of the various laws that dealt with debtors that the prisons were full to capacity; a problem exacerbated by the fact that wives and family could accompany debtors to prison. While imprisoning debtors caused chronic overcrowding, the hiatus in penal transportation placed an enormous pressure on a system already in crisis. Repeated calls for local authorities to build new gaols or expand old ones fell on deaf ears, while the central government was wrestling with a huge deficit and could not commit resources to the construction of two large prisons promised for London.[3]

In 1776, the Parliament agreed that the hulks of decommissioned warships could be used for convicts awaiting transportation, which they saw as a temporary expedient to last no more than two years, in full expectation that 'the usual mode of transportation might again be adopted'. Of necessity, Duncan Campbell had diversified his business interests and he had been contracted to supply the *Justinia* in August 1776, with an initial contract for 120 prisoners at £32 per annum for each prisoner. Six months later the contract was amended for Campbell to supply the hulk *Censor*, confining 120 more prisoners at £28 per annum. These two hulks were moored in the Thames, off Woolwich, where the felons were put to work raising sand and gravel from the bed of the river, and later on construction work on the Royal Arsenal. The concept of punishment by hard labour in the service of the state had always been resisted, although some of the bridewells had incorporated work approaching the factory system for paupers and minor criminals. The idea that discipline and hard labour were valuable tools for reforming the criminal mind was new and in this respect Campbell's project incorporated the most advanced penological thought of the day. Convicts themselves viewed the idea with such horror that some even petitioned to be hanged rather than serve a sentence on the hulks. Six years later, the two hulks with 450 convicts were still in the Thames, where they continued to alarm Londoners as the source of runaway felons and contagious diseases.[4]

✳

Two hulks made little difference to the overcrowded and parlous state of the prisons. When John Martin was sentenced in 1782, he joined thousands already under sentence of transportation, who were struggling for survival in fetid and disease-ridden jails. Eighteenth-century prisons were run on a private-enterprise basis. The prison governor and the turnkeys made their money by selling accommodation, procuring sexual favours, dispensing gin, accepting bribes and charging admission fees to a curious public. Most notorious was London's Newgate, an over-crowded, stinking cesspit that had been the focus of incendiary fury in the Gordon Riots. By the time Martin was received into Newgate, the prison had been rebuilt, but it was no less foul than before the rioters burnt it down. Its population had almost doubled without the jail being increased in size. Little had changed since John Howard had condemned Newgate in 1777. Poverty-stricken prisoners like Martin were held in disgusting conditions in the common wards. There were no beds or bedding, no proper sanitary arrangements, no medical attention and next to no food, except for the prison issue of a three-halfpenny loaf supplemented by charitable donations and a weekly ration of meat of a highly dubious quality. A prisoner had to depend for clothing, food, bedding and money on bribes being taken into the prison by the visitors who streamed into the jail. Without any work or exercise, the sole distractions for the prisoners were sex, drinking and gambling, all of which were rife within the walls of Newgate.[5]

During the day, the prison thronged with families, curious strangers, hawkers, prostitutes and accomplices. Wives managed to hide and stay overnight with their imprisoned husbands, pets were kept, spirits flowed freely (as long as one could pay), and sexual activity of all persuasions was openly indulged. With its rudimentary sleeping arrangements and unsanitary conditions, Newgate was only marginally worse than the poorest areas of London, the only real differences being that it was more densely crowded and closely confined. John Howard revisited the new jail in 1783 and was shocked to find that the stench of the prison over-whelmed him, just as it had six years earlier, while the sanitary condi-tions continued to breed epidemic disease. He warned that without more care, the prisoners would be in great danger of a deadly outbreak of typhus, a dangerously debilitating condition that caused high fever, vomiting and haemorrhaging from the gums, nostrils, mouth, which could readily spread into the rest of the London population. Although Newgate had an infirmary, medical practitioners could rarely be induced to enter it. The sick and dying were left untended. The only time the keeper of Newgate paid any attention was when a burial was required. As a stranger in England, without a family to provide the bare necessities of life such as food and bedding, Martin was condemned to a squalid existence that must have been utterly soul-destroying.[6]

Late in October 1782, Martin received a reprieve from the foul environment of Newgate when he was selected to go aboard the *Den Keyser* at Portsmouth. This ship had been chartered to take forty men and women to the island of Goree off the west coast of Africa. Earlier that year, another 350 convicts who had been reprieved on condition they become soldiers were formed into two independent companies and landed at the slave-trading fort of Cape Coast Castle in present-day Ghana. Supposedly, they were to defend Britain's slave-trade interests against attack by the Dutch, who had joined the alliance against England. Having been systematically starved by their corrupt and murderous commander, these soldier-felons created havoc at Cape Coast Castle. According to the governor of the castle, 'from the very day these convicts landed, their thoughts were turned upon rapine and plunder'. In a trice they picked the locks on the company storehouse and broke into the market stalls of the local Africans. Muskets and ammunition issued to them for an attack on the nearby Dutch settlement were sold to the Africans in exchange for brandy, while thirty convicts deserted to the Dutch and used their weapons to assist in the Dutch defence. Twenty-five men, who were embarked on a ship to go down the coast to relieve another fort, overpowered the crew and sailed away. Those who remained at Cape Coast were perpetually drunk. By the time the *Den Keyser* was ready to sail from England, only some thirty of the felon-soldiers were left alive at Cape Coast. Because the African Company, whose interests they were meant to protect, had lodged vigorous protest against receiving any more convicts, those on the *Den Keyser* were to be taken to Goree and dumped there.[7]

If Martin was anticipating, when he was embarked on board the *Den Keyser* on 1 November, a future of freedom and, possibly, a return to a long-lost homeland, he was to be sorely disappointed. He was seriously ill, probably suffering from typhus, which was rightly called 'gaol fever' for its highly contagious nature. Too sick to make the voyage and likely to infect the entire cargo, Martin was returned to gaol. Those who did make the journey had every reason to wish themselves back in the horrid confines of Newgate. They were landed without any provisions and no direction as to what was expected of them. The exasperated governor at Cape Coast Castle had no provisions to spare and ordered that they must look out for themselves or starve. He was not without sympathy, but at a loss for what to do for people 'landed naked and diseased upon the sandy shore ... seen dying upon the rocks or upon the sandy beach, under the scorching heat of the sun'. Three of the youngest and fittest male convicts did eventually manage to get back to England, where they were promptly arrested and retried for returning unlawfully from transportation; another hanging offence. Soon they were back in Newgate with Martin. Once more, these three were reserved as beneficiaries of the King's mercy and once more were sentenced to transportation to Africa.[8]

Sending convicts to Africa made a degree of economic sense. Slave ships from English ports usually sailed empty to the coast of Africa, so it would have been advantageous for them to be stocked with a profitable cargo of convicts, just as previously ships bound for America had carried convicts and returned with tobacco. Since 1776, however, legislation had made it impossible for a contractor to trade in the bodies of convicts, even though two illegal attempts were made to sell convicts in Baltimore during 1783. Contractors were no longer able to sell convict labour, nor could they transact with a convict to buy out servitude. Nevertheless, while convicts continue to be sentenced to transportation the potential for profiteering remained. Anthony Calvert of the slave-trading company Camden, Calvert and King was keen to be involved. The stumbling block was the refusal of the African Company to take any more convicts into its slave forts after the debacle at Cape Coast in 1782.

Despite the African Company's vehement opposition, the Home Office received unexpected support for an African solution from a previous governor at Cape Coast Castle, John Roberts, who put forward a radical plan to deport the country's accumulating felons. Recognising that 'the government must get rid of them some how or another', Roberts suggested that convicts should be sentenced to a life of hard labour on plantations established adjacent to Cape Coast Castle. 'There is not an island in the West Indies produces better cotton than we every day see growing spontaneously in Africa', he enthused. Land could be purchased cheaply from the free Africans who lived around the castle, and gangs of convicts could be set to clearing the ground for the cotton, under the supervision of drivers with whips. Essential to his scheme was the construction of a penal fortress with twenty strong, locked chambers each holding ten men under the surveillance of a driver armed with a musket. As well, there would have to be some authority invested with judicial power to hang any felon who tried to desert or shirk their work. 'No doubt many of them would soon die after they got there', he allowed, if not from fever then from hard labour under the harsh African sun. Still, he reasoned, 'this set of people are now got so numerous that it seems absolutely necessary for humanity to give way in some measure'.[9]

Roberts's utterly outlandish plan appears to have been taken seriously by the long-serving under-secretary of the Home Office, Evan Nepean. At the time that the Home Office was digesting Roberts's plan to turn convicts into plantation slaves at Cape Coast, Nepean was negotiating with Camden, Calvert and King to transport convicts to Cape Coast on the slave ship *Recovery*, then lying in the Thames. Arrangements were made with the Treasury to have convicts taken to Gravesend, where the *Recovery* was tendered with provisions for 150 convicts. When the judge advocate for the Home Office, Lord Sydney, proposed the plan to the committee of the African Company, they would not have a bar of it, insisting that more convicts 'would endanger their settlements'. Nepean was left holding a contract with Camden, Calvert and King. More pressure was applied to the committee of the African Company, of which Anthony Calvert was a member. Eventually it gave some ground; on 13 January 1785, some twenty-two convicts were loaded in the *Recovery* and shipped to Cape Coast Castle.[10]

Nepean then turned his attention to the island of Lemaine, about 400 miles up the Gambia River, thought to be able to sustain a settlement of some 4000 convicts. A convict settlement in the Gambia River was first mooted five years earlier by John Barnes, the then governor of Cape Coast Castle, who sent a description of Lemaine to the Home Office, emphasising that the area was extremely fertile, with good crops for animal foodstuffs. Nepean was moderately enthusiastic about the idea and it appears to have been revived by his friend, James Bradley, chief clerk to the newly formed India Board. Bradley had approached his two brothers about a business venture in Lemaine in late 1784, and subsequently informed Nepean that the Lemaine settlement could be organised and managed as a family enterprise. On 5 January 1785, Nepean authorised Richard Bradley to go to Gambia to negotiate the purchase of the island from its indigenous owners. At the same time the slave-traders Camden, Calvert and King indicated that they were eager to tender for the transport contract. Officials of the City of London were personally informed by Lord Sydney in January that convicts would indeed be sent to Africa. The judiciary swung into action to facilitate the process. On 3 February 1785 the convicted black sailor, Thomas Orford, appeared at the Old Bailey to have the destination for his sentence of transportation changed to Africa.[11]

It was apparent from the draft proposal for Lemaine that Lord Sydney sent to Treasury in February that the transported convicts were not to be put to work in any British enterprises on the West African coast, nor set to establishing cotton plantations. Instead, they would be left to their own devices, while provided with building materials, agricultural tools and seeds, to create some kind of a self-governing, self-sustaining society. An agent on an offshore vessel would be responsible for preventing them from interfering with the slave trade. The person appointed in this role was subsequently revealed to be the slave-trader Anthony Calvert, who held the contract to transport the convicts but otherwise had no interest in their welfare. The government's intention was to delay the voyage until the end of August or early September, after the rainy season had passed, and in the meantime to concentrate the designated convicts on one particular hulk. On 19 March, Duncan Campbell was able to inform Treasury that he had secured the hulk *Ceres* 'for a temporary reception of convicts under sentence of transportation to Africa' and that he had set about getting it ready. Campbell was well aware how eagerly prison governors across the country would embrace the offer of accommodation for their felons, advising the captain of the *Ceres* that the transportees 'will be forced upon us as quick as we can take them'. He also recognised that as soon the convicts discovered they were bound for Africa they would resist. 'I pray you as things are now situated to man your ships well for fear of any mutinous attempt', he instructed his captain.[12]

＊

Lord Sydney's determination that transportation would be resumed was a great relief to provincial officials in despair at the state of the country's prisons and the escalating rate of criminal convictions. A magistrate from the county of Lancaster reported to the House of Commons that the Manchester prison was so dreadfully overcrowded that it was a serious financial burden. Manchester was beset with unemployment as a result of the demobilisation around that city of four or five regiments, including the 4th, 47th and 63rd Regiments from America. This influx of idle men, suddenly cut loose from military discipline and without any paid employment, inevitably led to an increase in larceny and other crime. The city had no way of recouping the cost of incarcerating all these felons, the magistrate explained, because they were 'so closely ironed' they could not be put to work. Some convicts had been confined for three or four years waiting for transportation, and more were anticipated.[13]

One of the closely ironed felons in the Manchester jail was John Randall, aged 21, a black man from Connecticut. He had recently come from America as part of a regiment that had been demobilised and now 'lay about town'. Very likely, he had been a drummer with the 63rd Regiment of Foot. On 14 April 1785, Randall had been found guilty of stealing a watch-chain in the company of another black man named Charles Johnson. They were sentenced to transportation to Africa and sent immediately to join the *Ceres*.[14]

John Moseley had been in the condemned cells in Newgate Gaol for nearly a year when he reappeared at the Old Bailey on 3 March 1785 to have his death sentence commuted in favour of transportation to Africa. He must have been happy to be the subject of His Majesty's prerogative of mercy, but a sentence of transportation to Africa meant a separation as profound as death. While languishing in vile Newgate, Moseley managed to maintain a relationship with either his wife or a female inmate. There was no barrier to sexual intimacy in Newgate, and conception was a highly desirable outcome. For women prisoners in Newgate, being in a condition to 'plead the belly' was a significant weapon for the manipulation of mercy. A 'mulatto' baby of three months named Jane Moseley was baptised in the parish of Marylebone in November 1785. The child was almost certainly taken into Thomas Coram's foundling home of that parish, which took in infants from Newgate.[15]

✷

John Moseley, John Martin and Thomas Orford were among a hundred convicts from Newgate transferred to the *Ceres* in April 1785. Convicts were selected for the *Ceres*, the House of Commons was told, because they were judged to be 'of the most desperate and dangerous disposition, deserving for the sake of the public example of the greatest severity'. In May, George Francisco was among another group of convicts called before the bench of the Old Bailey to be assigned to transportation to Africa and sent to the *Ceres*. Caesar, sentenced to transportation in the Kent Assizes in the following March, was also put aboard the *Ceres*. From Winchester, a little to the north of Portsmouth, Janel Gordon was sent to the *Ceres*. He had been sentenced to transportation for stealing clothing. When Gordon was put aboard the *Ceres* he was judged to be around 50, the appropriate age range for the runaway from South Carolina called Jack Gordon listed in the *Book of Negroes* as embarked for Nova Scotia, but who had failed to arrive there.[16]

Duncan Campbell's mode of incarceration was more efficient and more humane than that of the keeper of Newgate. It was also much better regimented. The opportunity for intimate interaction was significantly more limited on the *Ceres*, if for no other reason than the cumbersome business of getting aboard a ship moored on the Thames. Nevertheless, families and friends hired lighters to take them to the hulks to bring money and clothing, as well as food to supplement the ration based on the naval allowance of bread, potatoes, pease soup, oatmeal, and small quantities of bullock head or beef. Though the food allowance was more substantial than in Newgate, the hulk diet was conducive to scurvy and other illnesses, compounded by damp, confined living arrangements. Between July and December 1785, sixty men died on the *Ceres*, almost certainly the result of typhus, which thrived among closely confined populations. John Moseley was mistakenly reported to have been among the deceased. He must have been misidentified as another black man, possibly John Randall's companion, Charles Johnson from Manchester. Moseley was still recorded on the *Ceres* a year later, but Johnson was not.[17]

All the convicted black men in London, with the exception of the youngest – John Williams, aged 16, and James Williams, aged 17 – had been put aboard the *Ceres* for Africa, regardless of the severity of their sentence. The eight black convicts waiting transportation to almost certain death represented 6 per cent of the men on the *Ceres*, in contrast to the prison population, where black felons constituted about 1 per cent. Perhaps they had been considered most likely to survive abandonment in Africa, although few commentators had any doubts that the place would make short work of one and all of those assembled on the *Ceres*. As Edmund Burke sardonically observed at the time Moseley received his commuted sentence, transportation to Africa was in reality nothing less than a 'singularly horrid' death sentence given 'after a mock display of mercy'. Gambia was 'the capital seat of plague, pestilence and famine', Burke told the House of Commons, where 'the gates of Hell were open day and night to receive the victims of the law'.[18]

Burke was one of the members of the House of Commons who had raised the alarm about the Lemaine proposal and persuaded Parliament to establish a committee to investigate the scheme in April 1785. One after another, experts told the committee that Africa was a place of disease and death. An army surgeon who had spent some years in Senegal said that two-thirds of the soldiers had died within a year of being sent there. Another who had lived on the west coast told the tale of 300 men who had been sent by the French up the Gambia River to work the gold mines. Only three had returned. Convicts sent to the Gambia River would 'either die from disease or at the hands of the natives', he stated flatly. The disastrous 1782 venture was still fresh in the memory of many witnesses, not just for the appalling mortality rate, but also for the riotous and undisciplined behaviour of the convicts that had caused problems with the Africans and destabilised the slave trade. Finally, and most damning of all, the committee heard evidence from Henry Smeathman, a botanist who had lived four years in Sierra Leone and married the daughters of two African chiefs. He reckoned that even if the convicts were landed 'in the most healthy part of the country', half would be dead within a month and 'only two at the most would be alive after six months'.[19]

Such evidence killed the Lemaine proposal. Nepean was more than a little disgruntled that 'from the mistaken humanity of some and the affected tenderness of others' the plan had foundered. He still had some cause for optimism as the committee had put forward another African possibility. Should the government persist in transporting criminals to Africa, the committee took the view that the only practical place would be one with no previous European contamination, 'between twenty and thirty degrees of south latitude'. They suggested a naval sloop, HMS *Nautilus*, be sent to examine Das Voltas Bay, the site of present-day Namibia. This region was seen to have many advantages. It had mineral deposits, the soil was fertile and the animals were plentiful. Convicts could be carried there on outward-bound slave ships that could then continue up the coast in their normal business. Encouraged that Africa had not been ruled out, Treasury drafted an order on 13 May 1786 appointing Africa as the place to dispatch 'sundry convicts under sentence to be transported to parts beyond the seas, still to be conveyed on transports', to which was attached a list of names that was drawn up while the committee remained in session.[20]

Although Lord Sydney remained committed to the African solution, he allowed himself to consider an even more radical proposition to create a convict settlement at Botany Bay, an impossibly remote place 13 000 miles distant, on the coast of the isolated southern continent that the explorer James Cook had named New South Wales. This spot was recommended by a refugee Loyalist from New York, James Matra, who had been a midshipman on Cook's voyage of discovery. It was after Matra's evacuation from America, with his prospects for advancement growing dimmer by the day, that he began to promote New South Wales as a wonderful new site for an imperial enterprise where Loyalists might be settled. At Lord Sydney's prompting, he incorporated convicts into the scheme, envisaged not as plantation slaves but as free yeoman farmers, provided with a small grant of land and the tools for its cultivation. Matra made three separate appearances before the parliamentary committee to explain his scheme. Neither Sydney nor the members of the House of Commons were much impressed. The obvious drawback was the absence of any established trading enterprise that could easily incorporate convict transportation. No trading ships were outbound for remote New South Wales, and without a lengthy detour to China or India, prohibited to most by the East India Company's monopoly, they would return with either a worthless cargo or no cargo at all.[21]

Lord Sydney had not entirely jettisoned Matra's scheme. In January 1786, Under-Secretary Nepean made a tentative request to Duncan Campbell that he should cost the transport of some 600 convicts to Botany Bay, as well as feeding and clothing them for a year and equipping them with farming tools. Campbell told Nepean that the journey would take fifteen months. Given that the ships would come back empty, the figure would exceed £50 per capita, he calculated, although this sum might be defrayed somewhat if the ships were to call at China on their return. With that monstrous expense in mind, Nepean's gaze remained firmly fixed on Africa. In June he was making arrangements with Camden, Calvert and King to ship 1000 convicts, of whom 150 were to be women, to Das Voltas Bay.

Lord Sydney was not the only prominent Englishman eyeing the coast of Africa as a place of settlement. The mercurial botanist Henry Smeathman, who had given damning evidence on the Lemaine proposal, was energetically promoting the possibilities of an agricultural settlement on the Sierra Leone River to produce export crops for Atlantic markets. This was the idea he presented to Granville Sharp, after failing to sell the plan to a raft of other potential backers, including Benjamin Franklin and the King of Sweden. Sharp in turn recommended Smeathman to the Committee for the Relief of the Black Poor, who were casting about for a suitable location to repatriate their impoverished charges. In order to win over the committee, Smeathman rhetorically recast his commercial proposal as an opportunity to create a 'Province of Freedom', under the protection of the British, to compete with the slave trade, as well as provide an alternative economic base in Africa where the black refugees could make 'a comfortable livelihood and secure relief from their former sufferings'. As a beacon of liberty, the colony would gradually absorb its slave-trading neighbours and 'change them into subordinate free states' and, by offering 'a sanctuary for the oppressed people of colour', would gradually abolish the slave trade. Neither Sharp nor members of the committee thought to ask Smeathman why, if he were so confident of a settlement on the west coast of Africa, he had given such damning evidence on the deadly prospects for a penal settlement there.[22]

Sharp's enthusiastic recommendation ensured that the committee embraced Smeathman's plan. A special handbill, directed to impoverished black people, pointed out that 'no place is so fit and proper, as the Grain Coast of Africa; where the necessaries of life may be supplied, by the force of industry and moderate labour, and life rendered very comfortable'. Those interested in going to this near paradise were directed to apply to Smeathman at the Office for Free Africans in Cannon Street. In the meantime, the Committee for the Relief of the Black Poor was paying out a weekly bounty to up to 700 people at its two relief centres. Word of the bounty travelled fast, over considerable distances. The recipients included numerous residents of Deptford like William Blue, now discharged from the army and attempting to make a living on the Thames. He was one of the first to sign on for the bounty, listed as number 50 of the 659 to whom payments were made throughout August 1786.[23]

Although there was an expectation that the payment was linked to the Sierra Leone project, accepting the bounty did not obligate a person to emigrate. Nor was there a requirement that everyone who received the bounty had to be present in person. Consistently, between April and August 1786, 'arrears' were paid to those unable to come in person to collect their allowance because of sickness or for some other reason. This was how this list of recipients came to include Caesar, who was at the time incarcerated upon the *Ceres* hulk moored upon the Thames River, awaiting transportation to Africa. His name was variously given as Thomas Caesar, John Caesar, and John Caesar Thomas, reflecting the indifference to the accurate use of first names that was so common in the eighteenth century, as well as the predisposition to call any black man either John or Thomas interchangeably. The different variants of his name suggest that the bounty was collected for him by friends, no doubt in the expectation that his sentence of transportation to Africa would actually allow him to go to Sierra Leone. The inclusion of incarcerated blacks in the Sierra Leone project was a matter of concern for the committee. In late June they received a petition from 'a poor black now under confinement ... who wishes to go to Africa'. The committee resolved to try to persuade the relevant authority to let the man 'go free in order to join the expedition with his wife and family'.[24]

By 7 June, the recruitment of settlers had begun in earnest. Those receiving relief were informed that the payment of the bounty would be conditional upon going to Sierra Leone. Some who had turned up for the bounty on that day said that they wanted time to consider, while others made it clear they would be happy to return to their home in America, but not to go to Africa. The Sierra Leone project was complicated in multiple ways by public awareness that the west coast of Africa had been selected as the site for a penal settlement. Indeed, Lord Sydney's description of the plan to purchase territory in Sierra Leone upon which to settle the black poor, 'also furnishing them with tools and implements etc., for the cultivation of the land, as well as provision for their subsistence, until it is supposed they will be able to raise food for their future support', sounded almost identical to the ill-fated Lemaine proposal.[25]

Just prior to embarkation on the ships for Sierra Leone, Captain Thompson returned to England in the *Nautilus* with the news that the Das Voltas region was 'sandy and barren and from other causes unfit for settlement'. This was unwelcome news. There were by now about 1300 convicted felons incarcerated on five separate hulks, and the government was more than anxious to be rid of them. As Lord Sydney acknowledged, it was imperative to solve the problem of the 'crowded jails and infectious distempers that may break out'. With that matter in the forefront of his mind, Sydney continued, 'His Majesty thought to fix on Botany Bay' as the destination for his unwanted felons. Shedding his previous objections, Sydney now expounded on the 'fertility and salubrity' of this place where hardly a soul had ever ventured, drawing on the evidence of Joseph Banks that its climate was healthy and the land fertile enough to produce 'any kind of grain', while cattle could be grazed on 'as fine meadow as was ever seen'. Sydney was especially enthusiastic about Botany Bay's location, so far away from England that 'it is hardly possible for people to return without permission'. Having sung the praises of this Elysium of the Antipodes, Sydney requested Treasury to provide shipping to transport about 800 convicts to its far distant shore.[26]

Having discharged his duty to investigate Das Voltas Bay, Captain Thompson was given the commission of escorting the Black Poor to Sierra Leone, ensuring that this expedition and the projected penal settlement at Botany Bay would be inextricably linked in London gossip. Although the Sierra Leone project should have been seen as a completely different concept from the mooted penal settlement at Botany Bay, the two were constantly connected in the press, in the popular imagination and in government business. Treasury and Naval Board discussions continually switched between the proposed settlements at Sierra Leone and Botany Bay, as if they were interchangeable. Government departments concerned with ordering supplies for the two expeditions found it convenient to deal with both in the same letter. The same firm was contracted to supply both expeditions and, in at least one case, supplies surplus to the requirements of the free black emigrants were transferred to the convict ships. A more troubling development was the widespread rumour that the Sierra Leone settlement would double up as a penal colony, or, worse still, that the black settlers were actually to be sent to Botany Bay. Such persistent misinformation undoubtedly contributed to the reluctance of people, including William Blue, either to sign up for the expedition or to go aboard the ships *Belisarius* and *Atlantic* moored in the Thames. After 4 September 1786, Blue's name no longer appeared on any of the lists of bounty recipients.[27]

The entanglement of the expedition to Sierra Leone with the penal settlement at Botany Bay heightened concern among the black poor about friends and relatives in prison or on the hulks. Soon after the planned penal settlement at Botany Bay became public knowledge, an unsigned letter 'from the Blacks' to the Committee for the Relief of the Black Poor requested the release of a certain prisoner, stating that they would not go to Africa without him. While deliberating this case, the committee was informed by one of the black corporals that there were five men and one woman incarcerated who also expected to go to Sierra Leone. The members of the committee attempted to meet these expectations by writing to the sheriff requesting their release.[28]

The half-truths, rumours and outright lies that surrounded the execution of the Sierra Leone scheme meant that the response of the black poor was underwhelming. By 29 November 1786 the Navy Board ruefully conceded that less than 300 were on board the *Belisarius* and *Atlantic*, with no more expected to embark. While the ships lay in the river, those on board grew increasingly restless. Anxiety about the expedition somehow reached the ears of the meddlesome Lord George Gordon, who made yet another of his peculiar public interventions. The *Public Advertiser* of 18 December 1786 reported that six of the black emigrants had come up to London to implore Gordon to use his influence to stop the ships sailing until Parliament would resume to consider their being forced to leave the country. This supposed deputation was, in all probability, a fiction, although there was discontent aboard the ships and some of the prospective settlers might have obtained an audience with the radical Lord. The anonymous newspaper report, no doubt written by Gordon himself, portrayed the Sierra Leone venture as a settlement presided over by a tyrannical military government, just as was proposed for Botany Bay. Gordon advised the deputation not to go to Sierra Leone, and the newspaper reported that subsequently some 400 people had quit, leaving only a few paid stooges behind on the two ships. In fact there was no voluntary exodus of the kind reported; those that left the ships did so in coffins, as a 'malignant fever' had taken hold on the *Belisarius*.[29]

By early January Gordon had turned his attention from the ships for Sierra Leone to the four refurbished transports that were now moored off Woolwich awaiting the reception of convicts bound for Botany Bay. Since the slave-trading firm of Camden, Calvert and King had shown no interest in transporting convicts to this remote corner of the globe, a Royal Navy contractor named Richards had taken the contract and was refitting his ships to carry closely packed human cargo made secure against mutinous outbreaks. One such ship, *Alexander*, moored at Woolwich, required reinforced hatches with 'bars and strong bolts', as well as a supply of 'security handcuffs'.[30]

When he heard about this, Lord Gordon wrote a letter to himself, which he passed off as a petition from prisoners in Newgate, to which he responded by visiting the supposed petitioners in gaol and warning them to 'preserve their lives and liberties and prevent banishment to Botany Bay'. As it happened, the felons earmarked for transportation were not in Newgate at all; they were on Duncan Campbell's hulks, *Ceres*, *Censor* and *Justinia*, which were not so accommodating to a visitation from the populist Lord. The government was taking no chance that the hero of the London mob might scuttle their latest plan. Gordon and the printer of the petition were convicted of libel and of inciting mutiny against sentences of transportation.[31]

On 6 January 1787, transfers from the hulks began. John Randall, John Martin, Thomas Orford, Caesar and Janel Gordon were moved to the transport ship *Alexander*. A wit in the London *Evening Post* pictured the forlorn procession of convicts in clanking chains as on their way to an earthly paradise:

> They go to an Island to take special charge,
> Much warmer than Britain, and ten times as large:
> No customs house duty, no freightage to pay,
> And tax free they'll live when in Botany Bay.

✳

However idyllic the popular perception of their final destination, none of the 184 put aboard the *Alexander*, black or white, could have taken any pleasure from their changed circumstances. They were in a pitiful condition. Some were so sick 'they were unable to help themselves'. John Moseley was not among those transferred from the *Ceres*; he must have been too ill to be moved.[32]

As the ships of the Sierra Leone Expedition waited in the Thames Estuary for more recruits, the people already embarked would have been aware that up river preparations were well under way for another fleet to take felons to Botany Bay. By the same token, information about the fleet for Sierra Leone moored off Gravesend could easily have filtered back to those incarcerated aboard the *Alexander*. Perhaps the black convicts nourished hope that they would still be permitted to join the Sierra Leone expedition. But these were to be dashed when the Sierra Leone ships set sail for Spithead on 11 January 1787.[33]

Further weeks of delay at Spithead and again at Plymouth caused high tension on the Sierra Leone ships. Captains were given orders 'to quiet the spirit of disturbance and dissatisfaction' among their passengers. Once again the expedition came under attack in the press, this time from a prominent black Londoner, who claimed that letters written to him from Plymouth revealed the prospective black settlers had been 'dragged away from London and carried captives to Plymouth, where they have nothing but slavery before their eyes'. He advised that they 'had better swim to shore, if they can, to preserve their lives and liberties in Britain'. Those on board should have heeded his call.[34]

The three ships and their escort *Nautilus* finally reached Sierra Leone on 10 May 1787 and 377 people went ashore on a mountainous peninsula on the southern side of the Sierra Leone River. They cut a track through the thick vegetation to a vantage point on a nearby hill, where the British flag was raised and the new settlers began the task of creating temporary shelter with the canvas the navy had supplied. Then the rain came. Delay in sailing had brought the fleet to Sierra Leone at the worst possible time. The canvas proved inadequate against the rain. Food became scarce. The ships sailed away. The list of passengers that Captain Thompson delivered to Treasury on 16 September 1787 made grim reading. His marginal comments indicated that 122 of the settlers were already dead, 'carried off by fever, fluxes and bilious complaints'. A few months later, a literate survivor took advantage of a passing slave ship to send a painful letter to Granville Sharp: 'I am sorry, and very sorry indeed, to inform you, dear Sir, this country does not agree with us at all; and, without a very sudden change, I do not think there will be one of us left at the end of twelvemonth.'[35]

5

BOUND FOR THE FATAL SHORE

The slap of unfurling canvas, the crack of ropes tensing with the strain and the coarse chanting of sailors were sounds familiar to the black convicts on the *Alexander* at Woolwich. Thomas Orford and John Martin had been seamen while Janel Gordon, John Randall and Caesar could have worked their sea passage to England. Yet as the *Alexander* pulled down river and set sail for the Motherbank, outside Portsmouth, they were not scampering aloft or heaving away on ropes; they were chained between decks with another 205 convicts filled with dire apprehension, listening to the bark of command and the clatter of running feet above their heads. If this was not something they had experienced before, then they had heard about it from those who had endured the Middle Passage on a slave ship. Were they now to be delivered into another kind of slavery at the end of the world, as Lord George Gordon had predicted? For months before their transfer, confused talk about the government's intentions had rippled through the hulk *Ceres*. Some felons had first-hand knowledge of what might be in store. John Martin could relate how he had only just escaped transportation to certain death in slave forts on the coast of Africa. Three men from that convict expedition had miraculously returned to England with horrendous tales to tell.[1]

When the *Alexander* reached Portsmouth and was once more at anchor, the convicts on board had some reason to feel relief. For sure, they remained bolted together in the cramped, dank space between decks and their monotonous meagre diet of salt provisions was unaltered, but their worst fears were not realised. However remote and strange their final destination, Botany Bay was not to be an outpost of slavery, so the expedition commander, Captain Phillip, had determined. From the outset, he insisted, the settlement in New South Wales would be run according to the laws of England and that one law, in particular, would come into effect from the moment their feet touched the ground: 'there can be no slavery in a free land, and consequently no slaves'.[2]

✳

Inevitably, disease broke out in the confined conditions below the *Alexander*'s decks, with the sick handcuffed to the healthy. Not only were many of the convicts poorly, the marines set to guard them were also falling ill and some had already died. News of a malady on the *Alexander* soon drifted ashore, alarming the town's residents. When the surgeon general for the voyage, John White, arrived at Portsmouth he was confronted by a deputation of town gentlemen come to tell him that the convicts on the *Alexander* had 'a malignant disease among them of a most dangerous kind'. White went below decks to find that the sick men's complaints were 'neither malignant nor dangerous'; most were chronically debilitated, mentally and physically, from the effect of long incarceration, while others were dressed only in rags and incapacitated by the piercing cold. He ordered warm clothes and made sure their rations would be supplemented with fresh meat and vegetables. The ship's master was instructed to bring up the men on deck to take fresh, clean air. Some time later, White had the bulk of the convicts taken off onto lighters, while the ship was thoroughly cleaned, smoked, sponged down with oil of tar and then whitewashed. Even with these welcome changes, eleven men died on the *Alexander*.[3]

In early March, two more black convicts from the hulk *Ceres*, John Moseley and George Francisco, were transferred to Portsmouth. They were sent by wagon, under guard, chained by the neck and ankles to other prisoners. Instead of joining their old compatriots on the *Alexander,* they were loaded onto the *Scarborough*, with another 206 felons from various hulks and prisons, including youths, James Williams and John Williams, who were known respectively as 'Black Jemmy' and 'Black Jack'. Later that month, the transport *Charlotte* arrived from Plymouth completing the fleet of transport ships. Confined on the *Charlotte* were more black convicts: John Coffin, a servant aged about 25, sentenced in Exeter in January 1786 for stealing some china and silverware from the house of his employer, and Samuel Chinery, aged 20, who had been sentenced at the Devon Assizes in August of the same year for stealing a linen shirt. Both of these men were probably recent arrivals in England, entering at the port of Plymouth. The convicts on the *Charlotte* had been held in appalling conditions on the hulk *Mercury* and were barely clothed when they were transferred, prompting the shocked Captain Phillip to demand they must be given new clothes as a matter of urgency.[4]

✳

By the end of March, all the convict transports were congregated at the Motherbank, where two naval vessels joined the fleet, in readiness for an immediate departure. Phillip had not yet arrived; he was still in London upbraiding the Navy Board for their dangerous presumption that so many people could be sent to the extremity of the known world with inadequate provisions, and no special supplements to retard the spread of scurvy during the long voyage. He would not permit the fleet to sail until the conditions for the journey were to his liking. A month's delay ensued as Phillip pressed his case with the authorities in London, while aboard ship at Portsmouth the convicts remained closely confined, with scant opportunity for exercise or fresh air. The women convicts on the *Lady Penrhyn* and the *Friendship* were not ironed and had more freedom of movement than the men, which led to reckless intercourse with the marines and sailors, much to the disgust of Ralph Clark, the prim lieutenant of marines aboard the *Friendship*, who was pining dreadfully for his wife.

The changes ordered by Surgeon White made a marked improvement in the health of both the hapless convicts and the undernourished marines. John Hunter, the acting commander during Phillip's absence, was galled to read newspaper stories that would have the world believe the ships were so sickly they were burying eight or ten people a day, when the convicts were in better health than they had ever been. Nevertheless, another five on the *Alexander* were buried before the fleet sailed. According to the ebullient Watkin Tench, captain of marines, the convicts were 'in high spirits', despite the 'slight appearance of contagion' on the *Alexander* and they, like him, expressed 'an ardent wish for the hour of departure'.[5]

On 3 May yet another forlorn group of convicts, mostly women, arrived from Newgate, bringing the final total to 582 male convicts and 193 female convicts with 18 children, plus 212 marines to guard them. That same day, many aboard the various transports would have heard the screams of agony emanating from the deck of the *Alexander* where a man was being flogged with the vicious cat o'nine tails, a lash made of nine strands of whipcord, each strand knotted in three places. The individual whose back was shredded was not, however, a convict, but a marine private, who had been given 150 lashes for 'unsoldier like behaveyour', so fellow marine private John Easty laconically recorded in his diary.

Possibly the convicts were martialled on deck, alongside the marines, to witness the gruesome spectacle, as each drum beat was followed by the sharp crack of the lash opening long cuts on the man's back while the deck was spattered with gore. What did they make of it? Even as slaves Caesar and Gordon might not have witnessed anything quite so brutal. Randall had seen that much and more in the British army, while Orford and Martin had experienced first-hand the regime of violence that ruled the seagoing world. Here was a foretaste of what they could expect in their new life governed by laws laid down by marine and naval officers – men who would order such savage torture without so much as a second thought.[6]

Four days later Captain Phillip finally arrived at Portsmouth expressing a determination to sail immediately, despite still not having received clothes for the women, nor any documentation as to the crimes and sentences of his charges. He had not, however, counted upon a militant adherence to customary rights among his lower-class labour force. The marines were outraged to be told that the daily allowance of grog would be available to them only during the voyage. Easty recorded the anger expressed by the *Scarborough*'s marine contingent on hearing that their 'rum should be takin from them att the time of dis embarken from the ships at Botany Bay'. The more literate among them, probably the two officers, wrote a petition to Phillip stating that the supply of rum was 'an indispensable requisite for the preservation of our lives'; they would not sail unless they were assured that there would be sufficient spirits for the whole of their tour of duty, as they had been promised on recruitment. Once they could be assured by their commander, Major Robert Ross, that they would have 'liquir for 3 years in the country', the order was issued that all the dogs on board were to be sent ashore and the full complement of water stowed in preparation for departure next morning.[7]

Now it was the turn of aggrieved seamen on the *Alexander* to refuse to sail, having been at work for up to four months without pay. They demanded the arrears and leave to go ashore to buy necessities before departure, as was the custom. The matter was finally resolved by swapping seamen with those on a ship whose captain could pay the wages, so that the fleet was finally able to weigh anchor at first light on 13 May 1787. After breakfast, the inquisitive Watkin Tench took a stroll below decks of the *Charlotte* to see how the convicts were bearing up. One of his duties in the previous months was to read the convicts' letters, and he had been struck that 'their constant language was an apprehension of the impracticability of returning home, the dread of a sickly passage and the fearful prospect of a distant and barbarous country'. Now that the ships were finally in motion toward their distant destination, he thought he could detect in their faces 'a high degree of satisfaction'. By noon the fleet was into the Channel and setting a course for Tenerife, sails billowing with a brisk easterly breeze.[8]

Almost immediately, seasickness overwhelmed convicts and marines alike. The smell of vomit and the rasping of involuntary retching invaded every ship. The unspeakable misery was far worse for the male convicts, who were still ironed together and forced to lie in slimy pools of vomit and bile. Two days into the voyage Phillip ordered the irons be struck off so they could remove their disgusting clothes to be free to wash and keep themselves clean. He had little fear: virtually all the convicts were so incapacitated by seasickness that they could barely move let alone mutiny. Among the unchained convicts were a few seasoned seamen who were not prostrate with extreme nausea. A small group on the *Scarborough* had managed to obtain some knives and tools and on the night of 18 May they attempted a break-out. It was hardly a serious or threatening mutiny. The guards were waiting for them, tipped off by a convict informant. The men received a paltry punishment of twenty-four lashes, though the two ringleaders were removed from the *Scarborough* and kept in double irons. Phillip was unperturbed by the incident, reporting to under-secretary Nepean that no one had 'any reason to be seriously alarmed'. One convict, however, had every reason to be alarmed; a fortnight later four men pinned down the informer below decks on the *Scarborough* and slashed his calf with one of the contraband knives.[9]

Even before the fleet had cleared the channel, there was another short-lived strike by seamen demanding an increase in their meat ration. In the moments between bouts of vomiting, Ralph Clark jotted down the particulars of this latest piece of lower-class effrontery. 'The[y] only want more provisions to give it to the dammed whores the convict women of whom the[y] are very fond', he fumed, neglecting to add that his fellow officers were also very fond of the convict women, many of them having already selected a companion for their bunk at night. Furthermore, the officers, including Clark, had each selected a servant from among the felons. Captain James Maitland Shairp, on board the *Alexander*, appropriated the services of a black servant, Caesar, who, being about six feet tall, was considerably larger than the bulk of convicts and was only too pleased to escape the close conditions below. By 3 June the fleet had reached Tenerife, where they loaded fresh water and the supplies of fresh meat and vegetables needed for the *Alexander*'s twenty-three ill convicts. John Powers, a white convict, decided he had had enough of being cooped up on this pestilential ship, and while the convicts were assisting with the loading of supplies, he slipped over the side into a rowboat and floated out of sight. His audacious escape was nearly successful, but he was recaptured just as the fleet was setting out for the long haul to Rio de Janeiro.[10]

The weather became increasingly hot and sultry as the fleet neared the equator. Desperate for water, one of the overheated women convicts mistakenly swallowed a vial of mercury, which nearly killed her. By 5 July the water allowance had been reduced to three pints for each person every twenty-four hours, causing Surgeon White concern that this measure would hasten the onset of scurvy and other maladies. His prognosis was correct. On 18 July he was summoned from his ship to the *Alexander* where a number of men were dangerously sick. The source of their illness was identified as the ship's bilge water, in which food waste, excrement, vomit and stale water had fermented to such a degree that the noxious gases thus emitted tarnished the officers' metal buttons. When White removed the bilge hatches 'the stench was so powerful that it was scarcely possible to stand over them'. Even though the source of the foul miasma was reduced by regularly pumping the bilges, five more men died before reaching Rio, where fresh meat, vegetables and fruit could again be purchased. Another nine had developed ulcers, symptoms indicative of the onset of scurvy.[11]

Scurvy was the horror of long sea voyages. It is caused by a lack of vitamin C in the diet, a necessary element for producing the protein that maintains the body's internal connective tissues. Because humans do not manufacture ascorbic acid, without an adequate supply in the diet, the body begins literally to fall apart: blood capillaries break down, bone tissue begins to unravel, teeth deteriorate and lose their hold. After approximately three months without adequate intake of the vitamin, the first symptoms appear, usually in loose and painful teeth accompanied by bleeding gums, accompanied by non-specific aches in the limbs and joints. If left without an infusion of vitamin C, internal haemorrhaging causes blotching of the skin and bones become so weak they are unable to support the weight of the body. Fractured bones come apart and old wounds reopen, causing excruciating pain. Without a change in diet the disease is irreversible and a horrible, drawn-out death inevitable. Every mariner in the age of sail dreaded scurvy; if they had not witnessed its ravages first-hand, they were well acquainted with the horror stories, such as Commodore Anson's ill-fated voyage when a fleet of 1900 men sailed from Spithead and only 500 returned, many of them physically ruined for life. As Ralph Clark scribbled furiously in his daily journal, he fretted equally about the absence of his wife and the fear that the scourge of scurvy would strike his ship.[12]

Scurvy was especially worrying at sea because sailors and marines were usually deficient in vitamin C when they came on board. Furthermore, the very conditions under which they worked accelerated the disease. At sea the body needs more of the vitamin, and sailors became prone to the disease even on a diet sufficient for the maintenance of healthy life on shore. By 1787 a remedy had been described by Gilbert Blane, an ex-naval surgeon. This involved the regular administration of lime or lemon juice to sailors at sea. But his preventative therapy was far from accepted and ships continued to operate with a dangerously haphazard approach to diet. For all the care and concern of Captain Phillip and Surgeon White, the First Fleet was no exception. The anti-scurvy remedies applied by the surgeons were next to useless and with months between ports it was impossible for the rations to include enough fresh fruit and vegetables to arrest the onset of disease. It would be another two decades before the Admiralty made a supply of lime or lemon juice mandatory on long sea voyages.

For all the sweet blood oranges and leafy green vegetables greedily consumed during the weeks the ships were resupplied at Rio, four months into the journey the signs of scurvy were clearly evident. Ralph Clark registered the first symptoms with a nagging toothache in early September. Unlike his fellow marine officers, he had not been consuming vast amounts of alcohol nightly and he was fastidious about his diet, so if he was showing indications of the disease then so must the vast majority, although the surgeons were probably not yet aware of the scale of the problem. At just this time the worst conditions for hastening the progress of scurvy overtook the fleet as the weather took a dramatic turn. On 11 September several diarists noted the sun was slowly enveloped in a thick haze and the waves grew heavy and dark. The tune played by the rigging began to change. During the night people were woken by the sound of shrieking ropes and the movement of violent rocking as the fleet was buffeted by sudden squalls. For the weeks that followed the sky was constantly shrouded in low, purple clouds and the oily sea was whipped into massive waves that crashed over the decks and poured through the portholes. As the shrieking ships rolled and shuddered in the monstrous seas, their passengers voided their stomachs in uncontainable vomiting. Desperate men and women were battered and bruised as they struggled to the top-deck for air, while one male convict was swept overboard. On one of the many nights that Clark was kept awake by the noise of the tortured rigging and the motion of the roiling sea, his ship pitched so violently the gunwales were submerged. Despite his alarm, he took some pleasure from observing the deluge of water that swept between the decks and washed the marines and their clandestine convict lovers out of bed.

Those with access to spirits consumed them with abandon as prophylaxis against the effects of the storms. Clark's fellow marine officers frequently got into drunken brawls late at night. On the *Scarborough* the marines tried to institute voluntary restraint, Easty confided, having 'drawed up an agrement amongst themselfs to punish any body as was in liquir'. It did little to curb their excesses. Meanwhile, the first indication of the onset of acute illness was noticed on the *Alexander*, where, on 4 October, the captain took the precaution of isolating the sick convicts from the healthy. On the same day, thirty convicts on the *Charlotte* were reported to be dangerously ill. The most worrying matter for the perpetually anxious Clark was that the *Charlotte*'s marines were also falling like ninepins; thirteen were severely sick and few were left upright to defend him from the potentially mutinous convicts.[13]

Whether from the terror of an agonising death of scurvy, or just sheer opportunism due to the incapacity of so many marines, four disgruntled sailors on the *Alexander* conspired with Powers, the bold young man who had almost escaped in Tenerife, supplying him with knives and pistols. The aim was to take control of the ship as they neared the Cape and desert once they reached Cape Town. It was hard to say how many convicts were involved in the plot. While there was doubtless a great deal of mutinous resentment among the convicts on board the *Alexander*, few of them would have entertained expectations of fair treatment at the hand of the Dutch East India Company (VOC). Certainly the five black convicts would have had no interest in escaping at Cape Town, which was an outpost of slavery. The plot was foiled when a convict informer revealed it to the ship's master. The conspirators were transferred to the flagship *Sirius*, where the seamen were flogged and Powers stapled to the deck.

If the disgruntled seamen and convicts of the *Alexander* held hopes of desertion at the Cape, they would have been quickly disabused of the notion when their sickly ship sailed into Cape Town harbour. Erected along the shore were an array of gruesome instruments of execution and torture: gallows, racks and spikes for impaled heads, as well as six wheels used for breaking the body that were elevated on posts about 9 feet above the ground. The surgeon Arthur Bowes Smyth observed with horror that they still held 'the mangled bodies of the unhappy wretches who hd suffer'd upon them'. With his usual understatement, the laconic Private Easty thought the Dutch a 'strict sort of people to ther own' given that they promptly hanged a sentry who had come on board one of the British ships. For more serious crimes, Easty observed, they 'rack them and break ther bones one by one and hang them upon a gibett like a dog'. This should certainly not have been a place where a deserting seaman or an escaped felon looked for shelter. Yet for all the fearsome symbolism at the town's entrance, five seamen did make a bolt soon after the fleet arrived.[14]

Marine Captain David Collins, who had been vested with legal responsibility as the judge advocate for the new settlement at Botany Bay, was very interested in the way the VOC regulated their remote settlement. Like Bowes Smyth, he observed with awe the broken bodies on display and he carefully wrote down the inscription over the courthouse: '*Felix quem faciunt aliena pericula cautum*', which was translated by his fellow officer William Bradley to mean 'happy is the man whom other men's misfortunes make wary'. Collins wondered just how wary such severity made the denizens of Cape Town. While it might be thought that the place was so sternly regulated that no one could escape justice, he was interested to see that the deserting sailors remained at large in the town, despite the Dutch authorities exerting every effort over the period of a month to find them, and only two were discovered before the fleet sailed in November.[15]

However forbidding and inhospitable the VOC at Cape Town appeared to be, the fleet was in desperate need of their help to secure water, freshly killed meat, fruit and vegetables to arrest the disease sweeping through the ships. They had arrived in the nick of time to prevent irreversible scurvy, Surgeon White believed. Even Bowes Smyth, who had been carefully brewing spruce beer to ward off the symptoms, was feeling the telltale ache in his bones. To compound the scurvy problem there was serious outbreak of typhus on the mephitic *Alexander*, as well as dysentery on the *Charlotte*. Yet it was nearly two weeks before the ships were able to obtain fresh meat, greens and decent soft bread. From that time the improvement in health was miraculous. The assistant surgeon from the *Scarborough* pulled many damaged teeth, but no one died, nor were any hospitalised ashore. By the time they sailed on 12 November, Collins had the satisfaction 'to see the prisoners all wear the appearance of perfect health'.[16]

Here was full justification for the extended stay in Cape Town, Phillip argued in his dispatch to the secretary of the Admiralty. He had also gained permission to load the fleet with as much livestock as could be stowed. Every ship took on the appearance of Noah's Ark with fowls, sheep, pigs, horses and cattle roaming the decks. Some of the stock had been purchased by the government, but most was bought privately by marine officers. Female convicts were moved to the *Lady Penrhyn* and the *Charlotte*, to provide accommodation for thirty sheep on the *Friendship*. Clark believed the livestock would prove 'much more agreable ship mates', than those 'dammed whores', although his opinion was unlikely to be shared by his fellow marines and sailors who were deprived of their sexual companions. The second mate was so disconsolate that he drank himself into a stupor and while trying to relieve himself he pitched overboard and was drowned. The *Lady Penrhyn* had to make room for displaced women convicts as well as seven horses with enough feed for an eight-week journey and 300 gallons of brandy for the thirsty marines.[17]

On leaving Cape Town with its gruesome display of mangled bodies and severed heads, Collins indulged in the melancholy reflection that 'the land behind us was the abode of a civilized people; that before us was the residence of savages'. This journey into the unknown took sixty-eight excruciating days through bitterly cold weather and dangerously turbulent seas on an inadequate diet of salt rations. The livestock crowding every ship was not to be used for fresh meat on the voyage, rather it was kept as breeding stock for the new settlement. It was with this in mind, Hunter explained, that the decision was taken for everyone in the fleet to 'live wholly on salt provisions so that as much live stock as possible might be landed on our arrival'. Immediately following the fleet's departure the livestock began to expire. Bowes Smyth noted that every new day presented them with '4–5 and 6 dead fowls'. Infuriatingly contrary winds pushed the ship further to the west, well off course, causing very slow progress. Then the rain began. To White's despair, epidemic dysentery took hold 'with violency and obstinacy' among the marines and convicts on several ships. Once again, scurvy was sure to follow.[18]

As the fleet battled against the easterly winds and wild weather, sea sickness reappeared among the poorest sailors, further weakening the body's capacity to repair itself. Ralph Clark, who had already lost a tooth to scurvy, was once again spending most of his time with his head in a bucket. Within two days his journal began to register nagging pains that disturbed his sleep and caused him to dream his arm was broken and his teeth fallen out. For the convicts unable to keep a journal who spent most of their time confined between the decks without a servant to clean up after them, nor even a bucket, the situation must have been exponentially worse. The young black convict George Francisco, on board the *Scarborough*, was a prime candidate for the disease. He had just come out of three years' imprisonment as a prisoner of war in France and his health was clearly precarious when he was sent to the *Ceres* hulk in 1785. Seriously debilitated by what now amounted to seven years' incarceration, followed by chronic seasickness and a steady diet of salt meat, it was a certainty that his teeth had loosened in bleeding gums, his muscles gradually degenerating to pulp, while old wounds festered and aching bones were barely able to support him.

On 25 November, the frustrated Phillip decided to split the fleet into two divisions taking the fastest transports *Alexander*, *Friendship* and *Scarborough* to accompany him in the small tender *Supply*. Battling gale force winds that shattered the *Scarborough*'s mast and ripped into the mainsails, the ships fought their way through mountainous waves crashing over decks. Trying to keep his journal steady on the *Scarborough*, Easty managed to record 'the heaveyst sea as ever I saw in my life'. On the *Alexander* the convicts were so alarmed that they broke out of their confinement into the main hold. Poor Lieutenant Clark on the *Friendship* was as sick as a dog, as were his preferred companions, the sheep. The new-born lambs died almost as soon as they could stand and by the time the ships sailed below latitude 40 degrees south, on 4 December, the sheep began to succumb to the bitter cold.[19]

The dead sheep meant that on Christmas day everyone was able to eat fresh mutton rather than the vile salt pork they had been subsisting upon. It was a boon to Clark, who was beside himself now they had run out of sugar and he had to drink his tea bitter. Never in his life had he lived so poorly. All the while his whole body ached. 'I wish to God that we had got to Botany that I might be able to get som greens', he wailed, 'for never was any body so sick of the sea as I am'. On New Year's Day, as the ship pitched through the heavy seas, all he had to eat was 'a pice of hard salt beef and a few musty pancakes'. Unlike his fellow marines, who were 'much in liquor' as compensation for their poor rations, the abstemious Clark had little other than his absent wife's picture to compensate for his miserable lot. Within a week, the sheep were dying at such a rate that it seemed they could eat mutton regularly, except the fuel was gone and 'we be obliged to Eat our Provision without cooking it', so all the fresh meat was wasted.[20]

Just off the southern coast of New South Wales on 16 January 1788, people in the fast ships got a taste of what they could expect in the new country. 'The sharpest lightening ever I saw in my life', wrote Easty, 'and the heaviest rain'. Two days later the fastest ship, *Supply*, sailed into Botany Bay. Those eagerly watching from the deck observed a steep shore with a powerful surf running onto it, surrounded by hills. Next day, the three transports arrived in fierce sunshine. Easty thought the bay 'as handsome one as I ever saw in my life'. He was thrilled to report that the *Scarborough* had not lost a man since leaving England, but there were plenty who were displaying the symptoms of severe scurvy. There were no convict diarists on the *Scarborough* or the *Alexander* to record their reactions, but no doubt they shared the view of Ralph Clark, who looked out from the *Friendship* and declared, 'I cannot say from the appearence of the Shore that I will like it the only thing I ask is that it may be a healthy place'.[21]

RECALCITRANT CONVICTS
AT SYDNEY COVE

'Heavily in clouds came on the day', wrote marine Captain Watkin Tench as his ship sailed into Botany Bay on 20 January 1788. He was quoting, as best he could remember, lines from Joseph Addison's much-admired play, *Cato*:

> And heavily in clouds brings on the day,
> The great, the important day, big with the fate
> Of Cato and of Rome.

This was surely 'a great, an important day', Tench wrote, hopefully the founding of an empire and not the disaster that had befallen Cato's Rome. No such lofty sentiments were felt by the convict aboard the *Alexander* named after Cato's nemesis. For Caesar, Botany Bay was just another prison.[1]

First ashore was Captain Arthur Phillip, who went with some of his officers to look for water on the north side of the bay. As their small boat approached its destination, a group of male Aborigines was sighted, calling out to the intruders 'in a menacing tone and at the same time brandishing their spears'. The Aborigines were entirely naked and their dark skin was scarred with raised weals on their chests and upper arms. Each man had his right front tooth knocked out, while several wore a bone through the cartilage of the nose, as well as ornaments of shell in their greased hair. For all the appearance of hostility, the men responded favourably when Phillip made signs indicating he wanted water, directing him 'to a very fine stream'. Tentative at first, the astonished Eora accepted the glass beads and mirrors that Phillip held out to them. They would have been even more astonished to know that this small pale man in his ridiculous uniform held the title of governor-in-chief and that in putting ashore he had assumed control of the entire region of eastern Australia. More naked warriors brandishing spears were seen the follow-

*

ing day, calling across the water: '*Warra, warra, warra*', later translated to mean 'go, or get away'.[2]

The strange visitors had no intention of going away. Over the next few days, Phillip explored his new domain with several officers in tow. They found that New South Wales was a place that deceived the eye, at first resembling a gentleman's park, with stately trees and grassy meadows, but in reality no landscape could have been more alien compared to the tranquillity of pastoral England. The grass was coarse and massive tree trunks rose straight up for 50 feet or more before extending contorted limbs to the sky, their drooping, narrow leaves providing little shade from the remorseless sun. All day the officers were tormented by flies crawling in their eyes and ears; as dusk fell, they were ready prey for swarms of mosquitos. The more closely they looked, the more bewildered they became. What they found at Botany Bay in no way resembled the edenic descriptions offered by Captain Cook and his crew.

Nevertheless, work had to commence in making this latest and most unruly outpost of empire fit for civilisation. Small work parties of convicts from the *Scarborough* and the *Alexander* were landed daily: their tasks to clear a site ready for settlement while cutting grass to feed the livestock. Happily, the Aboriginal inhabitants proved inquisitive rather than hostile. Some observers felt they were especially curious to discover a black man among the interlopers assaulting the landscape with their strange weapons. None of the fleet's many diarists recorded exactly which black convict landed with the initial work party, but possibly it was Caesar, who was reputed to be the strongest convict in the fleet. The naval officer William Bradley felt that the Aborigines were 'much pleased' to see a 'man of their own complexion' and he thought they were puzzled that the black convict failed to understand their language. This was Bradley's fanciful rendering of the unintelligible behaviour of the indigenous people. For the Eora someone from Africa dressed in a convict uniform would have appeared no less alien than those with pale faces dressed in the same peculiar clothes.[3]

As the governor and his retinue of officers continued their explorations, every fresh discovery brought further disappointment. When the straggly trees were cut, the timber was 'fit for no purposes of buildg or anything but the fire', one officer complained, with the soil beneath 'but a black sand'. In addition to these dissatisfactions, everything appeared to be 'covered with red and black ants of a most enormous size', each with a nasty nip. No one could locate the lush meadows of which Joseph Banks had boasted. On 24 January Phillip resolved to move the entire fleet a few miles north to Port Jackson. Ralph Clark was mightily relieved at this decision, confiding to his distant wife that had they remained at Botany Bay 'it would have been the grave of all of us'.[4]

Port Jackson had a magnificent harbour and the sheltered cove that Phillip selected for settlement was extremely picturesque, with a heavily wooded shore that promised fertile soil. At sunset on 26 January, the governor and his party briefly stepped ashore at the cove, now named after Lord Sydney, where they hoisted the Union Jack up the ready-made flagstaff. As the flag fluttered limply in the humid air, a detachment of marines fired several volleys, loyal toasts were drunk, and Phillip formally took possession of the continent on behalf of King George III.

The next day the men from the *Scarborough* were the first ashore at Sydney Cove, with orders to clear the site of trees in readiness for settlement. George Francisco was probably too ill, but the work party would have included John Moseley, as well as James and Jack Williams, the two young black seamen alternatively known as 'Black Jemmy' and 'Black Jack'. It was a relief to be walking on dry land after 258 days at sea, but one cruelly tempered by the unsteady gait of lurching sea-legs painfully weakened by scurvy-softened bones. Difficult as it was to hew these enormous trees under such trying physical circumstances, the task was made near impossible when they discovered the timber was so hard it blunted their inadequate axes and contorted their feeble cross-cut saws. Nevertheless, after two days of back-breaking work in searing heat they had cleared enough ground for the rest of the male convicts and marines to disembark and commence the work of setting camp among the tree stumps. The *Alexander* disgorged its complement, including the black convicts John Martin, John Randall, Janel Gordon (now called Daniel), Thomas Orford and Caesar. John Coffin and Samuel Chinery, two black men sentenced in Devon, came off the *Charlotte*.

A large number of tents were commandeered by Surgeon White to serve as a makeshift hospital for the many men debilitated by dysentery and scurvy. 'More pitiable objects were perhaps never seen', he lamented. 'Not a comfort or a convenience could be got for them.' Convicts still able to fend for themselves might, if lucky, find a billet in a tent. More likely, however, was a bed of leaves under the vast, star-studded sky. Samuel Chinery found shelter near the hospital in a hollow burnt into the trunk of a massive tree. A handful of convicts eluded the guards, bolting to the surrounding forest where the dense tangle of undergrowth promised concealment. Some were never seen again alive, though their remains were found later. A few staggered back, nearly demented with starvation, after many days at large in the bush.[5]

February brought electrical storms of terrifying intensity that swept in from the ocean accompanied by drum rolls of thunder and shards of lightning spitting in all directions, splitting trees from crown to roots. Squalls of rain turned the ground upon which they slept into a filthy quagmire. On 6 February, the full and final muster of convicts ashore numbered 732, after the 189 convict women were finally landed. The women were barely assembled on land and none of their tents were pitched when lightning rent the sky. Moments later, the settlement was pounded with drenching rain. While the officers huddled in their tents, terror-struck by the thought of incineration by lightning-strike, the male and female convicts, marines and sailors cavorted in the slithery and sensuous mud. Peering from their tents, the shocked officers were presented with a 'scene of debauchery and riot' that lasted all night. The governor, sheltering in his commodious canvas house custom-built in London, resolved that proper order must be established directly. Mid-morning the following day all were summoned to hear him give the orders.[6]

The officers flanked the governor as he read out his commission and the instructions to appoint a criminal court with a judge advocate, assisted by six military officers. Phillip then turned his attention to the bedraggled convicts who, encircled by the marines, sat caked in mud. He told them he was convinced many were incorrigible and 'nothing but severity would have any effect … to induce them to behave properly in future'. Any male convict attempting to gain access to the women's tents at night would be shot, he warned, and anyone who stole 'the most trifling article of stock or provisions' would hang. All the convicted felons needed to understand that they were in New South Wales to work; if they did not work, they would not eat. Their first labour would be the building of houses for the officers, next those for the ordinary marines, and lastly for themselves. After this 'harangue' the convicts were

dismissed and the officers retired to a large tent to dine on a cold colla-
tion of cooked mutton, which they found to their disgust was flyblown
and maggot infested.[7]

Phillip's words were a severe shock to his convict audience. Nothing
in their sentence implied that transportation equated to years of forced
labour. Yet Lord Sydney's instructions to Phillip on this point were
precise: the convicts' labour was assigned to the governor. Thus Phillip
was the master of a bonded workforce of over 700 people. Although
Sydney's ultimate ambition was for convicts to become self-sufficient
yeoman farmers, Phillip understood that all sentences be served at his,
the governor's, direction before the allocation of any land. Not that
Phillip knew when the convicts' sentences expired; that paperwork had
not been completed before the fleet had sailed. In actuality, John Martin
had only six months left to serve, while others had already completed the
greatest part of theirs. The governor was not, however, about to take the
word of thieves and vagabonds on the subject. He insisted he must
receive written proof of their sentences from England, a process that was
bound to take several years.[8]

Disturbed by the news that leisure was to be a scarce commodity the
convicts may have been, but they were not prepared to forego other
pleasures. Plenty ignored the governor's dire threat of summary execution for the crime of entering the women's tents. Prim and prurient Ralph
Clark moaned to his absent wife that a 'seen of whordome is going on
there in the womans camp – no sooner has one man gone in with a
woman but a nother goes in with her'. Of course, aside from the high-
minded Clark, the officers had taken their pick of the women, with little
the convicts could do about it. Ironically, Clark in due course followed
the example of his peers by choosing a mistress from among the convict
women. Second in the pecking order were the ordinary marines, while
the male convicts came a poor third. The convict men did their best to
keep the ships' crews out of contention, brutally beating any sailor found
near the women's camp.[9]

Marriage between convicts was promoted enthusiastically by the
governor and the chaplain. For those women not already spoken for by
officers, this appeared the best option in a society where men outnumbered women five to one, and married convicts were promised 'various
little comforts and privileges that were denied to those in the single

state'. In February John Randall, the black ex-soldier from Connecticut, married Esther Howard, and the following month the former sailor, Thomas Orford, married Elizabeth Jones (Osborne). Both of these women were white London pickpockets. They were arrested simultaneously and were prosecuted at the Old Bailey on the same day. Together in the horrid confines of Newgate for over a year, they were transported on the *Lady Penrhyn*. Doubtless they were close friends. Mary Hill, another of the *Lady Penrhyn*'s female felons, was convicted at the Old Bailey around the same time as Howard and Jones. She appears to have taken up with John Moseley.[10]

Marine Captain David Collins was appointed judge advocate for the fledgling colony. He had no legal training whatsoever, but he took his job seriously, unperturbed by his ignorance of the law. With assistance from those of his fellow marine officers who had agreed to serve on the court, Collins dolled out vicious punishments to the refractory convicts and wayward marines who came before him. On 29 February it was the turn of Daniel Gordon and 'Black Jack' Williams to face Collins's stern justice. They were accused of the theft of eighteen bottles of wine from the commissary store. On the day the wine went missing, two white convicts were found blind drunk. In return for a pardon they fingered the two black convicts as the true culprits. Gordon, a tailor by trade, insisted that he had altered the coat of one of his accusers, payment for which was the stolen wine. This he shared with his friend 'Black Jack'. The court chose not to believe Gordon. Both men were sentenced to death, but 'Black Jack' was pardoned immediately, due to being 'an ignorant black youth'.[11]

The middle-aged Gordon was led away to the hanging tree that stood between the male and female camps and the noose was fastened around his neck. As the chaplain intoned prayers for Gordon's soul, it must have seemed a paltry end for a man who had escaped the bonds of slavery, survived the scourge of smallpox and come unscathed through the siege of Charleston. In that excruciating moment, as the crowd waited for Gordon to utter his final testament, he was dramatically reprieved by the governor, on condition of being exiled to the South East Cape, at the bottom of Van Diemen's Land. Two other felons, whose execution had been held over from the previous day, were pardoned with the same proviso. The impracticality of executing the new sentence led to a further reprieve and a few days later Gordon and his two white companions were imprisoned instead upon a rocky outcrop in the middle of the harbour.[12]

Gordon and Williams were widely separated by age and experience. They had been tried in completely different parts of England, incarcerated in different gaols, housed on different hulks and transported to New South Wales aboard different ships. The close relationship forged between the two only a month after disembarkation suggests that the black convicts, as a distinctive minority, may have sought their own company above all others. Further evidence supports this notion: John Randall and Thomas Orford married women who were close associates; while John and Esther Randall shared their hut with John Moseley and possibly, as well, Orford and his wife Elizabeth.[13]

Undoubtedly other connections existed between the black convicts, but there were no convict diarists, and the scribbling officers, with one eye on the consumption of their narratives back home in England, rarely bothered to differentiate between one despised felon and another. Very occasionally, black convicts are glimpsed in the officers' musings, for example they were sometimes allocated to officers, officials and other men of standing as servants. One such who came free as a passenger onboard the *Lady Penrhyn* was assigned an unnamed black convict for a servant. Samuel Chinery was made servant to Thomas Arndell, the assistant surgeon, while Caesar was allocated to Lieutenant Maitland Shairp. Within the first year or so, John Randall was appointed game shooter for one of the important men of the colony, probably George Johnston, the governor's aide-de-camp. Johnston was one of a dozen officers who had served in the American Revolution, including David Collins, Watkin Tench, Robert Ross, Williams Dawes, John Hunter, Phillip Gidley King and possibly Maitland Shairp. Bonds forged during that war ran deep, and for black runaways from America who had served with the British, such as Randall, this connection would have stood them in good stead as they began a new life at the other end of the world.

Creating a settlement out of the antipodean wilderness proved to be a far more taxing undertaking than anyone had anticipated. The tools supplied were near useless. Clothing was quickly reduced to tatters, with mending an impossibility because thread had not been supplied. Shoes fell apart in weeks. The first huts that were thrown together from soft

cabbage palms, grass and mud, were woefully inadequate for the torrid
climate, disintegrating in the torrential rain that lashed the settlement
throughout the summer. All the heavy labour of clearing and construction was in the hands of the convicts, servants or not, who not only were
still suffering the effects of scurvy, but were also mostly drawn from the
urban slums of England and thus were unaccustomed to hard labour.
There were no beasts of burden; the task of carting the huge trees and
stones fell on the puny shoulders of the convicts. Here the black convicts
may have had an advantage, as they appear to have been taller and
stronger than most. At around six feet, both John Randall and Caesar
were each a head taller than virtually all the dwellers at Sydney Cove.
Judge Advocate Collins, another tall man, identified Caesar as 'always
reputed the hardest working convict in the country; his frame was
muscular and well calculated to hard labour'.[14]

Unfortunately the ration took no account of size or the amount of
labour undertaken. With remarkable fairness, Phillip had decreed that,
regardless of status, every man should have the same weekly ration:
7 pounds of beef, 3 pints of pease, 7 pounds of bread biscuit or flour and
6 ounces of butter. Within two months, the protein allocation had been
cut by 12 per cent. This was nowhere near sufficient to sustain someone
of Caesar's physique for eight back-breaking hours of labour per day. He
was always ravenous, Collins observed, 'for he could in any one day
devour the full rations for two days'.[15]

The governor intended that local game would supplement the meat
rations. However, the amazing creature that Captain Cook had called
'kangaroo' proved extremely elusive: the animal was acutely sensitive to
potential danger and moved with astonishing speed. The cumbersome
Brown Bess musket was virtually useless for hunting them, unless
handled by a first-rate marksman, so the best shots in the colony were
chosen as game-shooters. Phillip employed the white convict John
McIntyre as his shooter, while Major Ross employed Patrick Burn. John
Randall was the third convict licensed to shoot game. In May, Major
Ross's shooter caused some excitement when he brought in a massive
kangaroo weighing 96 pounds.[16]

The three game shooters were permitted an enviable freedom to
move as they wished through and beyond the settlement. Randall and
his two colleagues operated with little or no supervision, ranging at will

through the bush, tracking and shooting kangaroo. They were often out for days at a time, with bountiful occasion to procure fresh meat for themselves and their close associates. They were regularly included in the governor's exploratory sorties; their role to keep the explorers supplied with food. John Randall and John McIntyre were, almost certainly, the marksmen who, in April 1788, accompanied Governor Phillip, Lieutenant Johnston and a bevy of officers on the second expedition to Broken Bay, north of Port Jackson. They were probably the armed convicts who escorted Phillip and Johnston to Botany Bay in May 1788, while Randall was surely the black tent-carrier mentioned on the third expedition to Broken Bay in August 1788. This party landed their boats at Manly Cove, then followed the Aboriginal track overland to the southern branch of Broken Bay, upon which Phillip had bestowed the name Pittwater in honour of the prime minister.

During the expedition to Pittwater the party met with many indigenous people who proved both inquisitive and helpful. At an encounter with a large group ay Manly Cove, soon after landing, Randall gave one stocking each to two Aboriginal men 'with which they seemed much pleased'. But significantly there was no indication that they made any distinction between black Randall and his white compatriots. On their return from Pittwater, Surgeon White observed another group in 16 canoes who paddled up to the party, 'mimicking ... and indulging in their own merriment'. This had been the governor's third trip to Broken Bay, yet he remained sceptical about its potential for settlement. The party had located only 'several hundred acres of land free from timber and very proper for cultivation'.[17]

Phillip's indecisive expeditions were a fierce irritant to Major Ross, so much so that he wrote complainingly to London about these lengthy excursions. While at Sydney Cove hunger held sway, the peripatetic governor and his favoured officers escaped the squalor and misery of the settlement, while feasting sumptuously on wild duck and the occasional kangaroo in the name of exploration. For those who were not privileged enough to have access to the meat of the game shooters' labour, there was never enough to eat. The settlement may have been surrounded by water, but the newcomers were bewildered in this alien environment. Fish were abundant in the harbour, but none of them understood the seasonal movements of the shoals. The nets remained mostly empty. On shore they discovered a few wild berries and sweet leaves that concocted an interesting blend of tea, efficacious for alleviating the worst effects of scurvy but of little or no nutritional value. Within three months of landing, hunger determined the settlement's pattern of life.

On 30 April 1788, Collins's court heard several cases relating to the theft of rations, including a charge against Caesar. He was accused of stealing 4 pounds of bread from the tent of a fellow convict. Caesar denied the allegation, claiming the bread found in his bag was given to him by Lieutenant Shairp, who gave testimony in the case. However the trial record is fragmentary; Shairp's evidence, the verdict and sentence elude us. If guilty Caesar would have received the usual sentence for felons convicted of petty larceny: a flogging of 100 to 300 lashes depending on the mood of the court. He would not have been the sole victim of the flogger's art that day. One of the officers serving in court remarked the following day in his journal: 'we had a few trials and plenty of flogging, but I believe the Devil's in them, and can't be flogged out'.[18]

Those flogged could consider themselves fortunate; another convict found guilty of stealing bread was hanged. He was a mere 17 years old. Tench observed with distaste that instead of the required demonstration of terror and penitence, the youth met his fate with sardonic resignation 'which the grossest ignorance, and most deplorable want of feeling alone could supply'. Determined that the theatre of execution should not be mocked and that its power to strike terror into the heart of potential miscreants remained intact, Collins left the boy's body dangling from the branch, while beneath the soiled and purple-faced corpse, a procession of lesser offenders, Caesar probably among them, were lashed to the trunk and flogged insensible.[19]

Hanging was an unusual sentence. Flogging was the norm. It was an ordeal designed for psychologically emasculating offenders; a humiliating excoriation of the body that aimed to reduce the convict to the level of a trained animal with no will to resist. Stripped naked to the waist, the offender would be tied at ankles and wrists to a tree and struck with the cat o'nine tails to the solemn and steady beat of a drum. Each time the flagellator drew back he would run the cords through his fingers to dislodge the gore. To ensure the victim did not die under the lash – a very real possibility for men affected by scurvy – a surgeon always attended. Collins himself was present to oversee the state's legitimised violence. Three hundred lashes was an astonishingly brutal sentence, far in excess of the floggings meted out in the Royal Navy. A body could not endure such punishment in a single session, particularly as shortly after sentences were inflated to 500 or 600 strokes. Hunger made the lash a poor deterrent. Excessive sentences had, therefore, to be dealt out in stages. After 250 or so strokes, or the intervention of the surgeon, the near lifeless body would be cut down and taken to the hospital. Once the pulped back had healed sufficiently, those sentenced to further punishment would be strung up for a second, and sometimes third or fourth, dose of Collins's ineffective hunger remedy.

The bloody ritual of humiliation and pain rapidly became an all too common feature of life in the settlement as the number of lashes awarded spiralled ever upwards. Yet Collins himself admitted that the convicts were unused to living in a society 'where their conduct was to be regulated by written orders' and so offenders were often unaware of the rule they were supposed to have transgressed. His insight did not, however, temper the severity of his judgments; he had men flogged for the smallest infraction. The black convict John Martin was given twenty-five lashes because he and two others lit a fire in their flimsy hut to get warm.[20]

Collins's 'exemplary punishments' made convicts loath to implicate their fellows in any crime. 'There was such a tenderness in these people to each other's guilt', the judge advocate moaned, 'that unless they were detected in the fact, it was generally next to impossible to bring an offense home to them'. Collins's journal, with its litany of savage punishment, was published in England in 1793, prompting the penal reformer Jeremy Bentham to protest that in New South Wales the rights of Englishmen, enshrined in *Magna Carta*, the Bill of Rights and *habeas corpus* were illegally denied. Collins's interpretation of the law certainly made a mockery of the English fantasies that New South Wales would be an antipodean paradise.[21]

Governor Phillip was a humane man, in his stern naval way, and he took his prerogative of mercy very seriously, personally considering every sentence and issuing pardons or modifications to sentence. On the birthday of King George on 4 June 1788, Phillip gave all convicts under secondary sentence a full pardon. This extravagant show of mercy included Daniel Gordon, who was released from his rocky island prison to rejoin convict society at Sydney Cove. The King's birthday was celebrated with twenty-one gun salutes and an enormous bonfire that had taken two days to build. Every convict was allowed a pint of grog and let off work for the day. With the encouragement of grog, the convicts gathered around the ceremonial bonfire to give loud huzzas for King George. Their cheers did not mean, however, that they had the slightest enthusiasm for building a new society in the King's name. It was a source of dismay to Phillip that the convicts had no commitment to his project and would not work without brutal compulsion. Before leaving England he had insisted that in New South Wales there would be no slavery, but it could not have possibly escaped him that this outpost of empire, over which he had total control, bore some of the hallmarks of a slave plantation. The overwhelming majority of the settlers were at Sydney Cove against their will, while the sole weapon available to the few marine officers in their bid to compel compliance was the egregious infliction of violent torture to induce a submission born of fear.

If the governor hoped that his exercise of the prerogative mercy on the King's birthday would provide an incentive for the convicts to work harder and behave better, he was to be bitterly disappointed. After the bonfires' glowing embers dimmed to dust and the loyal toasts were drunk, a few convicts were discovered to have pilfered food and clothing from the unoccupied tents. One was a man whose back was still raw from a recent flogging. His suppurating flesh was not spared: he was sentenced to another session with the cat. The black convict John Coffin, who had stubbornly clung to the associations he had formed with other convicts on the hulk *Dunkirk*, was enraged to discover that the cakes and pies baked by him and his friends using their entire weekly ration had been stolen by some old hulkmates. A convict implicated in the theft of apparel bolted in terror, letting loose the settlement's small herd of cattle herd as he fled. Three weeks later an earthquake caused the fragile settlement to tremble for the briefest moment while massive trees shook like reeds in a wind. It was over in an instant, but was powerful enough to drive the terrified runaway back to Sydney Cove to face expiation. When he staggered back, 'his eyes were sunk into his head and his whole appearance shewed that he had been half starved', observed Surgeon White. He confessed to the larceny, but emphatically denied responsibility for the herd's escape. His explanation was judged implausible and the man was nursed back to something approaching health. Two days later, now strong enough to stand unaided, he was hanged. The cattle remained at large.[22]

The loss of the cattle was a calamity. As things stood, the natural produce of New South Wales could not sustain the settlement. Even the ebullient Tench was forced to admit antipodean nature's failings: the flora and fauna was either inedible or uncatchable; the soil was too barren to sustain European crops; and there was 'no stream in the country capable of turning a mill'. The sour Major Ross was certain that in this 'vile country' a century would elapse before the settlement achieved self-sufficiency. In a private letter to the Home Office he scornfully claimed it would be 'cheaper to feed the convicts on turtle and venison at the London Tavern than be at the expense of sending them' to New South Wales.[23]

Ross's scathing assessment was among a cache of letters and dispatches sent home on 13 July 1788 aboard a flotilla of the *Alexander*, the *Friendship* and the *Prince of Wales*. At the lookout on South Head, William Bradley watched them sail into the cerulean waters of the Pacific, anxious that those on board were 'in a distressed state ... both as to sickness and want of provisions'. The first two ships were bound for Batavia, but had only reached the Straits of Macassar when scurvy struck. The seamen were so debilitated they could not even raise the sails. All but four died on the *Alexander* and almost as many on the *Friendship*. The latter was scuttled and the survivors transferred to the *Alexander* to create a barely functioning crew. The *Prince of Wales* took a different course with equally terrible consequences. When the ship drifted into the harbour at Rio de Janeiro, Portuguese sailors were forced to bring the ship to anchor. The few glassy-eyed sailors on deck were incapable of lifting a rope between them. Ross's critical communiqué to the Home Office was inevitably delayed, by which time the Second Fleet was under way, while the Third Fleet was in preparation.[24]

Unaware of these maritime horrors, Surgeon White's despair had turned to alarm, for cases of scurvy were rapidly multiplying among the population of Sydney Cove, while an epidemic of dysentery had so weakened marine and convict alike that many were barely able to walk. With winter upon them and therefore the impossibility of cultivating fresh vegetables, White dreaded that scurvy would destroy them all. His return for October 1788 showed that over 100 had died since leaving England, more than half of that total at Sydney Cove. The hospital held 27 marines and 77 convicts, with a further 57 unfit for work. One of those who never recovered was the black convict George Francisco, who lingered fitfully among the living until August 1789. Such was the chronic shortage of workers, any able-bodied man who could stand upright and carry a load was pressed into labour. John Randall, a tall, strong man who had reaped the benefit of the fresh game meat he had shot, was put to work constructing the officers' huts. No doubt he resented this demotion to a life of hard labour; he and his work companion were charged on 17 October 1788 with disobedience to the master carpenter. The following day at court the carpenter withdrew the charge against Randall but not his workmate, who was duly sentenced to fifty lashes, a further indication that, for some reason, Randall enjoyed preferential treatment.

With or without Randall's labour, and in the face of hunger and disease, the camp at Sydney Cove slowly began to resemble a town. Bricks made from the local clay were used to construct a court house and barracks, a stone house was built for the governor, while the rough wattle and daub huts of the convicts ran either side of two rudimentary dirt roads. On the west side of the cove, where a small promontory jutted into the harbour, an observatory was constructed for Lieutenant William Dawes, who had been instructed by the Board of Longitude to take observations of a comet expected in the southern skies.

In December, a convict was found dead among the trees near the edge of the settlement where he had been cutting shingles. At first it was assumed he was a victim of murder, even though there were no obvious marks of violence. Post-mortem examination revealed he had died of malnutrition. Desperate to return to England on the expiration of his sentence, he sold his food rations to convict and marine alike for the purpose of purchasing a passage home. There were no shortage of buyers; at that time, food was Sydney Cove's most precious commodity. All grain crops had failed, while the produce of the gardens amounted to a few vegetables that helped ward off the scurvy for those in the hospital but did little otherwise to assuage hunger. Only one ship of any size, HMS *Sirius*, remained at the settlement and in desperation, the governor

＊

decided to risk sending the colony's lifeline 6000 miles to procure supplies at Cape Town.

By April 1789 the *Sirius* had not returned, nor had any supply ships arrived from England. The Eora, while not entirely ill-disposed to the newcomers, could provide them with no assistance. Smallpox had decimated the indigenous population, probably not brought by the Europeans, as first feared, but possibly introduced by Indonesian traders visiting the far northern coast of Australia. By a strange coincidence, smallpox reached Port Jackson at about the same time as the First Fleet. Having never been exposed to smallpox, Aborigines died by the score. All around the harbour, the coves and inlets became polluted with their putrescent bodies. The happy and numerous people Randall had encountered at Broken Bay were also decimated by the disease. The bewildered Europeans did what little they could to help, but few could be saved. The sole non-indigenous victim of the epidemic was a seaman from America. None of the black convicts succumbed to smallpox, which implies that either they had been exposed to the disease or had been inoculated against it. The British routinely inoculated those recruited into the army and navy, while during the American Revolution they had instituted an intensive program of inoculation among the black followers of the army. Thus Daniel Gordon was exposed to smallpox in South Carolina and was probably inoculated, while John Moseley had survived the epidemic that decimated Lord Dunmore's Ethiopian Regiment. The sight of the afflicted Aborigines must have awakened unbearable memories for both of them.[25]

Distressing though the smallpox catastrophe was, the focus of attention within the settlement remained firmly fixed on procuring enough to eat. Driven to back-breaking labour, the convicts grew ever more desperate to allay their hunger. On 29 April 1789, 18-year-old James Williams, known as 'Black Jemmy', was sentenced to 500 lashes for helping himself to the tobacco of a marine in charge of his work gang. Caesar was in court the same day for another charge of theft. Collins probably decided that flogging failed to deter or reform this man, and chose instead to extend Caesar's sentence of transportation from seven years to life, shrewdly guessing that while Caesar's powerful body could absorb the blow of the lash, the prospect of a life-time of forced servitude would strike terror in his soul. Vicious sentences were dispensed that same day,

a commonplace occurrence in Collins's court, reflecting his steely determination to cower the convicts into subordination. As the marine,
Private Easty, later observed, the convicts were 'the same as slaves all the
time they are in this country' and in this terrible situation the idea of
liberty became their obsession, with the convicts willing 'to try all
skeemes to obtain it'.[26]

Only a fortnight into his extended sentence, Caesar decided that the
terrors of the unknown hinterland were less fearsome than a penal system
arbitrated by David Collins. Armed with a musket stolen from a marine
and a cooking pot, he headed into the wilderness to take his chances. After
he was gone Collins noted an increase in robberies of gardens and that
someone had taken the lead weights from a fishing net to make shot for a
musket. A week later, just after provisions had disappeared from the brickfields, a mile west of Sydney, the discarded musket 'and a pot still boiling
on the fire' was found nearby. Collins was highly gratified when soon after
Caesar was caught by a young convict working at the brickfields.
Weakened by hunger, he offered no resistance to recapture.[27]

Reappearing in court, this 'wretch' further incensed the judge advocate by expressing complete indifference to his death sentence, claiming
that he would 'create a laugh before he was turned off', by playing some
trick upon the executioner'. What Caesar actually said, in the barely
intelligible argot of convicts, was 'if they should scrag him he would quiz
them all and show them some gig at the *nubbing-cheat*, before he was
turned off'. The subversive notion of hanging as pantomime gave Collins
pause. Hanging Caesar would not 'have the proper or intended effect', he
decided, as the execution of 'a mere animal' could not function as a
deterrent. The governor took it upon himself to pardon Caesar, on the
condition that he worked in chains on an island in the middle of the
harbour, the site of the settlement's first vegetable gardens. Here Caesar
was permitted to supplement his rations with the produce he grew.[28]

At the time that Caesar's sentence had been extended, his fellow
black convict, John Martin, had served nearly twelve months over and
above his original sentence, without any extension having been ordered.
Martin heard gossip about a woman whose term had just expired who
visited the judge advocate to be told that there was 'two years provisions
for her and she would not starve'. Martin spread this intelligence around
the settlement. On 28 July 1789, the judge advocate received a petition

written by John Calleghan on behalf of himself and Martin and four others whose time had expired, requesting that they be 'restored the privileges of free men'. Collins felt some sympathy for their situation, but with no documentation to confirm the expiry of their sentences, he determined that, if they were to be fed from the store, they would be required to work as directed until the paperwork arrived from England. No one had the capacity to be independent of the store, he reasoned, so 'there was little to be gained by them being restored to the rights and privileges of free men'. Calleghan disagreed that liberty was so insignificant an issue. He sought an interview with governor, to whom he claimed that Major Ross had told him he would be fed from the store whether he worked or not. Governor Phillip was also aware that Ross had despairingly uttered to Calleghan: 'would to God my time was expired, too!' Phillip was appalled by the ungentlemanly behaviour of his lieutenant governor, and insisted that such an unseemly and confidential statement should never again be uttered to a person of inferior social rank. Furthermore, for the purposes of maintaining discipline among the time-expired convicts, he charged Calleghan with uttering 'a gross and scandalous falsehood'. John Martin was brave enough to give evidence at the trial, but when his friend was sentenced to 600 lashes and then forced to work in chains for nine months, Martin saw the wisdom of compliantly accepting his lot.[29]

Two months later, Daniel Gordon was charged with theft using 'force and arms' of four bags containing provisions plus shoes and caps from the huts of convict workmen on the farm of the disaffected Major Ross. This time Gordon was certain of his fate: either the quick death of hanging or the slow death of the lash. When the court met to consider the case on 20 August 1789, Gordon had 'an appearance of delirium and wildness'; his tongue was lolling in his mouth and his eyes rolled back in their sockets. Even though evidence was given that he had been in his perfect senses only hours earlier, Surgeon White declared him to be in an unfit state of mind and, therefore, unable to stand trial. Proceedings were abandoned and, as Collins wryly observed, 'his fellow prisoners gave him credit for the ability with which he had acted his part'. Collins himself agreed that Gordon probably 'deserved their applause'.[30]

Collins saw no reason for applause on 14 November 1789, when he failed to secure a guilty verdict against John Coffin, another wily black convict who had been accused of stealing two quarts from the hospital, one of brandy and the other of wine. He was acquitted, having mounted the defence that the loss was attributable to a kangaroo that was kept in the store. Coffin had a key to the store, but he successfully argued that it was the boisterous animal who knocked the stop out of the casks. Six months later Collins was pleased that Coffin and one of his old friends from the *Dunkirk* were caught red-handed robbing the governor's garden. They confessed that in the past month they had made seven or eight raids upon the garden and had also killed and eaten an officer's pig. These should have been hanging offences, but mitigating evidence of some description was offered that resulted in the adjudgment that the two felons were public delinquents. Consequently they were chained together for several months.[31]

In December 1789, the 'incorrigible' Caesar made another bolt for the bush, having been released from his chains by his sympathetic marine guards. He had taken a week's provisions as well as the canoe used by the marines to get to and from the island. The man was 'insensible alike to punishment and kindness', Collins fumed. Three days later, William Bradley reported that in the night Caesar had stolen a musket from the settlement. He was at large for six weeks before he was carried back horribly lacerated by multiple spear wounds. Caesar told Collins's court that he had discovered the lost cattle, which were being tended by Aborigines. He was speared when he attempted to drive the Aborigines with the intention of escorting the herd back to the settlement. Collins was having none of this, declaring the whole story 'a fabrication (and that not well contrived) to avert the lash .... He was well known to have had as small a share of veracity as of honesty'.[32]

There may have been an element of truth in Caesar's tale since the herd was found five years later happily grazing about 20 miles from the settlement, but his claim that he attempted to drive the cattle away rang a false note. Had Caesar done as he described, he would almost certainly have been speared to death by the unerring aim of the Aborigines. The multiple wounds to the arms and legs suggested they were trying to drive him from their territory rather than kill him. William Bradley's journal indicates that he was present on the day of Caesar's surrender and casts the black man's actions in a different light. According to Bradley, Caesar said that even though he had no ammunition to shoot game he had survived because 'when he saw a party of natives with anything on or about their fire, he frightened them away by coming suddenly on them swaggering with his musquet'. As soon as he lost the gun he was attacked. There was no mention of cattle in this account. In a third variation to the narrative, Watkin Tench took a sympathetic view, insisting that Caesar had been trying to ingratiate himself with the Aborigines 'with a wish to adopt their customs and live with them: but he was always repulsed … and compelled to return to us in hunger and wretchedness'. Under sentence of death he was taken to the hospital to recover from his wounds until he was healthy enough to be hanged.[33]

Tench was not alone in his sympathy for Caesar's situation. Even the unbending Collins agreed that his ravenous hunger 'compelled [him] to steal from others, and all his thefts were directed to that purpose'. By this time, the court was overwhelmed with men in a similar situation, thieving food out of a desperation driven by hunger. No garden was safe from nightly raiders seeking cabbages and potatoes. One thousand strokes was now awarded for such larceny, yet, Collins noted with consternation, '[s]o great was either the villainy of the people, or the necessities of the times' that these excessive sentences had little or no effect. Collins despaired that he could flog men to death and it would make no difference. With no word from England and not a sign of any ships with relief provisions, the hunger and desperation would only get worse.[34]

In April 1790, Phillip was forced to reduce the ration to bare subsistence: 4 pounds flour, 2 pounds salt pork, 1 pound of rice a week. Recognising that no man could work ten hours a day on such meagre rations, he cut the hours of forced labour to between sunrise and one o'clock in the afternoon, giving the convicts the remainder of the day to work in their vegetable gardens, if they could muster the energy. Phillip knew the settlers could survive no longer than six months. The salted meat, now four years old, would last until August and the flour would be exhausted by December. The kangaroo proved to be as elusive as ever. A brooding silence descended on the settlement, with each person contemplating the hideous prospect of famine. All eyes turned toward the horizon, scanning for any distant speck 'on the tiptoe of expectation' that it would be a ship carrying supplies from England. For the anxious watchers, a puff of cloud on the horizon might be a vessel in sail, or the retort of a musket the sound of a ship's cannon. But no ship came.[35]

＊

THE DREAD OF PERISHING BY FAMINE

Life was not as hard on Norfolk Island, a small previously uninhabited island about 1000 miles to the northeast of Port Jackson, where a penal outpost had been established under Lieutenant Philip Gidley King in February 1788. King's reports spoke of rich soil that could support luxuriant gardens, as well as plentiful fish and game. In early 1790, to alleviate the looming famine at Sydney Cove, Phillip decided to send a large detachment of 186 convicts and two marine companies to Norfolk Island in the ships *Supply* and *Sirius*. After unloading at Norfolk Island, the *Sirius* was to sail to China to purchase further provisions. The expedition gave Phillip an excuse to deport serial offenders like Daniel Gordon, who had miraculously recovered his senses, the wily John Coffin and his chained companion, and, Collins sourly observed, 'the troublesome and incorrigible Caesar, on whom [the governor] had bestowed a pardon'. Phillip was also able to rid himself of the detested Robert Ross, whom he chose to act as lieutenant governor of Norfolk Island while King returned to England on leave. Ross, in turn, chose the peevish Ralph Clark to be in charge of one of the marine companies. They sailed on 5 March 1790 into a big swell. Soon everyone was prostrate with seasickness. Clark reported the strong whiff of vomit between decks 'a nuff to suffocate one'.[1]

A week later they arrived at Norfolk Island. As there was no harbour, the ships had to manoeuvre through treacherous surf to get as close as possible to the shore. The convicts were disembarked with difficulty from the *Supply* and they waded through the surf to the beach. For the next six days the roughness of the sea prevented the landing of stores from the *Sirius*. At midday on 19 March, Clark was waiting on the beach to have his trunk brought ashore when, to his horror, he saw the *Sirius* run aground on a reef. Near hysteria, he scribbled in his journal: 'gracious god what will become of use all, the whole of our provisions in the ship now a wreck before use'. Two convicts volunteered to swim out

*

to recover the rest of the livestock, but once on board, they broke open the spirits, got hopelessly drunk and set fire to the ship. As the island's lifeline blazed before his eyes the only prospect Clark could envisage was slow death by starvation.[2]

By organising a mass effort Major Ross managed to salvage most of the stores, but this was only enough to sustain the island's 500 inhabitants for a few weeks. What saved them from famine was the slaughter of petrels that nested on the slopes of Mount Pitt every winter. Clark kept a meticulous daily tally of the number killed; between April and July he counted 172 184 dead birds. As he later wrote to a fellow officer in Sydney, 'every body heer ous there existance to the Mount Pit birds'. When the petrels migrated, the short-tailed shearwater, which had the advantage of being very high in body fat, appeared in equally prodigious numbers. They tasted like boiled mutton, Clark explained, and so were called 'the flying sheep' or mutton-birds.[3]

Back at Sydney Cove, on 5 April 1790, Watkin Tench was compulsively scanning the seascape when he suddenly identified real sails on the horizon. Others had seen them too. With great excitement Tench, Phillip and Collins rowed out to the ship, now disappointingly identified as the *Supply* returned from Norfolk Island. As they pulled near they were alarmed to see the captain make 'an extraordinary motion with his hand'. Instantly, they understood that fresh disaster was upon them. The news of the *Sirius*'s wreck came as a terrible shock. It was 'almost sufficient to have deranged the strongest intellect amongst us', Collins recorded. All the settlement's hopes had rested on that ship's voyage to China. Lingering death now beckoned. 'The misery and horror of such a situation cannot be imparted, even by those who have suffered under it', wrote the dejected Tench. An anguished letter, also probably written by Tench and dated 14 April 1790, starkly revealed 'the dread of perishing by famine'; a dread made all the more excruciating by the sense of utter isolation felt by all the colonists – they knew as little of affairs in England as those upon the moon.[4]

Phillip could see no alternative than to send the little *Supply* over 4000 miles north to Batavia to obtain whatever supplies she could carry. It was a forlorn hope that the ship might return in time with sufficient supplies to ward off famine, but that slim possibility gave greater grounds for optimism than waiting upon phantom ships from England.

＊

In the meantime, Tench recorded, 'labour and attention were turned on one object – the procuring of food'. The basic commodity of flour had become 'more tempting than the ore of Peru'. The best marksmen among the marines, as well as the game-shooters, were directed to go out hunting kangaroo and deliver the meat to the commissary and they were allowed an additional weight of flour and meat as an incentive. Kangaroo were ever more scarce; and few, if any, believed that such a measure could save them.[5]

The penalty for stealing food was increased from an excessive sentence of 1000 lashes to an absurd 2000, as if heaping an extreme upon an extreme would make any difference. Furthermore, it was a completely illegal punishment that no man could be expected to with-stand. Collins was astounded to find that a man in the hospital recuper-ating from his first 500 lashes ready to receive the next instalment had somehow managed to get the irons off one leg and hobbled to the nearest garden to gnaw on a turnip. A new law was instituted stipulating that individual rations should not be bought or sold, yet the clandestine trade in food persisted, sometimes with tragic consequences. Tench observed a convict 'with a wild and haggard countenance who had just received his daily pittance' collapse in the street. He died at the hospital and the autopsy revealed that his stomach was completely empty. Some said that he had no utensils to cook his food, but others were convinced he had been selling his ration for rum or tobacco. As Phillip later explained to the judge advocate, the convicts found a ready market among those who had the capacity to pay the going rate of 'ten pounds of flour for a bottle of rum or thirty pounds of flour for a pound of tobacco', and he specu-lated that the buyers were marine officers 'who from their situation were not likely to be suspected'. Sure enough, Lieutenant Dawes was trading flour with a convict blacksmith who was brokering rations on behalf of other convicts. Dawes protested that he had been unaware that flour was part of the convict ration. The governor did not believe him, pointing out that Major Ross had previously warned Dawes about buying rations from the convicts. There was little Phillip could do about Dawes; as a marine officer he was 'not amenable to a general court martial in this country'.[6]

Very early on, the marine officers had insisted that whatever the offence they could not be tried in New South Wales, as the only authority that could empower a court martial was the Lord High Admiral. While immune to legal proceedings in Sydney Cove, several of these same officers acted as both judge and jury for convicts who were caught transgressing the governor's iron rules about food. Dawes was a member of the court that heard the case against Thomas Orford, the black convict charged with helping himself to potatoes from a marine officer's garden. Orford said he had lost his ration and was so hungry that when he saw the potatoes he could not help but pocket a few. He was sentenced to 2000 lashes.[7]

That Orford was in such desperate straits suggests he no longer maintained a close association with John Randall, whose household had broken up. Esther Randall died in August 1789, at which time she may have been separated from Randall, since she was buried under her maiden name. A daughter of Randall, named Frances, was born late in 1789 or early in 1790, to an unknown mother. Marriage was a fluid state in early Sydney; really no more than a mutually advantageous liaison of convenience that shifted as the tide of fortune ebbed and flowed. The official promise of 'comforts and privileges' promised to married couples amounted to practically nothing. Orford's wife, Elizabeth, who was Esther Randall's friend, appears to have taken up with John Moseley, who shared the Randall's hut, leaving Orford both literally and metaphorically out in the cold.

At the same court before which Orford appeared, 'Black Jemmy' Williams was charged with stealing biscuits on 11 April 1790. The court was told that he and a white convict had been rolling some casks from the wharf to the commissary store at the conclusion of their day's work, when Williams noticed one of the casks was broken. In his attempt to repair it, 'Black Jemmy' admitted he took the biscuits that had fallen out, believing he had the customary right to the spillage. For this he was 'found guilty of stealing under the value of twelve pence' and sentenced to have another 500 lashes laid on his back 'in the usual manner'. His companion William Lane said he was so hungry he was unable to resist taking some biscuit; 'some' in this case was 13 pounds. He, like Orford, was sentenced to 2000 lashes. Tench, who was also sitting in judgment that day, ruefully recorded 'the melancholy length to which we were compelled to stretch our penal system'. Orford received the first 800 of his sentence, while Lane could withstand no more than 250.[8]

It was a profoundly depressed David Collins who watched the *Supply* leaving for Batavia on 17 April. The ship departed with the hopes of those left behind at 'the lowest abyss of misery', he recorded. Collins failed to detect that 'Black Jemmy' was also on board, having stowed away rather than endure another 500 lashes on his cruelly furrowed back. As a former seaman he was almost certainly aided by crew on board the *Supply* and he was not detected until the ship was well under way. He sailed with the ship to Batavia and then was taken back as crew, returning to Sydney nine months later, by which time he had escaped the very worst of the famine and the punitive brutality it spawned.[9]

On the evening 3 June 1790 those people obsessively scanning the horizon were finally rewarded by the sight of the sails of a large ship flying English colours. Tench had abandoned the watch and was sitting dejectedly inside his squalid hut when a 'confused clamour' drew him outside to see 'several women with children in their arms running to and fro with distracted looks, congratulating each other, and kissing their infants with the most passionate and extravagant marks of fondness'. He ran down to the water and clambered into a rowboat that held the governor and the judge advocate. Exhorting the convict oarsmen onwards with cries of 'Hurrah for a bellyful, and news from our friends', these exultant officers drew level with the transport ship *Lady Juliana*, which had sailed from Plymouth ten months earlier.[10]

The *Lady Juliana* brought desperately needed food supplies and the welcome news that they had not been callously abandoned. The captain told how a large store-ship carrying two years of rations had been wrecked off the Cape of Good Hope. The *Lady Juliana* also carried 222 female convicts who were much less welcome. Women were once objects of intense desire, but to the sunken-eyed, hungry men they represented useless mouths to feed. Collins sourly observed that many were old and likely to require assistance rather than contributing much-needed labour to the infant colony. Tench could think of nothing but the mail. Torn open by trembling hands, the letters from home 'burst upon [the recipients] like meridian splendor on a blind man'.[11]

The store-ship *Justinian* arrived to scenes of jubilation on 20 June. As Tench recorded, 'rapture was doubled on finding that she was entirely laden with provisions' but carried no more convicts. Everyone was immediately restored to a full ration, which was the cause of much merry-making. As part of the celebration, the governor appears to have forgiven the remainder of Orford's life-threatening sentence. Nine days later, the *Surprize*, the *Neptune* and the *Scarborough* sailed into the harbour. There was, however, no jubilation at their arrival, even though they carried the soldiers of the New South Wales Corps, who were sent to relieve the ragged marine corps. The second in command, Captain Nicholas Nepean, was aboard the *Neptune*. David Collins was as enthused by the sight of the soldiers as any of the marines, yet he considered the circumstances of their arrival presented the infant colony with 'more horrid spectacles than had ever been witnessed'.[12]

The smell that accompanied the three ships gave an early indication that all was not well. The chaplain, Richard Johnson, who was by now conditioned to dreadful scenes, was shocked almost beyond belief when he boarded the first ship, *Surprize*. Going below he found a claustrophobic area without portholes. Hundreds of male convicts lay chained together, nearly naked and in a shocking condition, 'without bed or bedding, unable to turn or help themselves', he explained in a letter of outrage penned to the social reformer Henry Thornton. 'The smell was so offensive I could scarcely bear it.' Next, boarding the *Scarborough*, the chaplain was told it would be best if he did not go below. On the *Neptune*, where it was apparent conditions were 'still more wretched and intolerable', he made no such attempt. Johnson supervised the transfer of convicts, watching as horrified marines, gagging at the stench, received the cargo of emaciated bodies, crawling with lice and encrusted with excreta, who were 'slung over the ship's side in the same manner as they would sling a cask, a box, or anything of that nature'. Those whose hearts had failed them at the first exposure to fresh air had been thrown overboard, their bruised bodies washed upon the rocks by the tide. Others died in the longboats before they got ashore. Few of the survivors were able to walk and they were either carried through the shallows or else they dragged themselves on hands and knees. Of the 1006 convicts embarked on the three ships, 276 were dead. Johnson estimated that 'the landed sick were near five hundred'. A hasty burial pit was dug near the temporary hospital and at night the sound of the dingoes snarling and scrapping over the corpses was seared into the memory of the survivors who lay stupefied on the damp ground nearby.[13]

As chaplain Johnson walked between the rows of ulcerated, wasted bodies to minister to the dying, he observed that while scurvy was the most common problem, it was by no means the worst of the diseases suffered by the new arrivals; they also had typhus, dysentery and many were crawling with vermin. He claimed to have seen one man who had '10,000 lice upon his body'. Those convicts able to speak told the chaplain stories that were 'no less affecting to the ear than their outward condition was to the eye', he wrote to Thornton. Most terrible was the condition of those from the *Neptune*, a third of whom were dead on arrival. Of the few that landed in a fair condition, most were convict women who were transported unchained with ready access to fresh air. The men on the *Neptune* were far less fortunate. They had been kept ironed below decks the entire journey and had been systematically starved of rations. Some spoke of lying shackled to a corpse for as long as the stench could be borne in order to get the dead man's meagre ration. Everything they owned, even their clothes, had been stolen by the ship's captain.[14]

While conditions for the women on the *Neptune* had been less extreme, resulting in only twelve deaths, they too had been fed short rations and subjected to arbitrary brutality at the hands of the ship's master, Donald Traill. Convict women from the *Lady Juliana* searched for their friends among the barely conscious survivors, trying to ascertain who had come off the ships and who had already been thrown over the side. The contrast with their experience was painfully stark. 'It, to be sure, was a melancholy sight', one woman wrote home. 'What a difference between us and them.'[15]

All four transport ships were contracted by the same company, yet the *Lady Juliana* had landed her convict cargo in rude good health. The master of the *Lady Juliana* allowed the convicts to cohabit with the seamen during the voyage and, however exploitative this arrangement, it undoubtedly permitted a much healthier environment, providing the women with better food, protection, exercise and fresh air. Sailors from the *Neptune* later complained that they were enticed to sign on by the promise of access to the convict women, but when they requested Captain Traill to make good this promise, it was denied. Traill savagely flogged any crew caught speaking with the women, resulting in the death of one sailor, and he 'beat women convicts without mercy' if they tried to communicate with sailors. Only the first and second mate, the ship's surgeon, and the naval agent were permitted to select 'companions from among the female convicts with whom they cohabited as men with their wives', a sailor explained later at Traill's trial. The master's embargo, he said, had been the cause of 'great dissatisfaction among the crew as well as the female convicts who were mutually desirous of socialising with each other in the same manner as the officers and their females did'.[16]

Captain Traill had previously been the master of the slave ship *Recovery*, which was owned by slave-trading firm Camden, Calvert and King and had earlier transported convicts to Africa. Having shown no interest in the First Fleet, Camden, Calvert and King contracted for the four ships of the Second Fleet, but where the contract for the First Fleet was relatively generous at £54 000 for seven ships carrying about a thousand convicts and marines, their contract amounted to a mere £22 370 to carry 1226 convicts, plus an additional 200 or so soldiers. According to Captain William Hill of the New South Wales Corps, who travelled aboard the *Surprize*, the hideous conditions were directly attributable to the contract with the slave-traders. In an anguished letter to the abolitionist William Wilberforce, he described how the 'unhappy wretches' had been shackled in the same 'barbarous' way as a slave cargo, making it 'impossible for them to move but at the risk of both legs being broken'. Not just the method, but also the logic, of the slave-trade made this fleet infamous: Camden, Calvert and King were paid the same whether the cargo arrived dead or alive. Unlike slave cargo, the convicts had no value on landing, so there was little incentive to keep them fit and alive: 'The slave trade is merciful compared with what I have seen in this fleet', Hill concluded, racked with guilt that he had been unable to alleviate the suffering, although he had tried, and failed, to have responsibility for the convicts' care transferred from the brutish ships' masters to the senior military officers. Perhaps it was due to Hill's intervention that his ship, the *Surprize*, lost only 14 per cent of its human cargo, while both the *Scarborough* and the *Neptune* lost more than twice as much.[17]

On board the *Neptune* Captain Nicholas Nepean expressed no such concern about the disregard for humanity in the treatment of the convicts. He could not have failed to see what was occurring; the smell alone would have provided potent evidence. Nepean was the brother of Evan, the under-secretary at the Home Office. Nicholas's complaints to his brother about the captain's behaviour had resulted in the removal of the *Neptune's* original master. As the replacement, Traill sought favour with Nepean by providing him with an upper-deck cabin. The space originally allocated to Nepean was partitioned into two; a small cabin was created for Lieutenant John Macarthur and his wife, while the other side was given over to female convicts and 'their constant attendants – filth and vermin'. Nepean was happy to accept this advantageous arrangement, Mrs Macarthur reported: '[a]dopting the truly generous maxim, "Every man for himself".' In her account of the unpleasant voyage, Elizabeth Macarthur did not reveal whether Traill also obliged Nepean with a choice of female convict companion. The flamboyant D'Arcy Wentworth, who had scampered aboard as the ship was leaving in order to avoid the inconvenience of standing trial for the capital crime of highway robbery, certainly had the convenience of a convict companion for the journey.[18]

If the bodies of the convicts had no value to Captain Traill, their rations and clothing certainly did. The settlement had been without fresh supplies for over three years and once the wasted human cargo was offloaded, Traill followed instructions from Camden, Calvert and King to sell any unexpended supplies 'to the best advantage for our account'. Tench was shocked to see that Traill 'rioted on the spoils of misery' by setting up a store on the wharf to sell at exorbitant prices the provisions and clothing held back during the voyage, all of which were 'eagerly bought up'. Governor Phillip was livid, yet his report to the judge advocate contained only the mild criticism that the contractors crowded the ships and kept the convicts in irons. Phillip, who was so meticulous with the equitable distributions of rations, made no mention of the deliberate starvation of the convicts by Traill, nor his subsequent profiteering.[19]

None of the five ships of the Second Fleet brought release for John Martin, who was now two years beyond the expiry of his sentence. The papers relating to the sentences of First Fleet convicts had not been sent. Another convict in the same situation as Martin could no longer tolerate his illegal servitude and swam out to the *Neptune* as the ship was preparing to leave for China, willing to risk incurring a horrifying catalogue of abuse to get away. Because the ship was short-handed through desertions, the defector was taken on board, but he was later surrendered to marines searching the ship for stowaways. Technically this man was free to do what he chose with his life, Collins admitted when the judge advocate ordered a severe flogging, but he had 'taken a very improper mode of quitting the colony'. For his part Phillip demanded that Under-Secretary Nepean prosecute Captain Traill for allowing stowaways on his ship. Unless such action was taken, Phillip complained, the master of every ship that called at Sydney would 'carry off some of the best convicts'.[20]

Some good fortune came on board the *Neptune*. John Martin found a partner from among the women survivors: Ann Toy, who was trans-ported for pawning a violin stolen from a seaman at Greenwich. It was two years before Martin formally married Toy, but within two months the well-placed John Randall had married Mary Butler, an Irish woman convicted for stealing beans from a stall in Covent Garden. Mary Butler must have been among the convicts transferred to the second settlement at Parramatta, established 10 miles up the river from Sydney. It was here that most of the convicts who could summon the strength to support their own body weight were sent. The men were employed clearing the ground and preparing it for cultivation or else assisted the ships' carpen-ters in the construction of huts, while about fifty women were set to making clothing from the cloth brought out by the *Neptune*. When Mary Butler married John Randall on 5 September, she was the first of five women married that day at Parramatta, each with the same witnesses. In the weeks after the arrival of the Second Fleet, another twenty-five women were married in Sydney. In nearly every wedding, the groom was a First Fleet convict, soon to be emancipated, who, like John Randall, had good prospects and enjoyed the confidence of the governor.[21]

Nearly all of the convicts off the Second Fleet were sent to Parramatta in July. One group, however, was selected to join the threadbare commu-nity of convicts and marines that had managed to survive on Norfolk Island. Following the break-up of the *Sirius*, Major Ross had persuaded everyone to take an oath to support a survival plan. He then divided the convicts into small groups of six, giving each group an area of land to clear and cultivate in one of two different parts of the island. They were required to work for the government building roads and huts two or three days per week, while for the remainder they could work towards supporting themselves from their allotments. He allowed one pig to every three convicts. Each group would have 'two acres of clear land given them, properly stocked; and as soon as the corn on it is ripe and fit to house they are then to cease drawing any provisions from the public store'.[22]

Creating a sustainable life on Norfolk Island was daunting enough, given a scarcity of cutting axes and other tools, but there was the added difficulty that both marines and convicts had lost supplies of clothing, bedding and even cooking pots in the wreck of the *Sirius*. Ross complained to Philip that with respect to his marines 'not one of them have a shoe to their feet nor scarce a shirt to their backs; their situation at this juncture is truly deplorable ... there is not a bed or blanket among them that is fit to preserve the powers which sustain life'. As Ross was not a man to allow his men to fare less well than felons, the convicts were clearly in a much worst state. For their clothing, Ross grumbled, he had 'not a rag'. Despite the hardship, some responded enthusiastically to Ross's incentives to create an independent life.[23]

Caesar once again proved he was a strong and willing worker. Within months, he and a fellow convict had cleared 10 acres. Further to encourage self-sufficiency, Ross next instituted a policy that if a man undertook to maintain a woman, she would 'not be called upon by the public to do any work'. This proved attractive to Ann Poore, aged 23, sentenced at Maidstone in 1787 for stealing sheets and transported on the *Lady Juliana*, who became Caesar's wife. Over a period of three days, the Rev. Johnson, who had accompanied the convicts to Norfolk Island, married 'upward of one hundred couples'.[24]

The kind of independence Major Ross allowed convicts on Norfolk Island was almost unknown at Sydney Cove. One of the fortunate few metaphorically unshackled in the ironbound penal system was John Randall. At the time he married Mary Butler, he was still working as a game-shooter, although his terms of employment were about to change. Aware of Captain Nicholas Nepean's influential family connections, Governor Phillip ensured that the senior officer of the New South Wales Corps was made as comfortable as possible. He allocated Nepean a personal shooter and by all accounts this was Randall.

Working in the bush, Randall maintained good relations with the Eora – unlike his fellow shooter, the white convict, John McIntyre. For some reason McIntyre inspired a deep enmity among the Aborigines. During an expedition to Broken Bay, which included the three convict shooters, Tench noticed that McIntyre's attempt to make contact with

Aboriginal men was repulsed 'with every mark of horror and resent-ment'. He had observed that McIntyre elicited the same reaction in Aborigines who were living at the settlement. It was no surprise to him when McIntyre was speared on 9 December 1790.

The three game-shooters and a sergeant of marines were hunting on familiar territory at Botany Bay, south of Sydney. On previous trips they had constructed a hut of boughs after the Aboriginal fashion, and it was there that they sheltered overnight, waiting until dawn to hunt the wary kangaroo. Around midnight, they found themselves surrounded by Aboriginal men with spears. McIntyre told his companions: 'dont be afraid, I know them'. He put down his musket and walked towards them making expressions of friendship, while the warriors slowly retreated. Suddenly one of the Aborigines jumped on a fallen log and deliberately speared McIntyre in his left side. Randall and the other two white men were never threatened. McIntyre's offence was something greater than competition for the kangaroo; the weapon used was specially designed to cause the maximum damage. When friendly Aborigines examined the wounded man in Sydney they warned Surgeon White not to extract the spearhead, as death would surely follow. They also supplied the identity of the assailant, a man they called Pemulwuy. Despite their advice, the surgeon saw fit to remove the spearhead and discovered too late that it was serrated with a series of stone barbs, attached by gum resin, that broke off and lodged within McIntyre's body. A slow and excruciatingly painful death was guaranteed.[25]

Where Tench perceived that McIntyre had given serious offence to the Eora, Phillip insisted that the killing was entirely unprovoked and determined upon a massive reprisal. Tench was instructed to lead an expedition to Botany Bay and bring back Pemulwuy and to take the heads of another ten men. Tench was appalled at this order, but could only persuade Phillip to modify his request to six heads. More than fifty men left Parramatta at dawn on 14 December 1790, carrying muskets, hatchets for decapitation and bags for the heads. Randall and the other game-shooter were the guides for this grisly expedition. When the over-heated, insect-bitten party finally reached Botany Bay they were unable to find a single Aborigine. They trudged back to Sydney, only to be ordered out again. Tench knew he needed an element of surprise and instructed the guides to find the quickest route to Botany Bay, 'without heeding difficulty or impediment'. To save time, the game-shooters led them to a swampy area, which, they advised, 'was bad to cross, but might be got over'. Desperate for the advantage, Tench urged his men on, only to become mired in quicksand. He and his men would have been smothered had not the ropes intended for the Aboriginal victims been used to pull them free. Badly shaken and encrusted with mud, they continued a rapid march to the designated settlement. 'To our astonishment ... we found not a single native at the huts', wrote Tench, 'nor was a canoe to be seen on any part of the bay.' The Aborigines had been gone for days. Private Easty thought it was 'the most teadious march as ever men went'.[26]

Rather than teach the Eora a lesson about European superiority, Phillip's punitive expedition was a folly, although it did have the effect of enshrining the warrior Pemulwuy as a resourceful and dangerous enemy. One person who gained an advantage from these farcical events was John Randall. Having failed to lead the head-hunting marines to Pemulwuy, he incurred no personal enmity from the Eora and continued to hunt unmolested. At the same time, he had demonstrated his trustworthiness and loyalty to the governor, which stood him in good stead. He was permitted to live in almost absolute independence, armed and at liberty to move outside the settlement. When not hunting, Randall enjoyed the pleasures of a family life at Parramatta, which had now become a substantial village. As one of the 'convict families of good character', John and Mary Randall were permitted their own separate hut. It was here that Randall's second daughter, Lydia, was born in July 1791.[27]

It was not Aboriginal aggression but the supply of food that was the principal problem for the colony, even though a threatened famine was averted in May 1791 when the *Supply* returned from Batavia with a Dutch ship in tow, carrying supplies of flour, rice and salted meat. The *Supply* also brought back 'Black Jemmy', working his passage as crew. The captain of the *Supply* was so full of praise for him that Governor Phillip was inclined to forgive his outstanding punishment of 500 lashes, until persuaded that to do so would only encourage more stowaways. The sentence was cut in half and his back was again shredded with 250 strokes of the cat. His first-hand knowledge of the sea route to Batavia via Timor may have proved useful to a white convict at Sydney Cove.

✳

Early in the morning of 28 March 1791, William Bryant stole the governor's small cutter and with his wife, Mary, their two infant children and seven other convict men, sailed this open boat over 3000 miles to Dutch controlled Timor.

The Bryant family escaped from Sydney Cove not a moment too soon. A few days later, Phillip was again obliged to cut the ration. As Tench sardonically observed, it was a recurring pattern for rations to be cut at the end of summer 'when the gardens were most destitute of vegetables'. Made furious by hunger, Tench threw himself into a passionate denunciation of the cruelties of a penal system where convicts were forced to labour with next to nothing to eat. 'I every day see wretches pale with disease and wasted with famine, struggle against the horror of their situations', he wrote. 'How striking is the effect of subordination; how dreadful is the fear of punishment!' No human being could work without adequate food, he argued. It was inevitable that convicts would steal. In his carefully contrived narrative, Tench chose not to discuss his role as a member of the court that awarded these fearful and tyrannical punishments – the fruits of hunger. Only months before, he was among those who sentenced Thomas Orford to 2000 lashes. His belated insight into the relationship between theft and hunger may have tempered his future judgments, however. On 8 July 1791, Tench was one of the officers who heard the case of 'Black Jack' Williams. He was charged with stealing provisions, as well as powder and shot, suggesting he intended to follow Caesar's example and make a bolt for the bush. Where this was once a hanging offence, Williams was sentenced to 100 lashes, a mild punishment that was subsequently remitted.

The timely arrival of a transport Mary Ann carrying supplies, as well as 220 more female convicts, averted a repeat of the crime-ridden famine of the previous year. The Mary Ann also carried the unwelcome news that another fleet of ten ships, with many more convicts, was following closely. In future it was intended that New South Wales would receive two transport fleets a year. The infant colony had a bitter foretaste of what this meant when the ships of the Third Fleet followed the Mary Ann into Port Jackson and progressively disembarked another emaciated and scurvy-riddled convict cargo, almost half of whom were totally incapacitated. Once more the horrified colonists were presented with the terrible spectacle of human misery and callous abuse.[28]

✳

AN INCORRIGIBLY STUBBORN BLACK

John Martin was two years beyond the expiry of his sentence when the *Mary Ann* arrived in Sydney carrying the official records of the sentences from the First Fleet. Once the record had been checked, Martin and others like him were collected together by the judge advocate and informed that their options were to take up land as free settlers, or to sign on for further public labour in return for clothing and rations. Most expirees vehemently declared that they wanted to quit the place. Only a few gave their names as settlers and none signed on to work for rations. They were free to leave, Collins explained to them, if they could find a ship willing to take them. Here was the rub: few ships came to remote Sydney town and those that did had little need of fresh crew. When the *Atlantic* sailed for Calcutta to purchase food supplies in October, 'Black Jemmy' Williams stowed away. His sentence did not expire until May 1792, but he was not prepared to wait.

If John Martin wanted to quit the colony, the wherewithal eluded him. He stayed working for rations at Parramatta, where Ann Toy remained a convict. Thomas Orford's time expired in July 1791 and he too elected to work in return for rations. He was without a family; the woman he had married in 1788 was buried on 10 August 1791 under the name of Elizabeth Moseley, presumably because she had become the common-law wife of John Moseley. As a man with a life sentence, Moseley had still many years to serve, as did 'Black Jack' Williams. Samuel Chinery was living at Parramatta as Assistant Surgeon Thomas Arndell's servant at the hospital when his sentence expired in August 1791. He continued to work for Arndell in return for his keep. John Randall finished his sentence in April 1792 and also remained in Parramatta, working as a shooter for the commanding officer of the New South Wales Corps. With his wife still serving her sentence, and two small daughters, Randall was loath to leave a position that had served him so well.

*

The ageing Daniel Gordon lingered on Norfolk Island when his sentence expired in April 1792. He had found a niche for himself as a tailor, patching the ragged uniforms of marines that were literally falling off their backs. Caesar, now sentenced to life imprisonment, had been transported to the island with John Coffin, who had two years left of his sentence to serve. Both were among the convicts who had cleared enough ground to be self-supporting. Ralph Clark proudly wrote to his fellow officers at Sydney at the end of September 1791 that everyone was in good spirits as the crops had survived attacks by grubs and gave 'every apparence that there will be a most plentiful harvest'. Major Ross's radical plan for survival on Norfolk Island appeared successful, but Clark was concerned that there were 'worthier friends' in Sydney who would 'endeavour to throw every drop of cold water on it' to ensure the scheme's failure. One of those 'worthier friends', Phillip Gidley King, returned in early November 1791 when the *Atlantic* called at Norfolk Island en route to Calcutta.[1]

Once he resumed his role as lieutenant governor of the island, King wasted no time demolishing the system Ross had created. Knowing that Ross had the ear of under-secretary Nepean, King damned his predecessor's plan with faint praise. While he believed the scheme was 'laudable, and end much to be wished for', the main thrust of his account worked to discredit the system. Contrary to Clark's description of pride in achievement, King could report only 'discord and strife in every person's countenance, and in every corner and hole of the island'. He told Nepean that over 150 convicts had sent him a petition protesting that Ross had forced them into an independence they did not desire. As a consequence, King explained, he was obliged to cancel the allocations of land and to call in the pigs, which he redistributed to the retired marines who had opted to take land as free settlers.[2]

Most of the convicts were allocated to the public works or assigned as labour to settlers and soldiers. John Coffin did not appreciate the change of circumstance; his mutinous behaviour caused him to be worked in irons for two months and he was subsequently given 100 lashes for neglecting his government labour. On the other hand, the new arrangements probably suited Gordon. He was kept so busy making new uniforms from the supplies of cloth that arrived with King, he continued working as a tailor when his time expired. Caesar was one of a few favoured convicts to benefit from King's concession that permitted them to raise their own food. He was allocated one acre of land and permitted to work there for three days a week. At this time he was living with Ann Poore and their daughter Mary-Ann, born in March 1792.[3]

When the *Atlantic* called at Norfolk Island to off-load the lieutenant governor, the naval agent was aware that 'Black Jemmy' Williams was on board. He had managed to survive undetected by the authorities on the three-month journey to the Ganges, suggesting that the crew were complicit in his defection. However, the naval agent at Calcutta refused to accept that 'Black Jemmy's' term had expired and insisted he be returned to Sydney to verify his status. He arrived back on the *Atlantic* on 20 June 1792, still insisting upon his status as free man. The judge advocate checked the record to find 'Black Jemmy' was, indeed, free. Collins determined that further punishment was unnecessary and the young man was 'at liberty to get away in any ship that would receive him on board'. With recent experience as a seaman and excellent recommendations from the ship's captain, 'Black Jemmy' was better placed than most to secure a berth. Almost certainly he was one of two ex-convicts who left on the *Atlantic* when it sailed for England in December 1792. One way or another, he made good his escape from New South Wales, albeit to a perilously uncertain world where black seamen were constantly at risk of being snatched by man hunters and sold into slavery.[4]

Fear of re-enslavement may have influenced the choice of ex-seaman John Martin to continue in the place of his incarceration. After all, there was no slavery, as such, in New South Wales, however brutal and coercive the penal system. In August 1792 Governor Phillip further restricted Martin's choices by indicating that only a select few of the ex-convicts would be permitted to leave and then only if they carried a certificate to that effect. A new clause was inserted into shipping contracts to penalise the master of any ship that took away anyone who did not hold such a certificate. That same month Martin confirmed his future in the colony by marrying Ann Toy, who remained under sentence.[5]

Martin's decision to work for the government in return for rations became less and less viable as the store-ships from England failed to arrive. By July 1792, the ration issued by the commissary contained neither flour nor meat. Richard Atkins, an ageing drunk who had been

exiled to the distant colony by his illustrious family, was bemused to
find that New South Wales remained entirely dependent on stores from
England, rather than harvesting the abundant resources at hand. 'The
quantities of fish in the harbour is amazing', he wrote, 'I should imagine
the fishery under proper regulations might be of great advantage.' He
watched helplessly as convicts recently arrived in the Third Fleet,
already weak from their traumatic journey, died at a terrifying rate for
want of adequate food. 'If the convicts had but an opportunity to fish',
he despaired, 'but there is no trusting of them with a boat.' As the
magistrate at Parramatta, Atkins found the daily business of his court
even more distressing as he administered rough justice to any 'number
of poor wretches, whose emaciated looks, denote poverty and misery in
the extreme'. He found himself 'obliged to punish those whom hunger
drove to steal a few cobs of corn or a turnip'. However wasted, the
convict men were still required to do work, 'yoked to draw timber
twenty-five in a gang', as one Irish convict later recounted. 'The sticks
were six feet long; six men abreast. We held the stick behind us, and
dragged it with our hands.' This when being fed a few ounces of salt
meat a day. 'Men used to carry trees on their shoulders', the man
recalled. 'How they used to die.'[6]

Of particular concern to Atkins was that the fundamental staple of
flour was absent from the convict ration. The substitute, Indian corn,
was 'little use in point of nourishment', he wrote; 'they have no mills to
grind it and many are so weak that they cannot pound it'. Since a fishery
was not in operation, the only means to survival on such a severe ration
was to cultivate a garden. Atkins noted with approval that ex-convict
settlers who had taken land grants on the northern boundary of
Parramatta provided plenty of vegetables and Indian corn, as well as
several pigs, for their families. And this they had managed within ten
months. If periodic starvation was to be avoided, he concluded, one
must have the capacity to become self-sufficient. He promptly secured a
land grant for himself in August 1792 on land that had been cleared of
timber by the 'poor wretches' whose desperation kept his court so busy.
John Martin reached the same conclusion. In November 1792 he took
up a 50-acre grant on the northern boundary of Parramatta.[7]

It was surely no coincidence that on the same day Martin received
his grant, Randall was given a grant of 60 acres adjacent to Martin,

'eastward of the Northern Boundary Farms'. The term 'farms' in this case was a complete misnomer; the land in question was a tract of virgin bush. Grants of between 30 and 60 acres were given to emancipated convicts, with the larger grants for those with families, on condition that the grantees cleared the land and raised enough crops for their subsistence, being provisioned from the store during the first eighteen months only. After five years of cultivation they would receive freehold title, and after ten years their grant would be subject to an annual quit rent of 1 shilling. Those taking up the grants were given two pigs as initial livestock. To assist in clearing the land, they were supplied with a hatchet, a tomahawk, two spades and a shovel.[8]

Around Parramatta the eucalypt trees reached a hundred feet into the unclouded sky, while the undergrowth was a tangle of bushes armed with hidden prickles. Areas of open vegetation might appear to be grassy sward on which stock could graze; in actuality it was clumps of razor-sharp spear grass that hid snakes with venom potent enough to kill a pig in minutes. Even when the huge trees were felled, the stumps were too unyielding to be grubbed out and their extensive root system bound the soil into an uncompromising mass. Civil officials, such as Atkins and Arndell, had the advantage of convict labour to clear their acres and plant their crops, while emancipated convicts had only their bare hands. There were dim prospects that a man with no experience of rural labour could wrest a viable farm out of this blighted wilderness, Tench concluded, just months before Randall and Martin took up their grants. In a year or so, he predicted, the inexperienced ex-convict would 'have the honour of returning to drag a timber or brick cart for his maintenance'.[9]

This was not the first time Martin and Randall had to fell massive trees, nor the first time they built huts from rudimentary material, even if they had no prior farming experience. It was not so much their inexperience, as the weather, which was against them in the first few months. Between December and March the daytime temperature hovered between 102 and 114 degrees Fahrenheit, in the shade. The ground was littered with the bodies of birds that had dropped lifeless from the sky. The men struggled to clear enough land to plant a garden and to sow a crop in the face of fierce winds that blew from the west like a blast from an oven. On 7 December 1792, a wildfire swept through the tinder-dry bush, threatening huts and destroying gardens. Fanned by scorching westerly winds, it spread across the Sydney basin, speeding through the tops of the eucalyptus trees with a deafening roar as it greedily consumed the highly combustible, oily leaves. Atkins tersely described the situation in his journal: 'at 12 o'clock 107 in the shade, the whole country was in a perfect blaze'. The fire was beaten back from the farms around Parramatta, but on Assistant Surgeon Arndell's farm, a spark from the burning treetops flew into the thatch of the hut he had built to house his convict workers. Such was the intensity of the roaring inferno, Collins reported, 'the hut with all the out buildings and thirty bushels of wheat just got into the sack, were in a few minutes destroyed'. Arndell's servant, Samuel Chinery, had once made his home on the hollow of a burnt-out tree and may have again had to resort to such shelter. It was a summer of disaster. On 13 February 1793, in a week when the temperature gauge registered between 112 and 116 degrees, John Randall and his wife Mary buried their infant daughter Lydia.[10]

After recovering from the fire, settlers desperately needed to sow crops before the winter's onset as once more the colony was feeling the pinch of approaching famine. The increasingly desperate situation required drastic measures: the Indian corn seed with which the settlers were issued was soaked in urine to prevent it being eaten instead of sown. Martin managed to establish a few acres of Indian corn on his grant in time to benefit from the rains that broke in the autumn of 1793. Randall was lucky to be employed as a game-shooter for the commander of the New South Wales Corps, which would have helped him supplement his family's ration. He had given up on farming, preferring instead to invest his energy into his client relationship with the senior officers of the New South Wales Corps.

The New South Wales Corps had been raised specifically for this post, and its commanding officer, Major Francis Grose, finally arrived in Sydney in February 1792. Grose immediately sought to augment the corps's strength by recruiting a second company from among those discharged marines who had chosen to remain in the colony. Grose determined that Lieutenant George Johnston on Norfolk Island would command this company, and Johnston had little difficulty enlisting thirty-five men from among the disheartened ex-marine settlers on Norfolk Island, and was thus rewarded with a commission as captain.

The retired marines returned from Norfolk Island in May 1791, carrying scandalous stories about Lieutenant Governor King's new order. Easty was shocked to hear from his old comrades that 'the Iland wich was reconed the most flourishing of any Iland in the world all most turns out to be a pore mersable place'. Tales of chronic food shortages and a regime of brutality led Easty to conclude that King 'behavs more like a mad man then a man in trusted with the goverment of an Iland … belonging to Great Bretain'. King's own reports indicated that circumstances on Norfolk Island had greatly deteriorated since Clark's rosy assessment. Convicts had been on short rations for months, King admitted in September 1792, and as a consequence there was a persistent problem of food theft. More troublesome were a handful of recently arrived Irish convicts who had run off to the bush from where they made night-time raids on the gardens of the officers. Without adequate judicial powers he felt unable to control such desperadoes. Governor Phillip agreed that he could send 'the most notorious characters' back to Sydney. [11]

On 21 March 1793, the *Kitty* arrived from Norfolk Island with 172 male convicts, including Caesar, without his pregnant wife and daughter. According to the documentation from King, these included 'every convict from the gaol and many from the lockup house' as well as those who had 'served their time'. King may have been persuaded that Caesar had served his time, as his original sentence expired in March 1793 and he may have been unaware that during his absence from the colony, Caesar had been given a secondary sentence of life, as well as twice being sentenced to death and pardoned. If this were King's explanation for Caesar's repatriation, the judge advocate would have to be involved. Collins, who regarded this 'incorrigibly stubborn black' as his particular *bête noir*, merely observed of those on the *Kitty* that the lieutenant governor 'desired to get rid of any such characters as might be dangerous or troublesome to him'. There was no record that Caesar had been 'dangerous or troublesome' during his time on Norfolk Island. Rather it was likely to have been the anticipation of trouble that saw this hardworking convict torn away from his family. [12]

King appeared to be taking pre-emptive action when he sent so many men back to Sydney in March 1793. There could not have been that many convicts in the gaol; King himself acknowledged that there had been no dramatic increase in the crime rate and that for the past six months no house had been robbed, nor any vegetables stolen. The problem was more complex. When the unruly soldiers of the New South Wales Corps replaced the marines on the island, King was faced with demands from the soldiers for preferential treatment. Convicts like Caesar who had been permitted to cultivate land for their own use were now turfed off it 'in order to give the non-commissioned officers and privates an opportunity of providing themselves with vegetables', King explained. In addition to preferential treatment in the allocation of land and convict labour, the soldiers wanted the women. As King was later to complain, they became 'very intimate with the convicts, living in their huts ... and perpetually enticing the women to leave the men they were married to'. Such an emotionally volatile environment invited violence. By removing so many of the men from contention, King was reducing the potential for conflict that threatened to destabilise completely his small, isolated world. If this was his strategy, it was unsuccessful. Conflict over women erupted into a serious mutiny within a year. Meanwhile, Caesar was hauling carts in Sydney like a beast of burden.[13]

On 11 December 1792, Governor Philip had sailed for home on the *Atlantic*, probably with 'Black Jemmy' among the crew. The acting governor was Major Francis Grose, commander of the New South Wales Corps, whose very first decision, made on the day after Phillip's departure, was to abandon the policy of equitable rations, ordering a higher allowance for his soldiers. In the weeks that followed, Grose abolished the sitting of civil magistrates and substituted an entirely military government. The new governor's determination to privilege his officers and men was unequivocal. He gave each officer a grant of 100 acres freehold, assigning at least ten convicts to clear the land and plant crops, with three more to work as domestic servants, all on the government's time. Enlisted men were allowed 25 acres and one or two convicts (sometimes more) to work the land. Grose was adamant that the New South Wales Corps were 'the only description of settlers on whom reliance can be placed', and he informed the judge advocate he intended to encourage their non-military pursuits as far as he had the power. As governor his power was absolute.[14]

The ne'er-do-wells who took commissions in the New South Wales Corps were a rapacious bunch whose exile to this godforsaken place promised profit over glory. Even under the austere Phillip's watch, they grasped every opportunity to speculate on food shortages by pooling regimental salaries for chartering the store-ship *Britannia* to purchase livestock in India that could then be sold in Sydney. When the American ship *Hope* arrived with a large shipment of rum on Christmas Eve 1792, Grose directed the commissary to buy the entire shipment, all 7597 gallons of which was handed to the officers of the corps to dispense. In a self-justifying account to the Home Secretary, Grose 'lamented on this occasion being obliged to purchase spirits, without which [the captain] would not agree to the disposal of his provisions'. He gave stern instructions that rum must not get into the possession of the convicts, though he might have saved his breath. The officers of the New South Wales Corps were no respecters of persons when it came to turning a profit. Having watered down the rum and decanted it into wine bottles, they sold to all and sundry at a profit of 400 per cent. Grose also directed his officers to use the rum as barter to concentrate livestock in their hands. This was achieved by purchasing the sheep Phillip had diligently distributed among the settlers shortly before his departure.[15]

For all of Grose's lamentations about the necessity of buying spirits, the purchase from the *Hope* was merely the first of many speculative trading ventures that brought rum to Sydney. The spirit was available to anyone, for the barter of goods or the issue of promissory notes. Landless labourers would work for rum, soldiers happily handed over their 25-acre grants in return for 2 or 3 gallons of the spirit, and farmers exchanged their produce for it. Thus all the benefits of trade accumulated in the hands of the officers of the corps. Convicts were strictly forbidden spirits, but as the disapproving Collins observed, they 'preferred receiving liquor for labour, to every other article of clothing or provisions' and they would 'go to any lengths to procure it'. The New South Wales Corps was happy to oblige. In next to no time, the colony was awash with 'this pernicious American spirit'.[16]

The rapaciousness of the officers of the corps and the havoc caused by their liquor trading was a cause for comment by many diarists. A visiting naval officer sardonically observed how the 'United Company of Traffic Merchants' kept the flow of spirit unchecked by generously extending credit, then calling in their debt at the most auspicious time for their profit. In just such a way a neighbour of John Martin lost his farm at the northern boundary, when officers called in their debts as his promising wheat crop was due for harvest. Once a crop was harvested, the corps acted as the broker, buying grain in return for rum, or taking it as repayment for debt, and then reselling it to the commissary at a considerable mark-up.[17]

In reality, the 1793 harvest was barely good enough to stave off famine. In May 1793, Grose drastically cut the flour allowance, issuing instead Indian corn-on-the-cob that was still to be husked and ground, even though the colony was without a properly functioning mill. By the time the *Britannia* returned from India in June, three-quarters of the cargo of livestock purchased by the corps had died on the voyage. Grose was forced to charter the ship one more time to take a letter back to the governor of India, Lord Cornwallis, begging for supplies on the British government account. The ship also took Captain Nepean, whose health was poorly, and who was not prepared to endure life at the end of the world without even the barest of necessities. When the ship departed there was only enough food in the store to last about six weeks; everyone knew the round trip to India took about eight months. As the hottest summer gave way to the coldest winter to date, the convicts and settlers anxiously scrutinised the weather, as they had once scanned the horizon for sails, desperate for a good harvest in the following season.

When Nepean quit the colony, John Randall transferred to Sydney to be the shooter for Grose. Randall exemplified a problem that had preoccupied Governor Phillip in the days before he left: grantees who failed to work their land, seeing it rather as capital. Randall was not residing on his grant in October 1793 when four Irish convicts armed with clubs broke into his hut and nearly killed the two men who were living there, before they were driven away, empty-handed. At that time, he was in Sydney with his wife Mary, who gave birth to another daughter in early December. The two men living at Randall's hut were likely to have been convicts who, for their refusal to co-operate with the runaways, were violently assaulted. As a trusted employee of Major Grose, Randall would have been allocated convicts to work his land, on the same principle that Grose assigned convicts to work the land of his regular soldiers. Grose had expropriated almost all the convict labour in the colony for the use of his officers and soldiers, the subsequent governor found to his chagrin. With no paperwork to document this transfer of public labour to private use, it was impossible to know who or how many were 'scattered about the country, and employed by private persons'.[18]

Although Randall had a home in Sydney, he was required to travel considerable distances into the bush as the kangaroo had become scarce close to the settlements. A Spanish visitor in March 1793 noticed that kangaroo were extremely difficult to procure; even with the additional aid of dogs it required a hunter of 'much agility and nimbleness' who could pursue the game 'running for five or six miles'. Given the difficulties of procuring game meat, it never offered a serious alternative to the salted provisions that were the staple of the weekly ration for those 'on the store'. The visiting Spaniard became heartily sick of eating kangaroo at almost every meal, but then he was sitting down at the tables of Captain Nepean and Major Grose, who were supplied with this luxury by Randall. The pinched and pale convicts hauling timber on their wasted shoulders at Parramatta and Toongabbie, or staggering under loads of rock on the public roads in Sydney, were not repasting on dinners of fresh game.[19]

By Christmas 1793 there was food to last only a few short months, even at the drastically reduced ration. 'There is every appearance of distress taking place among the convicts', Atkins recorded. ''Tis true we have wheat in plenty but neither sufficient thressers to send it to the store or have we mills to grind it.' Alcohol compounded the problems of a poor diet. Another of Martin's neighbour's died as a result of excessive drinking and the surgeons grew desperate as the hospitals overflowed with people sick with 'fever and dysentery' brought on by the combination of starvation rations and alcohol abuse.[20]

The colony hovered on the brink of famine until early March 1794. By then the salted meat was completely depleted. Nearly all the livestock was in the hands of the New South Wales Corps, and no one expected they would willingly share their fresh provisions with the colony's despised felons. It seemed to the judge advocate that bloody and terrible conflict was inevitable. Just how long, Collins wondered, would the convicts sit 'quietly down on their return from labouring in the field to their scanty portion of bread and water, and ... [look] patiently on while others were keeping want and hunger at a distance by the daily enjoyment of a comfortable meal of fresh viands?' Thankfully, he did not have to ponder long upon this awful prospect. On the very day the commissary closed its doors, the sails of an English ship were sighted: the first of two fully laden store-ships carrying supplies from England.[21]

The constant threat of famine persuaded Grose that he could not keep feeding those time-expired convicts who remained on the store. Atkins reported in May 1794 Grose's order that these people 'should give their names so they could be sent home'. Such a prospect may have persuaded Thomas Orford he would be better off working his own land. On 1 April 1794, he took up a grant at Bulanaming north of Sydney. Meanwhile, months of near starvation had pushed Caesar beyond endurance. In July 1794, after four years of good conduct, he once more made a bolt for the bush. He survived for a brief period before being caught and punished 'with some severity'. The episode proved to Collins that Caesar was 'still incorrigible', not so much for absconding as for his refusal to be cowed. Bloody and flayed, Caesar still managed to treat his old adversary to a bravura display, telling the judge advocate 'with exultation and contempt' that 'all that [flogging] would not make him better'.[22]

By July the full ration was restored after several more ships arrived from India and America carrying food, commodities, and many more gallons of rum, all of which Major Grose felt obliged to buy. Atkins looked upon these particular transactions as an unmitigated disaster. 'Instead of giving a spur to industry by those who have farms being enabled thereby to employ labourers ... it will only increase the general depravity', he wrote. Much as Atkins himself was an incorrigible drunk, he was horrified by the effect of spirits on the lower classes: 'Gaming, whoring and drunkenness stalk in broad day without the least check ... and I am sorry to say, sanctioned.' Atkins was delighted with the news in September 1794 that Captain John Hunter would be returning to Sydney as the new governor, promising an end to rapacious military rule. Responding to this, Major Grose made immediate plans to leave, further increasing Atkins's delight. Even so, not all the events of that month brought such pleasure. Atkins was pained to record that the public granary at Parramatta burned down consuming the 2400 bushels of husked corn in the blaze, some of it John Martin's hard-won crop.[23]

Although Martin was now off the store and in his second year as a farmer, life on his grant continued to be precarious. If poisonous snakes, wild fires, desperate convicts and drunken neighbours were not trouble enough, another threat had been added to the catalogue. The Eora had become more aggressive in asserting their right to the land in response to the rash of settlement spreading out from Sydney and Parramatta. During the summer a group of settler women were attacked on the track between their farms and Parramatta, and Eora raids on settlers' ripening crops became so numerous that Atkins believed the Aborigines had developed a craving for corn. He had no comprehension that their persistent assaults on the cornfields might be a strategy calculated to force the settlers to quit their farms, but he did understand that the raids threatened the viability of the whole agricultural enterprise. If the colony were ever to prosper, he concluded, it was 'absolutely necessary ... to take fatal steps with them'.[24]

By 1794 a patchwork of farms worked by ex-convicts and a few free settlers fanned out in a 20-mile radius west from Sydney. They had felled the trees, fenced the grassland, driven away the kangaroo and kidnapped Aboriginal children for farm workers. In short, they destroyed the capacity of the indigenous people to exist in the land they had occupied for over 40000 years. The establishment of new farms 25 miles east of Parramatta on the Hawkesbury River was the trigger for concerted Eora retaliation led by the warrior Pemulwuy. Large parties of Aborigines converged on the new settlers' huts stealing provisions, clothes and whatever else they could lay their hands on. As with the persistent raids on the ripening corn at Parramatta, Pemulwuy's strategy was not to inflict serious injury, but to drive the settlers away. It was obvious to him that the newcomers regularly encountered episodes of starvation that pushed them to acts of desperation and that the colony was over-dependent upon the grain crop. Moreover, two Irish runaways living among the Eora supplied him with intelligence about the precarious state of the colony as well as appropriate military strategies.

Murderous conflict followed soon enough. In late summer 1794 two Aboriginal men were killed during a confrontation at a cornfield near the Northern Boundary Farms at Parramatta. Another group of Aborigines were shot by settlers from the Hawkesbury in September 1794. The following month an Aboriginal boy was caught by a group of settlers and dragged several times through a fire, before being doused in the Hawkesbury River and finally shot through the head. Two settlers implicated in this incident were killed by Aborigines in May 1795, instigating reprisal by the New South Wales Corps. This was met with a counter-reprisal by Pemulwuy. Both actions left combatants on each side dead or grievously wounded. Collins summed up the gruesome situation with laconic indifference: 'the natives at the Hawkesbury are murdering the settlers, [the New South Wales Corps] are in turn murdering the natives (but it cannot be avoided)'. So great was the murderous disruption to farming on the Hawkesbury that it appeared the area with the colony's richest soil would have to be abandoned.[25]

At the same time the commissary store was once more completely depleted of flour and the stock of salt meat, sugar and dried peas was dangerously low. The acting governor, Captain William Paterson of the New South Wales Corps, determined that only his soldiers and civil officers were to be issued these essentials in their rations, while everyone else was forced to make do without meat or dried peas. Collins, who had been in the colony since its inception, perceived the potential for trouble, especially when the convicts' miserable ration included the despised dhal as a substitute for flour. He 'lamented that necessity ever existed, of forcing upon them such trash' and held high hopes that the new governor, when he arrived in September 1795, would terminate the excessive privileges of the military.[26]

Governor Hunter did no such thing. Rather than rein in the officers of the New South Wales Corps, he sought as his confidant John Macarthur, the powerful and overbearing paymaster, who also held the important position of inspector of public works at Parramatta. Having secured the unpaid labour of convicts, Macarthur wished to maximise the amount of work he could extract from them, and encouraged Hunter to reorganise the convict schedule. Where previously convicts were required to work for the government in the period between dawn and one o'clock, now they were to work from sun-up to sundown, with a break of two-and-a-half hours. Collins pronounced himself pleased with the change, since its effect was to reduce the 'idle time the prisoners before had and which, emphatically they terming *their own time*, they applied as they chose'. The more regimented and hard-pressed they were, the better, in his view. Only those in the New South Wales Corps would have agreed with him. The convicts lost their capacity to work for payment and the settlers lost their pool of labour – to make matters worse – at harvest time. Enraged on that account alone, Atkins watched with fury as the governor capitulated to the New South Wales Corps's demands to be fed a full ration at the expense of the rest of the hungry colonists. 'We shall see how this end[s]', he wrote ominously, late in November 1795.[27]

Caesar was not prepared to wait to find out how things would end. In December 1795 he 'once more fled from honest labour to the woods', so Collins recorded. This was an inauspicious time for the colony: not only did famine loom as ever-present, but bloody confrontations between settlers and Aborigines at the Hawkesbury were escalating in intensity, with the two Irish bolters successfully advising Pemulwuy on military tactics. Collins had no expectation that Caesar had run away to join forces with Pemulwuy, even though he regarded him as 'a savage of a darker hue, and full as far removed from civilization'. Collins hoped that the notorious and powerful black convict would prove a match for the Eora leader. Indeed, Caesar was almost redeemed in Collins's eyes when he was reported to have shot and killed Pemulwuy. This 'one meritorious action' caused him to mollify his distaste for Caesar. But, as it transpired, Collins was mistaken. Although there probably was an armed confrontation between the two in which Pemulwuy was seriously wounded, he was not killed. The Eora warrior abruptly disappeared for over a year before reappearing at the head of a large party of Aborigines in the streets of Parramatta.[28]

Caesar was able to obtain firearms and ammunition from sympathetic ex-convict settlers in the district, among whom was Thomas Orford, his old companion from the *Ceres*. They were happy to illicitly provide him with the arms they had been issued for their own protection. Nor was Caesar the only outlaw thus supplied. Collins reported that Caesar was the model for and leader of 'several other vagabonds', who had formed into an armed outlaw gang. When the commissary conducted a survey to establish the whereabouts of nearly 300 muskets belonging to the crown they found that less than fifty could be accounted for. In Collins's view, the unrestrained activities of these *banditti* presented a threat to the penal colony far more dangerous than Pemulwuy.[29]

In an attempt to nip this new threat in the bud, at the end of 1795 Governor Hunter made an offer of conditional pardon to Caesar, to which Caesar responded 'that he would neither come in or suffer himself to be taken alive'. The governor would not tolerate such effrontery. On

29 January 1796, he published an official notice: 'Whoever shall secure this man Black Caesar and bring him in with his arms shall receive as a reward five gallons of spirits.' Many days went by and still Caesar remained beyond official reach, rapidly acquiring the status of a celebrity. 'Scarcely a morning arrived without a complaint being made to the magistrates of a loss of property supposed to have been occasioned by this man', Collins's wrote testily. '[E]very theft that was committed was ascribed to him.' Collins believed that soldiers had stolen a case of salt pork from the new mill-house they were guarding and they found it very convenient that 'the theft was fixed upon Caesar'. Exasperated though he was, Collins was confident that such a lavish reward would bring quick results.[30]

Caesar was true to his word; he was not taken alive. John Winbow shot and killed him on 15 February 1796. In making an explanation to the authorities, Winbow claimed that he had not deliberately ambushed Caesar but had shot in self-defence and had a witness to prove it. Governor Hunter repeated Winbow's story when he told the secretary of state that Black Caesar was killed when he 'attempted to shoot the man who spoke to him, but there being two of them together, the other, in self defence, fired and shot him'. Collins gave much the same account, supplying the additional information that Winbow had been hunting for Caesar 'for some days'. Both the governor and the judge advocate passed over without comment the awkward fact that a convicted felon still under sentence spent days roaming unsupervised in the bush with a gun and ammunition. Winbow had been a highwayman in England. The inescapable conclusion was that he was himself one of the *banditti*, which is why he was armed and knew where to find Caesar. Any sense of fraternal loyalty Winbow might once have felt to a fellow convict had been extinguished by the soul-searing experience of transportation. As the Rev. Johnston was pained to observe at the time the Second Fleet discharged its pitiful cargo, the survivors had thoroughly absorbed the maxim of the pampered Nicholas Nepean: 'Every man for himself'.[31]

SPORTSMAN TO GENERAL GROSE

Word of Caesar's death was carried to the *Reliance* when it sailed from Sydney a week later, on 21 February 1796. On reaching Norfolk Island only one of Caesar's old companions-in-chains was still around to hear the news. Daniel Gordon was working as a tailor at the settlement at Queenborough, but John Coffin had left a year earlier, having secured a berth on a ship, bound for India, that came into Norfolk Island short-handed after putting three crew ashore in Sydney. Ann Poore received the information about her husband's death only a few weeks before she herself died from an unknown cause on 25 March, leaving 4-year-old Mary-Ann and 2-year-old John as orphans. The children were adopted by their mother's old friend from the *Lady Juliana*, Mary Randall.[1]

Back at Sydney, Judge Advocate Collins was supremely satisfied that the long battle of wills he had waged with this 'incorrigibly stubborn black' was finally resolved in his favour. Six months later he left the colony for England, confident that without an alluring role model like Caesar, the dangerous precedent of convict resistance had been snuffed out once and for all. Governor Hunter was equally confident when he assured the secretary of state that the death of this 'notorious offender' would have a salutary effect on the 'turbulent and refractory' colony. Hunter's report on this matter would have been one of the few communications that the secretary of state was happy to receive from New South Wales. It was his lofty view that nothing was more likely to endanger the infant colony than the idea 'that such a *banditti* could exist with impunity'. That was not how it appeared to the settlers struggling in New South Wales. For them the real *banditti* were not runaway convicts but the grasping officers of the New South Wales Corps whose actions appeared immune from censure or restriction. Settlers who had not already lost their farms to these officers-turned-traders were deeply indebted to them and forced to pledge their crops for several seasons to come.[2]

*

Governor Hunter took the view that the endemic indebtedness and pauperism among settlers was a result of an inherent bent toward indolence and drunkenness in the ex-convict population. It was nearly five years before he was forced to scrutinise the officers of the New South Wales Corps, who had long since abandoned military pretensions (other than duelling) to form a ruthless trading monopoly. In February 1798, Hunter received a petition from a group of disgruntled settlers at the Field of Mars in which they insisted the evil which beset the settler population was not of their making and that the remedy lay in his hands alone. The settlers complained of the exorbitant prices charged for every commodity imported into the colony. Tobacco – 'more in use in this colony than even in Virginia' – headed a long list of items, including sugar, tea and spirits, commodities that were purchased off the ships by the officer cartel and sold at ten times cost price. At the same time the settlers were forced to sell their crop to the cartel at rock-bottom prices, knowing that the grain would be sold to the commissary at a hefty mark-up. The hard-hitting allegations were reinforced by an investigation into settler conditions by two magistrates from Parramatta who found crippling debt and poverty at every place they visited. In the Northern Boundary District the only farmer who remained from the original grantees was John Martin, 'a sober and industrious man, yet very poor'; the rest were 'gone to ruin', or like John Randall had left their farms for other employment.[3]

Finally, the spineless governor was forced to acknowledge that the New South Wales Corps must be curbed. Even so, Hunter was not prepared to restrict the mercantile monopoly of the military; he was having trouble enough recovering unauthorised convict labour from their farms. Early in his term of office, Hunter lent a sympathetic ear to John Macarthur's claims that officers needed large numbers of convicts to work their farms. He therefore felt it reasonable to demand two convicts be returned from every officer's farm and 'one from others who may have hitherto been allowed some assistance'. Even so, locating all the convicts and getting them into government work gangs proved an intractable problem. It was only by removing assigned convicts of small-fry like John Randall that the governor eventually got enough labour to repair the parlous state of the public works and build the strong gaols required at Sydney and Parramatta.[4]

*

At this time John Randall was still in the employ of the senior military officer of the New South Wales Corps, technically as the shooter for Lieutenant Colonel Grose, who had lived in England since 1794. In reality, Randall was most probably in the employ of Major William Paterson and, after Paterson's departure in 1796, of Captain George Johnston, who became Governor Hunter's aide-de-camp. Second only to the paymaster John Macarthur, Johnston was the most successful entrepreneur in the corps, who for some time had control over the allocation of convict labour at Parramatta. As well as benefiting from the officers' monopoly of trade, Johnston had been granted many hundreds of acres and he had been accused of appropriating cattle from the government herd for his land. By 1799 he was the wealthiest man in the colony. Randall was known to Johnston, who had previously employed him as a shooter. Indeed, Johnston may have known Randall from a long time before when, as a mere boy of 14, Johnston took a commission in the regiment of his patron, Lord Percy (late Duke of Northumberland). The regiment was stationed in New York and Lord Percy particularly encouraged black recruits into his service, several of whom he took back to England when he left America in 1779. Even if Johnston had not personally encountered Randall, he must have become familiar with the runaway slaves during this formative period in his life.[5]

Randall no longer lived at Parramatta having moved to Sydney where, on 28 May 1797, John Randall Jr was born. Randall may even have been living at Government House. On the evening of Wednesday, 5 June 1799 a servant at Government House intercepted Randall carrying 'sundry plates and glasses' between the kitchen and the gate to the sentry box. Randall gave an ambiguous explanation for this behaviour and the items were returned to the kitchen. That would have been the end of the matter, except that at ten o'clock that night the constable on duty saw Randall sneaking out of the house with more kitchenware. After making a tackle, the constable arrested Randall, the evidence surrounding him on the ground: five whole and two broken glasses.[6]

The case came before the court a few days later, when the judge advocate took a very dim view of the felony. It was common knowledge that early in Hunter's term his principal servant had been engaged in a criminal racket fencing items stolen from Government House. The judge advocate's letter to the governor about Randall sternly advised 'the propriety of ordering exemplary punishment' and implied that Hunter should not encourage a perception that criminal activity was officially encouraged at Government House. Hunter's response was delivered the following morning. He abjured punishment, explaining that he had received 'a petition from Black Randall expressing his sincere contrition for the robbery attempt'. He politely requested the judge advocate to 'take the trouble to order him to be liberated'. Randall was illiterate and had been incarcerated in gaol for four days. Some well-placed person must have interceded on his behalf: Captain George Johnston, perhaps.[7]

Even if Randall retained his most powerful patron, this incident signalled a gradual fall from grace, from where he lost his cosy niche in the colonial order. He may have continued in his accustomed position for a few months, with Hunter's indulgence, but his circumstances undoubtedly changed in November 1799 when Colonel William Paterson returned as the senior military officer. Paterson brought from England orders to clean up 'the abuses which are practiced and countenanced by the officers of the New South Wales Corps'. Tales of officers purchasing entire cargoes of spirits and retailing them at extortionate prices had reached the ears of Prince Regent who demanded a stop to any activities 'pernicious to His Majesty's Service'. While Hunter consistently deflected orders to institute an inquiry into the irregular trading activities of the officers and refused to arrest any found dealing in spirits, Paterson was determined to make a show of disciplining his officers. The man most immediately in his sights was Hunter's aide-de-camp, George Johnston. Paterson complained to Joseph Banks in England that the governor would not co-operate, even after he was recalled by the furious Duke of Portland. Paterson was obliged to keep his powder dry until the replacement governor arrived.

Phillip Gidley King, protégé of Joseph Banks and the lieutenant governor of New South Wales, stepped ashore on 16 April 1800. Within two days of establishing himself in Paterson's quarters, King began a campaign of harassment designed to oust Hunter from Government House and establish his own authority over the colony. By referring ostentatiously to his royal instructions (which, in fact, did not exist), King left Paterson in no doubt that he was here to purge the colony of its basest corruptions. On 3 May 1800, Johnston was under arrest for selling over-priced spirits. Hunter, who refused to vacate either his residence or his office until a suitable ship was made available to transport him back to England, insisted that it was an impossibility that his aide-de-camp be tried by a colonial court. Johnston was also, therefore, to return to England, where protection against adverse judgment lay in the power of his patrons.[8]

At the time of Johnston's arrest, Randall had been living back in Parramatta for at least four months. He had not yet fallen on hard times, as was apparent when he appeared as plaintiff in a criminal case against a recently arrived Irish convict accused of stealing a pound of tea from his house in the town. Randall stated in his evidence that a woman named Kit Murphy had come to his house asking for 'a gill of spiritous liqour' which she drank. She then requested more and Randall obliged. While he and his wife Mary were visiting a neighbour, Murphy was left alone in the house with John Randall Jr, who gave evidence that she broke into his father's box and stole more rum, a pound of tea and a pinafore. In her defence, Murphy said Randall, had 'ill used her and had attempted to be carnally connected with her against her will'. He had given her tea – to a market value of around four guineas – as inducement for sex. The constable at Parramatta testified that he often saw the prisoner 'in the habits of intercourse with Randall and she was frequently at his house'. Another witness said he was passing the accused's house when he heard her cry out and on entering her dwelling found her in a dishevelled state, hair wildly disordered and clothes torn. She told him 'Black Randall had been beating her and offering her tea to sleep with him' and saw a man running away, who may have been Randall. The assistant surgeon, D'Arcy Wentworth, said he found marks of violence on her thighs and knees.[9]

The case was dismissed. The magistrates obviously believed that Randall had the capacity to make such an expensive gift, as well as liberally provide large quantities of spirits to a person who called at his house. This in turn suggests that Randall was a retailer of commodities and spirits on behalf of the New South Wales Corps. The officers always used soldiers and trusted ex-convicts for this purpose, as gentleman could not be seen to engage in anything as tawdry as trade. In just this way Simeon Lord, who was the ex-convict servant to the military adjutant, became a wealthy man.

If retailing for the New South Wales Corps was how Randall kept his family comfortably housed and supplied with the best goods, then his situation became precarious when Johnston was arrested. With a wife and three children to support, Randall was hard-pressed to return to farming on his land at the Northern Boundary Farms. After a relentless drought, bushfire, hailstorm, and a plague of caterpillars, harvests were so meagre that his neighbour, the 'sober and industrious' John Martin, was unable to grow enough food to keep his wife off the store. Nevertheless, Randall had little option but to move back onto his land. In the 1800 *Settlers Book*, he was listed with four pigs, five goats, and 4 acres planted. But he, his wife and three children were all dependent upon the store. Worse still, he was imminently facing a demand for the payment of quit rent on his land. Forced to consider his future, Randall looked to the solution he knew best: the New South Wales Corps.[10]

Colonel Paterson had returned from England with an increase in the pay for privates, as well as instructions to recruit soldiers from within the colony. For the past decade, the recruitment of time-expired convicts had been encouraged if they were military veterans and Randall had every reason to expect that he would be a suitable candidate. Unfortunately, concern in high places about the probity of the military meant that Paterson was specifically instructed not to recruit time-expired convicts unless 'the good behaviour of individuals may justify a departure from the general rule'. Those purloined Government House glasses, in Randall's case, made such a 'departure' most unlikely, added to which he required a well-placed person to write him the 'good and sufficient recommendations' to show he was a fit and proper person to be taken into His Majesty's service.[11]

Randall discovered a solution in the unlikely form of the transported Irish rebel Joseph Holt, who had just arrived in the colony on the same ship as William Cox, the New South Wales Corps' latest paymaster. Cox, like the previous paymaster John Macarthur, was an enthusiastic entrepreneur. Unlike Macarthur, trade did not suit: soon he was heavily in debt due to ill-judged trading ventures using regimental payroll as capital. He was forced to resign his commission. In 1800, before Cox's spectacular fall from grace, Holt was managing his farm, which happened to be close to the Randall and Martin grants. Holt had never met Randall, but when a 'six foot high, well-made and straight' black man called on him in November 1800, he knew by reputation this was 'the sportsman to General Grose'. Holt agreed to Randall's proposal that he should buy Randall's grant at cut price in return for sending a recommendation to Colonel Paterson.[12]

Paterson was, of course, well aware of Randall, knowing him to be an expert marksman and guide. But Randall had more to offer. As Holt noted, 'the black played on the flute and tambour [drum]', skills more highly prized by Paterson than straight shooting and a good sense of direction. For the commander had grand ambitions to establish a regimental band and to this end he had ordered musical instruments from England. Randall was readily accepted. On 10 November the deed to transfer Randall's land to Holt was registered and a week later Randall was in Sydney to enlist with the New South Wales Corps. He was paid a recruitment bounty of £5 10s in addition to his salary of 1s per diem and placed in the company commanded by the long-absent Grose. Since both the captain and his lieutenant were on extended leave in England, Randall's company was effectively without a commanding officer.[13]

By the time Randall entered the third phase of his career in New South Wales, the colony had dramatically changed in size and character. In 1801, Sydney was not only a substantial town, but its cove had become a mercantile hub, largely thanks to the entrepreneurial spirit of New South Wales Corps. No longer was there a need for a lookout on North Head, sails were now always seen in the cove. Transport ships from England came regularly – four or five a year – but these represented only a small portion of the shipping in and out of Sydney. Ships came from the Cape, India, England and the United States with merchandise to sell, as well as American whalers that were working the waters off New Zealand and beginning to exploit the fur seal population in Bass Strait.

There were new opportunities for people with capital. By 1800 the officers no longer held a trading monopoly, nor was the commissary the only storehouse for goods. In 1798 the Scottish-born merchant Robert Campbell was induced to open a branch of his Calcutta trading firm in Sydney and he built a wharf and storehouses on the western side of the cove. A few years later Campbell acquired land at Dawes Point and constructed even more imposing storehouses. He had had excellent foreign trade connections and substantial capital reserves that allowed him to extend long credit on better conditions than the corps. In 1800,

Campbell was permitted directly to import goods into the colony and, at about the same time, a group of free settlers combined to form their own cartel having successfully persuaded Governor King to allow them to purchase the entire cargo of a visiting merchant ship. In the meantime, officers of New South Wales Corps remained vigorous mercantile participants, particularly where spirits were concerned.

Governor King's avowed intention to curb the unbridled spirit trade was less than resolute in practice. While some cargoes were turned away, he allowed an enormous amount of spirit to be landed in 1800 and 1801. He even gave dispensation to officers and soldiers to purchase large quantities at a very low price, which was an open invitation to engage in the trafficking he had been ordered to suppress. Nevertheless, in encouraging other powerful interests to enter the market, King effectively destroyed the trading monopoly of the military.

The town of Sydney had a population of 2200 adults of whom only 40 per cent were convicts under sentence. They lived largely cheek-by-jowl in an urban environment that was entirely dependent on the importation of household necessities such as tea, sugar, tobacco, soap as well as manufactured goods and spirits. Many of the emancipated convicts without land, as well as convicts with families, lived in the Rocks, a jumble of ramshackle dwellings linked by a web of steep footpaths that had sprung up along the rocky ridge behind the hospital and commissary store. The houses were built in haphazard fashion without survey, lease or formal title. The lack of valid legal ownership, planning or forethought, combined with the steep and rocky topography, determined the higgledy-piggledy aspect of the Rocks and also made it impossible to know who was or was not an inhabitant. This elevated, streetless neighbourhood, with its commanding view over the harbour, was fast becoming the commercial centre of Sydney. Housed within the hotchpotch of one- and two-roomed huts was a growing population of tradesmen and labourers, as well as enterprising men and women who ran bakeries, laundries, forges, pubs and shops from their homes. Below them, at the edge of the cove, more imposing commercial enterprises were taking shape. The same year that Robert Campbell constructed his wharf and warehouse, the ex-convict Simeon Lord, who had grown wealthy as the corps's main retailer, opened a large warehouse by the Hospital Wharf at the foot of the Rocks.

✳

When John Moseley received a conditional pardon from the governor on 3 April 1800 he moved to the Rocks, where the wharves and storehouses of the new merchant-traders provided him with more employment options than were available to his friends John Randall and John Martin eight years before. Moseley was nearly 40 when he was emancipated and without a female partner, commonplace in a town where the ratio of men to women was four to one. As a single man, he may have been sharing his accommodation with John Randall's family, as he had done in the earliest days of the colony. Married soldiers like Randall lived within the Rocks, which was about half a mile from the parade ground. Several non-commissioned officers were well-known residents who doubled as publicans in their 'leisure' time.

Given that a soldier's pay was insufficient to feed a family of five, Randall and his wife Mary probably played a role in the disorderly commerce that gave the area its dubious reputation. Their children Frances, Mary and John might have been part of the multitude of noisy ragamuffins left to fill their day in unsupervised play who prompted the disapproving governor to shake his head at parents who would expose their tender offspring to 'every kind of wretchedness and vice'. Yet the Randall children were not left entirely wild and untutored: the military provided some education for the soldiers' children. The profligate paymaster, William Cox, among his other duties, was the school-teacher.[14]

Although Randall was merely an ordinary soldier, he held a privileged position as a member of the regimental band formed in September 1801 when the musical instruments arrived from London. Traditionally, the officers paid for the band instruments by subscription, but in this case Paymaster Cox paid the large bill out of the public accounts. In 1802, a curious French visitor noted that 'a numerous and well composed band' was in concert every morning at the parade ground in front of the officers' barracks, where the entire Sydney garrison would muster to parade arms. Nearby he noticed a kind of coffee-house which provided the officers with various diversions like billiards. This was the officers' mess, which, like the band instruments, was traditionally paid for by subscription, though in all likelihood it too was financed from the public purse. The most important diversion for the officers was the formal mess dinner, where they and their guests would eat, drink and carouse, while the regimental band entertained. These dinners could be fairly uninhibited affairs and Randall's regular attendance would have afforded him a more intimate interaction with the officers than a private might normally enjoy.[15]

The other ranks displayed remarkably strong bonds of loyalty to the officers of the corps, strengthened by the economic benefit of the trickle-down effect from the trade in spirits, and they appreciated that the officers closed ranks to protect soldiers from being exposed to criminal charges. For just such reasons, John Macarthur was immensely popular among the soldiers, while George Johnston, who had been sent to England for court martial, was idolised. Randall would not have been alone in rejoicing when Major Johnston returned to Sydney in December 1801 on board the *Minorca*. Thanks to his patron the Duke of Northumberland, the charges against him had been quashed, though he did not immediately resume his role as second-in-command.[16]

Under Governor King the endemic disputation and posturing among the officers and between the military and the governor steadily worsened. King was stubbornly locked into a bitter dispute with the majority of the officers, who were under the influence of John Macarthur. By the time Johnston returned, Macarthur had been sent to England for court martial, not for bartering spirits, rather for the near-fatal wounding of his commanding officer in a duel. Colonel Paterson was bed-ridden as a result of his tryst with Macarthur, but even so he was careful to keep Johnston under gentleman's arrest at Annandale, about 4 miles from Sydney, where Johnston lived with his ex-convict wife and children. It was not until October 1802 that Johnston was formally reinstated.

Johnston did not take command of Randall's company however, which remained in a limbo with no active commanding officer. The ensign who had nominal command was under a kind of suspended arrest for engaging in spirit trading and refusing to make an appearance at his trial. Six months later the same officer was in court charged with circulating scurrilous and defamatory rhymes about the governor; a case that ignited further conflict between the officers, as well as a bitter stand-off with the governor. Doubtless the constant feuding between the gentlemen of the colony had an impact on the morale of the military rank-and-file, but John Randall had other matters to occupy his mind.[17]

*

In July 1802 Mary Randall died in childbirth. The tragedy came at a time when Randall was on reduced income because all members of the regiment were forced to make a 'voluntary' contribution to the Royal Military Asylum. Nevertheless, there is reason to believe that Randall found other ways to supplement his income. He was probably able to keep his family together, with Frances aged 15 and Mary aged 13 looking after the house. His fortunes must have improved from January 1803 when Major Johnston became acting commander-in-chief, and finally took full control later that year when Paterson was despatched to the new colony of Van Diemen's Land.

On 4 July 1803, Governor King chose the celebration of the King's birthday as the occasion to deflect attention from his increasingly futile struggle with the entire officer class. He decided upon an extravagant show of mercy that he hoped might create another class of people to check the unbridled power of the New South Wales Corps. It was an ambitious program of emancipation for deserving convicts. He bestowed conditional pardons on 'sixty seven very deserving objects', including 'Black Jack' Williams, who was emancipated after almost twenty years of servitude. He was still only 34, strong and healthy, but possessing no fixed idea about how to use his new-found freedom. Nine months later he still lacked steady employment and was seen lurking about the streets after dark in a suspicious manner, which earned him a few weeks in the gaol. This experience may have persuaded 'Black Jack' to return to the seafaring of his youth. His choices were limited because a conditional pardon did not permit him to leave New South Wales. Several Sydney merchants, pre-eminently Robert Campbell, but also the emancipated convicts Simeon Lord, Joseph Underwood and Henry Kable, had ships engaged in the coastal trade between Sydney and the other penal settlements of Van Diemen's' Land, Norfolk Island and Newcastle, in addition to local sealing and whaling operations. Once the Colonial Secretary had been assured that 'Black Jack' had no outstanding debts, he signed on as crew of the *Sophia*, a French prize converted for the sealing trade by Robert Campbell, which left for the sealing island in Bass Strait on 28 April 1804.[18]

The departure of 'Black Jack' from Sydney was soon followed by that of Thomas Orford, who had long since served his time. Orford had permission to leave New South Wales. Remaining in the colony were

John Martin, still struggling to be self-sufficient on his farm near Parramatta; Samuel Chinery, a landless labourer in the Hawkesbury area; Daniel Gordon, returned from Norfolk Island and living near Chinery, probably employed as a hut keeper; John Moseley, employed carrying goods from wharf to warehouse at the foot of the Rocks in Sydney town; and the privileged soldier John Randall, who was playing in the band.

TUGGING AT THE OARS;
PLAYING IN THE BAND

When the *Minorca* returned Major George Johnston to his regiment in
December 1801, it also disembarked almost a hundred male convicts,
among them William Blue, the black veteran who had fought with Wolfe
at Quebec. Although Blue was over 60 and had already spent five years
in the hulks, he was still a strong, vigorous man, described in later years
as 'a very Hercules in proportion'. Blue's exceptional strength and fitness
allowed him to work, prior to his arrest in October 1796, as a lumper on
the ships from the West Indies in the River Thames. Lumpers were
employed to unload the cargo of the merchant ships moored side-by-
side in the Thames in tiers of seven or eight. All cargo was offloaded
onto lighters and taken to the riverside warehouses, so speed was of the
essence. Lumping was a dangerous occupation – lifting and swinging
heavy loads, manipulating winches and cranes, hauling on ropes – which
only the strongest and fittest could undertake without the certainty of
severe injury.[1]

This life-threatening work was among the lowest paid in London;
ship-owners did not even provide food or drink for the lumpers, requir-
ing them to go ashore, taking time out of their paid labour.
Compensation for such a poor lot was small-scale plundering, referred
to as drainage, spillage or leakage; hence the other connotation of
lumper – to pilfer the cargo. A couple of regular trips ashore during the
day gave lumpers the opportunity to take with them small amounts of
the cargo, which was regarded by all involved as an element of the wage.
It was acknowledged in evidence to the parliamentary committee enquiring into the port conditions in London, taking place at the time Blue was
arrested, that 'which used to be called plunderage was, at least in a
considerable degree, a mode of paying wages'. Generally merchants
allowed up to 2 per cent of the shipped weight to disappear as spillage.

*

Taking more on a regular basis *was* regarded as plunder, which was how William Blue came to grief. He was charged with four separate counts, each for stealing 20 pounds of raw sugar from the *Lady Jane Halliday* on a single day in September 1796.[2]

In his deposition, Blue explained that as well as being a lumper, he traded as a chocolate-maker in St Paul, Deptford, where he lived. Chocolate was made by grinding cocoa beans into a paste that was then mixed with sugar and spices to form a bar. The bar was not eaten; it was melted into hot water and served as a drink, usually in a coffee house, although in the homes of the better sort it might be prepared by the servants downstairs for consumption in comfort upstairs. More expensive than coffee, chocolate was a much more powerful stimulant, especially if the sugar level was high. For the labouring poor reduced to the back-breaking work of unloading ships and forced to go ashore to get sustenance, a quick, hot drink that boosted energy while suppressing hunger was in high demand. Chocolate-making was simple, if laborious; it required no apprenticeship and, as long as the ingredients were readily available, might be manufactured within a small household. Presumably Blue also worked as a lumper on the West Indian ships that imported cocoa beans from plantations in Jamaica. For 80 pounds of sugar, another 100 pounds of cocoa ground from a large quantity of beans was required, producing as much as 180 pounds of chocolate – nothing less than a serious commercial enterprise. A chocolate-maker on this scale was usually involved in a coffee shop, but might otherwise be an independent retailer of the product to a variety of outlets.[3]

Blue was the type of lumper of whom West India merchants deeply disapproved: someone engaged in vertical integration, able to create a commercial opportunity from lowly, life-threatening labour on their ships. Evidence to the parliamentary committee heard tales of a lumper who kept a mistress and a horse 'out of the profits of his delinquency', even though common knowledge had it that lumpers were unable to survive without dipping their hands into the cargo. Blue alluded to the customary rights of spillage when he protested on arrest that while he had taken the sugar 'all the lumpers had some sugar' too. He was singled out because he took too much, too often. On several occasions on Monday, 26 September 1796, the mate of the ship, had taken a 20-pound bag from him as he was leaving the ship to go ashore. On the last occasion the mate found a bag concealed under the voluminous smock worn by Blue. On Tuesday the mate refused him permission to come aboard and an altercation ensued upon the lighter. He was returned to shore and a constable was called. Early on Wednesday morning, Blue was arrested at a pub on the docks where lumpers were recruited, as he was about to start work. When the case came before the Kent Assizes, the judge and jury were reasonably well disposed, although they did not believe that Blue was guiltless. Unlike several of his confreres, who came before the Old Bailey around the same time, he was not acquitted, being found guilty of one charge of stealing sugar to the value of 8 shillings.[4]

Blue's vertical integration as lumper and chocolate-maker casts doubt upon the claim made in his 1823 petitions to a 'whole lifetime spent in his Majesty's Service' prior to sentence. True, he appeared not to be in His Majesty's service in September 1796, a time when England was engaged in an exhausting war with France. Blue was over 55 when the French Revolutionary War began and so was too old to serve. There is, however, evidence that he served the King in another capacity during the 1790s. Much later in his life, Blue explained that the nickname – 'the commodore' – by which he was universally known was given to him 'for being in charge of the old Enterprise at Tower Hill'.

HMS Enterprise was moored on the Thames just below the Tower as a hospital ship. From December 1793 to 1806, it was also a receiving ship for impressed sailors. At first glance there would seem to be little connection between employment related to these activities and the appellation 'commodore', except that the term also had a non-naval connotation in 1790s' London. A 'commodore' was a name given to the man who was in charge of gangs of men labouring in the warehouses lining the Pool of London. By the same dint, it was used by sailors to describe the leader of a gang of sailors ashore, so Blue must have been in charge of the press-gang that operated in and around Deptford for the Enterprise. There were about eight such gangs in operation, made up of local men known for their strength and aggression. It was disreputable, casual work, but it could be profitable. The 'commodore' of the gang answered to a Navy Board employee carrying the rank of lieutenant who paid in cash for each man pressed into service. From 1793 business was brisk in Deptford and the money Blue earned would have been good. During the period prior to Blue's arrest some 34 000 men passed through the *Enterprise,* where they were held in restrictive custody for a day or so, before being transferred to their ships. Impressed men were not subject to the Articles of War until they joined a ship, so if they escaped, there was no scope for prosecution. Doubtless Blue was employed at both jobs in September 1796, given that lumping was casual, seasonal work and since the beginning of 1796 there was a sharp drop in the returns from the Impressment Service. Prime Minister Pitt's introduction of the Quota Acts, required each city to provide a set number of men for service and London's quota was 5704 men, a figure achieved largely by reprieving convicted criminals of serviceable age if they agreed to serve. The number of impressed men on the *Enterprise* in 1796 was less than half of what it had been in previous years. By the time the Impressment Service returned to strength, Blue was part of a different gang: the hulk chain gangs put to work raising gravel from the bed of the river.[5]

It was after nearly five years on the hulks that Blue finally embarked on the *Minorca* for New South Wales. His companions between decks throughout the 176-day voyage to Sydney included William Redfern, a young naval surgeon. Redfern would have been ill-disposed toward 'the commodore' since he had been a significant figure in the mutiny of sailors at Nore in 1797. Redfern was sentenced to hang from the yardarm, but was subsequently pardoned on account of his youth. Later to distinguish himself in Sydney as a compassionate and intelligent surgeon, Redfern's presence among the convicts possibly contributed to the ship's low mortality rate. Governor King was delighted to report that the cargo was landed 'in high health and fit for immediate labour'. Redfern received a pardon from the governor on the King's birthday in 1803, about six months before Blue was freed, having served his full sentence.[6]

When William Blue attained his freedom he moved into a small house in the steepest part of the Rocks, where he applied his energy to various small-time enterprises, including collecting and selling oysters. Above all, it was the dazzling azure waters of Sydney Cove that enticed him. Where once the denizens of the shore saw the beautiful, deep harbour as nothing more than an alluring prison moat that separated them from home, by 1803 it offered boundless opportunities for exploitation. In addition to being a place of leisure and recreation, it was

✳

the focus of increasingly complex mercantile activity. At the time Blue moved into the Rocks half-a-dozen ships that had sailed from London, New York, Providence, Calcutta, Madras and China were at anchor in the cove. Once their merchandise was unloaded, their holds were refilled for the return leg with whale oil, seal skins and timber. In the shadow of these large sailing ships, which represented the infant colony's lifeline to the outside world, there were several smaller colonial vessels that plied the coastal routes between Sydney, Newcastle and Hobart. Among the hulls of these sea-going vessels, a plethora of small craft bobbed and weaved over the water, transporting people and goods hither and thither. In this unregulated watery space Blue sought to make his mark, setting himself up as a waterman, ferrying passengers and goods from ship to shore and back again. With the growth of trade in the cove such boatmen were a crucial element of the burgeoning maritime economy. Blue was one of about twenty-five self-employed watermen plying their trade in and around the cove, most of whom were emancipated convicts.[7]

By July 1804 Blue was living with Elizabeth Williams, a woman of 26 who arrived at the end of June on the female transport *Experiment*. Governor King encouraged free men to look for partners among the new arrivals as a way of accommodating the relatively small number of female convicts arriving in the colony and, if Joseph Holt is to be believed, the governor's *modus operandi* revealed his penchant for vulgarity to poor advantage. When a female transport ship arrived, Holt reported, King instructed the bellman to ring the bell through the town and announce that 'if anybody wanted mares or sows that they should be served out to them.' Whether or not such crude insensitivity facilitated the coupling, there can be little doubt that Blue took up with Elizabeth Williams straight off the boat. She moved into his small dwelling in the turbulent Rocks where their courtship was assailed by violent disturbances from both sides. In July, the couple were woken by the cries of a neighbour being savagely beaten by her husband. Soon after they were again kept from sleep by a drunken brawl at another house where a man was murdered. They married on 27 April 1805, and their witnesses were Edwin Piper, a convict with Blue on the *Minorca*, and his wife Dulcibella, who came free. Blue's daughter, Susannah, was born shortly after.[8]

From his work in the cove, Blue could look up and see his house. On the morning of 31 July 1805, he was 'tugging at the oars', bringing a sailor ashore, when he sensed something was amiss at home. According to his passenger, Blue asked him to mind his boat, then hurried away to discover his wife had been raped, or so he said in his charge against a man named in the *Sydney Gazette* as D. McKay. The paper reported the case's dismissal and was scathing in assessment that the black man had attempted to frame the innocent McKay. According to the editor, evidence for the defence by witnesses, together with glaring inconsistencies in Blue's testimony, 'left no doubt that Mr Blue's center was several shades darker than his superficies'.[9]

The case was heard by the old inebriate Richard Atkins, who was now judge advocate. He was assisted by a bench that included Major George Johnston, John Harris, the surgeon of the corps and superintendent of police, and Thomas Jamison, the chief surgeon. Blue explained that on the day in question he was 'looking towards his house he saw his wife struggling with someone'. On rushing back to the house he found his wife 'walking about with the baby in her arms' and she told him that 'McKay had carnal knowledge of her without her consent.' Dulcibella Piper, was visiting at the time and Blue demanded to know from her 'how she would suffer such an act in her presence?' Dulcibella's reply, according to Blue, was that 'she could not help it'. Elizabeth Blue maintained that McKay called by her house and after some conversation pulled her to the floor and raped her. Dulcibella Piper's official testimony contradicted her friend, asserting that McKay 'took [Elizabeth] by the waist and she fell down and some conversation passed between them'. McKay remained in the house for 10 minutes, she continued, and he had called Blue 'a second wooden Jo'. Her evidence that no carnal conversation took place was supported by George Darling, who claimed to have been with McKay at the time, so if a rape had occurred 'he must have seen it'. He also reported that McKay remained for 10 minutes and 'when he saw Blue he said he was a second wooden Jo'. A neighbour, John Ajar, gave evidence that he overheard the incident, confirming that McKay was in the house for 10 minutes and 'what he heard McKay say to Mrs Blue was that he [Blue] was a second wooden Jo'. Additionally this neighbour reported that later Blue had commented to him that McKay wanted to send him to gaol and that Blue 'would find some method to be revenged'. Several days after the incident Ajar heard Blue beating his wife. 'I will. I will. I do not like to be beat', Elizabeth implored. In her evidence she was emphatic that 'she had not been beat or struck by any person'. Finally Chief Constable John Redman reported a conversation he had had with Blue on the way to see magistrate Jamison. Blue said that on entering the house 'he saw his wife lying on the floor with her petticoat up' – a different story to that offered the court by Blue.[10]

It was downright foolhardy for a recently emancipated man to force his convict wife to concoct a rape case in the face of two eye-witnesses, especially considering the man who was accused. Daniel McKay was an emancipated convict who lived nearby and who earnt his corn retailing spirits for the corps. He had a lease on land next to Simeon Lord at the Hospital Wharf, where he owned a public house kept by his common-law wife, a convict who had arrived on the *Experiment* with Elizabeth Blue. This man could well threaten Blue with gaol: he was the town gaoler, possessing the well-deserved reputation of a hard man. In addition, Chief Constable Redman was a long-time associate of McKay's, while all the members of the court who heard the case, with the possible exception of Atkins, had business entanglements with him. Dulcibella Piper was a free woman, but her husband remained a convict, as was the man who corroborated her evidence, George Darling. He happened to be the clerk to John Harris in his role as the collector of the gaol fund. These witnesses had good reason to give overly consistent testimony contradicting Blue's evidence and carefully repeating McKay's insult that Blue was 'a second wooden Jo', a sly Scots reference to Blue being an old black man and a cuckold to boot. Presumably the insult was meant to imply that Elizabeth Blue was free with her sexual favours.[11]

For all that the charges were adjudged groundless, Blue suffered no retribution other than the scorn heaped upon him by the *Sydney Gazette*, while Daniel McKay ceased his horizontal conversations with Elizabeth. Blue's challenge to McKay may even have worked to his advantage, as some in Sydney would take it as a sign of integrity and strength of character. Certainly, Blue was able to get financial backing and the governor's approval to advance from being one of many watermen in the cove to running a substantial business. Two years after the court case, the *Sydney Gazette* of 2 August 1807 carried an advertisement 'respectfully inform-ing the public' that William Blue was 'the only waterman licenced to ply a ferry in this harbour'. He promised a 'tight and clean boat, and active oar and an unalterable inclination to serve those who honour him with their command'. Clearly Blue did not author this notice.[12]

For Blue to have obtained a coveted licence to operate the only ferry in Sydney Cove suggests he had acquired a literate patron with the ear of the new governor. Someone interceded with Governor Bligh on Blue's behalf, either by word or petition, and the most obvious candidate was the merchant Robert Campbell, who became the Naval Officer when Bligh stripped John Harris of this important office in May 1807. Harris wrote letters bursting with outrage to England complaining that Bligh had not only deprived him of all his offices, but also had removed Jamison from the bench in September, while incarcerating Daniel McKay in his own gaol 'for some weeks past'. Governor Bligh, who was not known for a soft heart, explained that he had removed McKay from his post as gaoler 'out of motives of humanity'.[13]

As Blue was eased up the ladder of opportunity, life was taking a happy turn for another black resident of the Rocks, Private John Randall. In 1807 a son was born to Randall and his new partner, Fanny. In this third union, Randall was not married by the colony's chaplain, nor was there a record of the child's birth and baptism. The woman who called herself Fanny Randall may have been a Catholic, as no official record was kept of Catholic marriages and baptisms, despite there being a priest in the colony. By the same token Randall might have been infected by the anti-clerical temper that permeated much of the New South Wales Corps, thus choosing not to marry in a church. It was more common than not that relationships in the corps went unsanctified, much to the disgust of the Rev. Samuel Marsden. Major Johnston had not bothered to marry the woman with whom he had cohabited for the past twenty years.

In 1807 Randall's household included Fanny and her new baby, as well as John Jr, aged 10. His 18-year-old daughter Frances had taken up with a black sailor named John Aiken, who arrived as a carpenter on the *Marquis Cornwallis* in 1796 and had a grant of land at the Field of Mars; Mary, aged 14, was living with her father's old friend and neighbour, John Martin, whose first wife died in February 1806. Martin still held his 50 acres at the Northern Boundary Farms, where more than half were sown in grain while two sheep and a dozen pigs roamed his property. As well as working his farm, Martin was the local constable for which he was paid and victualled from the store. He could, therefore, afford to employ a convict and a free man. Randall's grandchild, also named John, was born in November 1807.

If William Blue acquired a patron in 1807, Randall's history implies that he had always had one. His life in the New South Wales Corps was singularly untaxing; to all intents and purposes, playing in the band was all that was ever required of him. Randall was never rostered on guard duty, though other band members were; when members of his company were detached to Parramatta or Norfolk Island or Port Dalrymple, Randall always remained in Sydney, lounging about the barracks, or engaged in some informal activity not recorded in the regimental ledger. His company almost permanently lacked a senior officer in charge, since most of those officers appointed to that role were either on extended leave or under arrest awaiting court martial. Yet some senior officer ensured that Randall's soft billet continued. It is possible that his patron remained the long-absent commander-in-chief, General Grose, but a more likely candidate was acting commander-in-chief, Major George Johnston. Significantly, all the officers transferred to Randall's company were from Johnston's company.[14]

Randall played in the band on ceremonial occasions and at the parade-ground muster every morning. He no longer played at the officer's mess, because the dinners had been abandoned, a casualty of the conflict between Governor King and the corps. The governor's efforts to impose his will on the officers through a series of aborted courts martial had caused an absolute breakdown in civility between the military and his office. After years of persistent and bruising strife, it was the governor who was eventually defeated. Humiliated by his failure to secure punishment for those officers who traded in spirits, and held him up to ridicule, King's recall to England was as unceremonious as his predecessor's.

By 1807, Randall's company had a commanding officer who managed to remain with them for long enough to inspire fierce loyalty among the rank-and-file. The acting commanding officer, Major Johnston, was their idol, but soldiers like Randall would never have extended their loyalty to the new governor. Bligh, like his despised predecessors, was a naval officer, lacking in grace and manners. The other ranks in the New South Wales Corps may have been rough and ready, but they were trained by officers who had little else to do than make their fortunes through trade and indulge in exaggerated displays of gentlemanly honour. As such, the rank-and-file were unprepared to tolerate a bluff sea captain whose abusive and intemperate language had driven his own naval officers to rebellion. Bligh displayed 'violent torna-does of temper' that not even the spectacular mutiny on the *Bounty* had taught him to curb. Prior to his departure for New South Wales, Bligh was court martialled for his 'ungentlemanly behaviour' and although acquitted, he was warned to be more careful in the conduct of his expression. However, it was barely days after his arrival in Sydney that Bligh delivered a vituperative tongue-lashing to John Macarthur. 'Jack Boddice', as the scurrilous gossips dubbed Macarthur, had resigned his commission in England and returned to be the premier landholder in the colony. Because Macarthur was the son of a corset-maker, he was over-sensitive about his status as a gentleman, and framed his behaviour accordingly. It was not long before he had become Bligh's implacable enemy.[15]

For his part Bligh believed that the jumped-up fellows who formed the self-appointed colonial elite hardly merited his respect. 'You can have no idea of the class of persons here who consider themselves gentlemen', he wrote to a well-placed contact in England. By the time John Harris was writing angry missives to England in October 1807, Bligh had alien-ated all but a handful of the colony's 'good' and 'great' by employing the 'most vile and abusive language and degrading epithets'. But it was not only would-be gentlemen like Macarthur who were abused by the gover-nor. The soldiers took exception when Bligh roared admonishments that they were 'wretches', 'tremendous buggers', and other words 'too gross to be repeated'. Tactless abuse was not, in itself, enough to instigate rebellion among the rank-and-file. Rather, it was Bligh's threat to their property that triggered mutiny.[16]

The town that had sprung up around the cove in higgledy-piggledy fashion offended Bligh's sense of order. He sought to impose the regu-lated, classically minded vision of Phillip. In November 1807 the gover-nor had his surveyor draw a detailed plan of Sydney and ordered all the leaseholders to bring their deeds to Government House. Those leases that encroached on the governor's domain and other places he felt should be kept as open space were to be revoked. Houses already built were torn down. One belonging to a soldier was demolished in an area known as the cricket ground. When the house was rebuilt, Bligh ordered it torn down a second time. Sergeant-Major Whittle, whose house and garden was near the Hospital Wharf, received a personal visit from the governor to demand the dwelling be removed. When Whittle protested that he had a lease with six or seven years to run, Bligh 'bawled out in a very violent manner (and all the neighbours heard it) that ... he would have the house down by 10 o'clock ... it shall be all [the governor's] house, and ground, and all'. Whittle signed his lease over to Major Johnston to stay Bligh's hand. Meanwhile, an extension to John Redman's house opposite the gaol was demolished, and part of Daniel McKay's garden was forcibly resumed. Richard Atkins reported the town was buzzing with anxiety about the destruction of homes. Everywhere he went he heard the same refrain: 'my turn will be the next'.[17]

Bligh indicated that he also desired the church be surrounded by open Crown land, upon some of which ground John Macarthur happened to hold a lease. Macarthur was himself facing a trial on a trumped-up charge, but provocatively he surrounded his lease with a fence on 12 January 1808, announcing his intention to commence construction forthwith. Bligh responded the following day by ordering the demolition of the offensive fence, and in so doing he unintentionally forged a powerful bond between Macarthur and disgruntled soldiers, who filed out of the barracks under Sergeant Whittle's command to mend Macarthur's fence and, literally and figuratively, to defend his ground. In a gesture of comradeship Macarthur instructed Whittle to draw up a list of deserving soldiers to whom he could distribute some excellent Cape wine at the very low price of 5 shillings per gallon. Ten days later, as his trial date approached, 'Jack Boddice' had Wilkes-like become the hero of a dangerously resentful military, for whom the governor was now the sworn enemy. As one private later recalled, it was safer 'to praise Bonoparte, than to speak respectfully of Governor Bligh'.[18]

It was in this highly charged atmosphere that the officers decided to reconvene the mess dinner, symbolically choosing 24 January, the birthday of the late Whig leader Charles Fox, another defender of English liberty and property. By all accounts, the dinner was a highly convivial affair, which gave Randall and his fellow bandsmen their first formal opportunity in years to play non-martial music. Macarthur was not a guest at the mess that night, although his son and business partner were. According to him, he remained outside on the parade ground where all could see him, walking up and down, enjoying the music. Inside the mess, the officers and their guests danced, drank and refused to talk politics. 'No parish business' was a traditional mess protocol on which Major Johnston fastidiously insisted. Randall may have observed, as did a fellow bandsman, that Anthony Fenn Kemp, the paymaster, was highly intoxicated. Johnston was forced to confiscate his bottle, saying 'look here, Kemp; recollect tomorrow.' The following day Macarthur's trial began.[19]

Randall was likely to have been one of the many beneficiaries of Macarthur's excellent wine, since Sergeant Whittle also happened to be the drum major. He was possibly one of the grim-faced soldiers who lined the courtroom on 25 January as six of their officers were sworn in to hear the case against Macarthur, including the current commander of Randall's company and three others who had briefly served as his commanding officers in the past. Major Johnston was not in attendance, having suffered a carriage accident after the mess dinner. Before Judge Advocate Atkins could be sworn, Macarthur rose in the dock to deliver a stirring speech which he concluded by addressing his former comrades sitting on the bench: 'Now gentlemen, for God's sake, remember you have the eyes of an expecting public upon you, trembling for the safety of their lives, liberties and properties.' With the room in uproar, Atkins was forced to quit, declaring there could be no court without him. 'We are a court', shouted the now sober paymaster, Kemp, to the whoops and cheers of the soldiers. Released on bail by the de facto court, Macarthur was then escorted to his Sydney house by a military guard. Across the town at Government House, Bligh took the view that usurping the authority of the court in this fashion was tantamount to treason. When Major Johnston refused to leave his invalid's bed to deal with the matter, Bligh ordered Macarthur taken to gaol and all six officers arrested for treason.[20]

At dawn the next morning, the richest man in the colony was igno-miniously incarcerated among the common felonry. At the officer's barracks, the usurpers digested the news that they were expected to join him in detention, or be hanged. It was John Harris who informed Major

Johnston that the agitation in the town following Macarthur's arrest was such that 'an insurrection of the inhabitants was to be feared'. As the injured Johnston drove into town with Harris, he was well aware that if his six officers joined Macarthur in the gaol it would ignite such fury among the soldiers that even he would be unable to contain their rage against the governor. No doubt he was also aware that the soldiers had been freely indulging in Macarthur's excellent wine for much of the day. Arriving at the barracks in the early evening, Johnston was greeted by a number of the town's merchants who told him that, unless Bligh was arrested, insurrection and certain massacre would follow. Johnston believed that negotiating with Bligh was pointless; the man could not be trusted to behave like a gentleman. Anointing himself with the title of lieutenant governor, Johnston signed a warrant to release Macarthur from gaol, but was far from resolute about the actions he should take against the governor. 'God's curse!', he is reported to have cried. 'What am I to do?' It was Kemp who persuaded him that if they were all going to hang for treason, mutiny was the only course left to them.[21]

At that point the freshly liberated John Macarthur took control. He quickly penned a letter to be signed by nine of the civilians who were present, in which he implored Johnston to put Bligh under arrest and assume command of the colony. He told Sergeant Whittle to order the call to arms. At the sound of the fife and drum, anxious townspeople came out of their houses and ran toward the parade ground, either because they were curious or because they shared the soldier's mutinous anger against the governor.

At Macarthur's instigation, the band struck up the strains of 'The British Grenadiers', as 400 soldiers with bayonets fixed, fell in behind to march down Bridge Street, across the Tank Stream, and on to Government House. During the several hours it took Whittle and his men to locate Governor Bligh (he was eventually found hiding under the bed in one of the servant's rooms), Randall and the band remained outside with John Macarthur. No one noticed whether or not they were still playing the jaunty refrain.[22]

Bligh was placed under arrest. For a day or so it was unsafe for civilians to be out of doors unless they indicated their support for the new order or had posted signs in their windows saying 'Johnston for Ever'. Daniel McKay, who was immediately reinstated as the gaoler, paid effusive homage to Major Johnston, a fellow Scot. Outside his pub he hung the drawing of a Highland soldier, sword drawn, with a snake at his feet and the legend: 'The Ever Memorable 26th January 1808'. John Moseley may have been among those shouting approval. William Blue was probably at his work in the cove, among the small craft working on and around the ships at anchor, a safe distance from the exultant McKay. On 28 January, Sergeant-Major Whittle had his troops gather up firewood in carts and wheelbarrows to build an enormous bonfire for a celebration that evening where Randall had another opportunity to entertain, as the officers and their ladies mingled happily with the excited soldiers and common folk. Blue would have heard their huzzas wafting across the water on the balmy evening air as the band struck up the tune 'Silly Old Man'.

While some of the soldiers were building bonfires, others were kept busy bringing people from the Rocks to the barracks to sign the petition that Macarthur had written imploring Johnston to arrest Bligh. There were nine signatures on the document when the troops marched out for Government House, yet when it was presented as a justification for Johnston's actions, there were 150, including in neat and fluent letters 'William Blue'. Someone had forged his name, probably without his knowledge or consent, since he was completely illiterate and could only sign his mark. Subsequently, others whose names appeared on the document claimed they were unable to remember signing it, or, having been told to sign, that they had no clue to its contents. Although Blue was more than capable of opportunism, he had every reason to disapprove of Johnston's action. Rather than join the chorus of assent, Blue was more likely to follow the lead of Robert Campbell. The merchant had been dining with Bligh on the night of his arrest and was immediately stripped of his post as Naval Officer and as a magistrate. But he was far too significant a figure to be victimised. He kept his head down, his opinions to himself, and his mind focused on the conduct of his mercantile business, waiting for the jubilation to pass and the recriminations that would inevitably begin.[23]

The reign of the New South Wales Corps came to an end on the morning of 31 December 1809, when Lachlan Macquarie stepped ashore at the Government Wharf. He led the 73rd regiment on an unsteady march towards the parade ground where the outgoing New

South Wales Corps presented arms while the band played. Private Randall was not present. He was on the sick list; sick at heart, perhaps, that the way of life he had enjoyed for so long had come to an end. Everyone knew that the New South Wales Corps was to be replaced by the 73rd. Randall's cosy career was finished. He was not eligible to join the Veterans Company, established by Macquarie for men who had both 20 years of military service and a bond with New South Wales so strong that they lost any desire to return to England. Nor did a transfer to the 73rd suit; he was too old to start the business of proper soldiering. He was discharged on 24 April 1810. George Johnston was in England facing court martial. For the first time since arriving in New South Wales Randall was bereft of a patron and forced to rely solely on his own resources.[24]

Randall continued living in Sydney with Fanny and his two infant boys. His eldest son, John Randall Jr left home in 1810 as a seaman on a coastal trading ship. In December 1810, Randall secured a lowly position as one of the constables appointed to patrol the town at night in Macquarie's new police system. In each of five newly created police districts six constables were appointed, all of them responsible to Chief Constable John Redman, who had been reconfirmed in this job by Macquarie, even though Daniel McKay was removed as the gaoler. At the apex of the scheme was D'Arcy Wentworth, newly appointed superintendent of police, as well as the colony's assistant surgeon. It was a curious role for a man who had fled to the colony to evade trial for highway robbery and was generally held in particularly low regard by the few members of Sydney society that might be judged respectable.

Randall lived in the Rocks, so he was probably assigned to the first district, which stretched from Dawes Point to Surrey Lane, including the docks, wharves and warehouses, as well as the Rocks, with its concentration of brothels and public houses. The job of the constable was to keep an eye out for disorderly and suspicious characters, to ensure that places licensed to sell spirits were shut by nine o'clock at night, and to arrest anyone found drinking in brothels or other unlicensed premises. For a man with Randall's history, this was rather like expecting the fox to look after the henhouse, especially as the modest pay of a constable would never support a family of four. For reasons unknown, Randall was abruptly dismissed on 24 August 1811. His fall from grace might have been connected to the public notice that appeared soon after pronouncing that officers of the government would immediately be dismissed should they 'be discovered in pillaging or robbing, or conniving at others committing such plunder'.[25]

Deprived of his client relationship with the New South Wales Corps, Randall rapidly slid into destitution. In 1813, he and his family were living on a small farm at Kissing Point with 4 or 5 acres of corn. In 1814, they were all dependent on the store. Randall's descent was not nearly as spectacular as that of Daniel McKay, the ex-gaoler and hard man of the Rocks. Within eighteen months of Macquarie's arrival, all of McKay's buildings, household effects, land and leases had been sold off by the bailiff. Randall himself put his Kissing Point land, with house and furniture, up for auction in February 1814, probably to repay debts. In the muster taken nine months later he was listed as a landowner, which he no longer was, but with no other occupational description. Soon after, he accepted employment as the resident manager of a remote 700-acre property at Broken Bay (near present-day Mona Vale) that belonged to Robert Campbell Jr. Despite his age Randall was a good choice for this position, having been part of the early exploration of the region, as well as a renowned bushman.[26]

A short item in the Sydney Gazette on 20 July 1816 provides a glimpse of the manifold difficulties Randall faced at Broken Bay. The paper reported that 'two fine boys, one eight and the other nine years old, sons of John Randall, in the employ of Mr. R. Campbell, jun. were drowned in attempting to cross Manly Beach in a boat, a tremendous surf being on at the time, which rendered their feeble exertions unavailing'. The report continued that after nine days only one of the bodies had been recovered. Nothing more was heard of John Randall. In 1822, a destitute Fanny Randall petitioned the colonial secretary for her two daughters, Eliza aged 9 and Ann aged 6, to be taken into the Orphans' Institution in Sydney.[27]

THE OLD COMMODORE

William Blue emerged as a winner from Macquarie's reorganisation of Sydney. The governor created a rudimentary authority to monitor the workings of the harbour and, on 17 August 1811, he announced that Blue was appointed the watchman of the Heaving Down Place at the cove. His duties would include acting as a water-born constable and guardian of the shore touching upon the Government Domain. With the new position came a hexagonal stone house at the edge of the domain, where Blue and his growing family lived contentedly and rent-free for the next eight years. In this role Blue answered to the newly created harbour master, although ultimate authority rested with the Naval Officer, who also collected import duties. Macquarie reinstated Robert Campbell in this position, but soon expressed concern that this created a conflict of interest with his mercantile business. Campbell resigned in favour of a captain from the 73rd regiment, although his nephew Robert Campbell Jr remained Assistant Naval Officer.[1]

Blue's ferry business did not interfere with his role as constable and watchman, as he was at pains to assure the governor when he petitioned him to establish a ferry to Lane Cove. The man employed as an assistant was 'fully competent to the concern of the ferry boat', the petition insisted, so Blue's 'sole attention will be ever directed to the faithful discharge of the duties attached to [his] present situation'. That he was diligent about his job was apparent in the magistrate's court on 4 March 1815, where Blue laid a charge against the master of the *Marquis Wellington* for a breach of port regulations. Two seamen from this ship had landed a boat near Blue's house to take women aboard. When the sailors refused to pull away as ordered, Blue 'jumped into the Boat and mark'd the broad arrow on it'. The court supported Blue's action and the boat was forfeited to the government. Sometime later, Blue claimed to have also regularly intercepted and impounded goods illegally landed to avoid the payment of duties, though these never came to court.[2]

*

Although Blue employed an assistant, he himself was always at the oars when it came to ferrying the governor and his family about the harbour, or up the river to Parramatta. By 1814 it was well known that he had become a favourite of the governor and his wife. Blue personified Macquarie's vision of the reformed convict, the figure who would become the backbone of the orderly and respectable society he aimed to create in New South Wales: a hard-working entrepreneur who had, with all propriety, married his convict partner and bestowed legitimacy upon his children. For Elizabeth Macquarie, the governor's strong-willed wife, Blue was a guileless, rough-hewn man, the no-nonsense type she most trusted. He proved an excellent companion for their adored child. Yet there was something more profound in the governor's friendship with this illiterate ferryman; a bond of shared experience between the professional soldier and the 'sable veteran'.[3]

Blue was never too shy to boast of his military service in some of the most extraordinary campaigns of the eighteenth century. The sweeping extent of Blue's experience combined with his intense fidelity to the cause of His Majesty would certainly have endeared him to the governor. For Lachlan Macquarie had served in the same or similar places. He began his military career in 1777 aged 15, and saw service immediately in America. Commissioned as an ensign in the 84th, he had joined a regiment raised in New York from veterans of Highland regiments disbanded after the Seven Years' War. He may have been with one of the companies of the 84th at the invasion of South Carolina in 1779, but at the commencement of 1781 he was a lieutenant in the 71st Regiment of Foot, a Highland regiment which first saw action in the invasion of New York in 1776 and later served at the garrison at Stony Point where Blue may also have been stationed. It is unclear where Macquarie was serving throughout 1781, but it is known that several companies of the 71st marched away with Cornwallis to disastrous defeat at Yorktown. It is feasible that Macquarie and Blue were both caught in the dreadful siege of Yorktown and were among the lucky few evacuated by ship to New York.

This was a formative period in Macquarie's life – as for George Johnston – and doubtless these traumatic events were indelibly stamped on his psyche. Even if Macquarie had never before set eyes upon Blue, once he boarded the black man's ferry in Sydney Cove in 1810 it was enough that Blue was able to recount stories about soldiers from the Highland regiments at Quebec and later in Portugal, or soldiers from the 71st who had shared the bombardment, starvation and ignominious defeat of Yorktown, for a unique bond to be forged between them. Blue provided a glimpse of this relationship when he gave evidence in a court case in 1832. He and the governor 'were always together', he told a court, and it was a relationship of equals. 'I was just the same as the governor. He never countermanded any orders of mine … he built the little octagon house at the corner of the domain for my especial accommodation.' By way of explanation for this attachment, Blue added: 'I was with General Wolfe in the American war, and with Lord Howe.' The sense of intimacy was captured in his observation that 'the Governor had a bit of the "old brown" in him'.[4]

This reminiscence also provided Blue with the opportunity to describe the exchange in 1814 when he asked the governor to give him land for his ferry terminus at Millers Point.

> 'Poh, poh!' says he. 'Billy, you have got land enough, you can use as much as you want.'
> 'Please your honour' says I, 'I want a landing place.'
> 'Well come,' says he, 'Show me the place.'
> And so, when I showed him the place, 'Jemmy,' says he to [Surveyor] Meehan, 'run the chain over the Commodore's land.'
> Lord bless you. We were just like two children playing.[5]

Blue was well into his nineties when he gave this evidence. He ended the intriguing vignette by dissolving into laughter, which might have encouraged the magistrates to think it was a piece of tomfoolery. Not so. In the colonial secretary's correspondence, dated 23 April 1814, was a letter from Macquarie to say that Blue was to receive a grant of 80 acres of land and although the location was not specified, other evidence suggests that Blue owned land at Miller's Point. On 11 June 1814 Blue was among those listed in the *Sydney Gazette* as eligible to receive cows from the government herd, presumably put to graze on his land there. In October 1816 Blue's government duties and remuneration were increased when he was formally appointed the keeper of the Government Domain, and three months later he received another 80 acres for his ferry on the opposite side of the cove, which he named

Northampton Farm (now called Blues Point). This made him a relatively substantial, and very well-appointed, landowner, while the number of his little ferry boats had grown to seven or more. 'Why Billy, you have a regular fleet!' Macquarie was reputed to have exclaimed. 'I'll have to call you Commodore.' That story was apocryphal. Blue had had the nick-name from his arrival in the colony, as he himself explained in the same court case in 1832: 'I got the name of the old Commodore for being in charge of the old *Enterprise* at Tower-hill'.[6]

Blue had clandestine sources of income in addition to his public duties, ferry business and farms, as became apparent in the early hours of the morning of 10 October 1818 when Blue was apprehended by Chief Constable John Redman as he was rowing his boat toward the wharf of George Williams, a spirit dealer. The day before, when two constables were patrolling Williams's wharf, they detected suspicious signs of 'some casks having been rolled up the yard from the water side'. Having been tipped off that some spirits were to be illegally landed, they went into Williams's premises and found 'two casks which were not yet dry'. After informing the chief constable, a plan was hatched for four junior constables to lie in wait near the wharf that night. About three o'clock in the morning the waiting constables noticed a flurry of activity as one of the ships at anchor in the harbour was lit up and the sound of tackle was heard, suggesting 'the people on board the ship were getting something over the side'. Half an hour later the lights were extinguished and the rhythmic splash of oars drifted over the water toward them, while simultaneously signs of frantic activity were discerned at Williams's wharf. Intercepting the boat, the constables discovered the man at the oars was none other than Constable William Blue. Lashed on either side of the bow, level with the gunwales, were two barrels contain-ing 120 gallons of rum.

When questioned by Redman, Blue explained that he had inter-cepted smugglers in the cove who, on being challenged, fled the scene, leaving behind two barrels bobbing in the water. Like the dutiful consta-ble everyone knew him to be, Blue insisted he had sequestered the booty for the chief constable. Redman was incredulous; being ex-navy he knew that it was 'utterly impossible for any one person to have so lashed casks of the magnitude which these are in the manner in which they were found'. After taking possession of the casks in Blue's boat, the chief constable then paid a visit to Williams's warehouse to recover the other two casks. Later in the day one of the junior constables visited Blue at his house on the Domain, trying to persuade him to inform on the person who had inveigled him into carrying smuggled goods. As the constable later told D'Arcy Wentworth, the superintendent of police and magistrate, Blue drew the side of his hand across his throat in a quick motion, saying 'I would suffer this first'.[7]

The *Sydney Gazette* report of the court case hummed with outrage about this double-edged fraud on the people of Sydney, who were cheated of the benefits the revenue would bring, while paying the price for the smuggled rum as if duty had been paid. As for 'this unfortunate man Blue ... a man of colour with a very large family, who has been very much indebted to the humane feeling with which his Excellency the governor has for many years been pleased to view him', the crime 'was more than usually criminal'. Blue was a constable, after all, appointed 'for the purpose of *detecting* or *preventing* smuggling'. After inveighing against Blue's manifest delinquency, the editor changed tack to observe that a small player with as little money as Blue had 'a vast deal more of personal character at stake than his trifling profits', implying that Blue was the victim of the entrepreneur who possessed the capital, contacts and infrastructure to run a successful smuggling enterprise. The reader might presume that the identity of such a person was suspected, but the pity was, the editor lamented, Blue had so far refused to give any names.[8]

The frustration of the judge advocate about Blue's obstinacy to 'make confession against the parties to whom he has so improperly and illegally lent himself' was evident in a letter sent to the governor on the day of the hearing. Judgment against Blue had been deferred in the hope that the deceived patron could bring to bear 'a higher influence' on Blue's sense of duty and obligation to get him to expose the real miscreants and avoid a criminal sentence. If Macquarie did make an intervention, it was to no avail; Blue remained tight-lipped. Having been caught red-handed, he inevitably was found guilty of 'aiding and assisting in illegally landing a quantity of spirits, with intent to defraud His Majesty's revenue of the duties'. On 24 October he was dismissed from his government positions and sentenced to twelve months' imprisonment.[9]

This was a curious case. Smuggling was a major problem for Macquarie; its persistence deprived his government of substantial revenue. After the embargo on spirits was lifted in 1814, Macquarie sought to control the trade by levying a hefty import duty of 7 shillings per gallon. Six months before Blue was apprehended, the governor raised this import duty to 10 shillings per gallon which, Macquarie ruefully acknowledged, had increased smuggling 'to a very considerable extent'. Despite the reorganisation of policing, he had no adequate regulations to deal with the problem, other than confiscation of the smuggled goods. Blue was the only person ever brought before the bench to answer charges.[10]

The arrest of Blue looked like a set-up. The constables had been tipped off about the spirits and probably knew who it was they were lying in wait for. But why was Blue set up and by whom? Blue tendered a written statement in his defence, but it was removed from the papers relating to the case. Clearly the authorities believed there were more significant figures than George Williams behind the illegal transaction. Williams himself merely suffered the confiscation of the two casks that were found at his warehouse. Suspicion of receiving smuggled goods was not enough to establish any sort of *prima facie* case. Although he was regarded as a rogue, he appears to have suffered little or no harm from the incident: he did not lose his spirits licence and he continued as the purveyor of spirits to the military and to serve on juries. Captain Nicholls, master of the suspect ship the *Portsea* from Calcutta, suffered no penalty other than being ordered to quit the harbour without landing any goods 'in consequence of his illegal and clandestine practices', and he was forbidden, and prevented, from landing goods at Hobart.[11]

On the face of it, Blue's determined silence could be read as loyalty of the criminal class to their accomplices. However, a glance at the commercial world of Sydney in 1818 suggests a more sinister reading. The captain of the *Portsea*, Captain Nicholls, had been in trouble before for 'illicit and contraband trade' and at that time his employer was Garnham Blaxcell, a business partner of D'Arcy Wentworth, the superintendent of police who sat on the magistrates bench to hear the case against Blue. Another of Wentworth's partners was Alexander Riley, whose brother Edward was their Calcutta agent for the importation of 10 000 gallons of rum. Edward Riley had recently arrived in Sydney and established a business as agent for the importation of Bengal spirits. As well as the partnership with Riley, Wentworth had a longstanding

*

BLACK FOUNDERS

commercial arrangement with the third magistrate, Simeon Lord, described by a previous governor as a notorious smuggler. Lord, in turn, had a business relationship with George Williams.

Any of these Sydney merchant traders had reason to be smuggling large quantities of Bengal rum in 1818. Sydney was just emerging from a six-year depression which had ruined Blaxcell and driven him from the colony. It almost forced Robert Campbell's business into liquidation, and Riley's fortunes were strapped by financial hardship. Lord's business was barely managing to survive through auctioneering and small-scale trading. By the middle of June 1818 the spirit market, which was an excellent barometer of commercial health, was on an upward trajectory and demand for quality Bengal rum was becoming increasingly healthy. At exactly this time, as the traders were struggling to recoup massive losses, Macquarie increased the duty on spirits by over 25 per cent. The owner of the four unclaimed casks stood to make a huge profit from the evasion of duty. Other than the men on the bench and their business partners, the only other merchant trader with the capital and resources to finance a smuggling operation on this scale was their arch-rival, Robert Campbell. However the rum was not unloaded at Campbell's wharf, nor did he have any obvious connection to the *Portsea* or business dealings with George Williams.[12]

The most plausible contender who was relying upon Blue's integrity was one or more of those sitting in judgment upon him. As the hand across the throat signified, he knew he had a better chance of survival keeping quiet than spilling the beans. As it transpired, the magistrates were so influenced by the weight of Blue's previous public service, and so concerned for his large family, that they submitted the case to the governor with a strong request for mercy. Macquarie appears to have pardoned Blue's custodial sentence, at the same time as dismissing him from all his positions and evicting his family from the pleasant stone house.[13]

Though it proved impossible for the authorities to point the finger at anyone other than Blue, his prosecution provided the impetus for tightening regulations and surveillance. Within days, the governor had posted an order in the *Sydney Gazette* that no boat, of any description, could land duty-laden goods, night or day, at any wharf other than the Kings Wharf without special authority. The first to apply for an exemp-

*

tion was Campbell, whose application could be read as an object lesson in the power possessed by a substantial merchant, which also explained why residual sympathy existed for small-fry like Blue. Having expended an immense amount on his premises, Campbell explained, he should be permitted the use of his own wharf and in addition should also be exempt for wharfage charges, as was 'the ordinary and usual custom in the ports of Great Britain as well as in His Majesty's other colonies'. Such an exemption, that would allow him indiscriminate use of his own facilities, would neither damage the revenue nor fair trade, Campbell assured the governor. Doubtless Macquarie did not share this confidence, but Campbell was allowed full use of his premises, upon payment of a bond, although the wharfage charge remained.[14]

In his disgrace, Blue still had his ferry business and his land, although at some stage he was forced to sell a large portion of the Millers Point holding. He even managed to regain the friendship of the governor and his family in the few short years before Macquarie's recall in February 1822. Once Macquarie quit the colony, the sharks began to circle Blue's enterprise. William Gore, who was once provost marshal, made the first overt move against Blue's ferry business. Gore had accumulated a 600-acre property on the northern shore, at a place he called Artarmon. On 22 September 1823, he petitioned the local magistrate Edward Wollstonecraft, who was a free settler with a large business in the colony and massive landholdings on the North Shore, that the ferry be put in the hands of more a trustworthy person than Blue. Gore insisted that Blue's ferry was the reason that the lives of his family and his property were exposed to a raft of 'armed dangerous and suspicious individuals who constantly infest and perambulate in the surrounding forest'. As Wollstonecraft was foremost among those who regarded the emancipist class with distaste, he responded enthusiastically to Gore's request. To this accusation, Wollstonecraft added his own view that Blue was the main cause of lawlessness in the region. The complaint was laid before his fellow magistrates, Edward Riley and D'Arcy Wentworth. They agreed to remove the licence from Blue and appoint the two 'fit and trustworthy persons' identified by Gore to manage the ferry.[15]

Blue fought back. He may have been illiterate but was a match for William Gore when it came to deploying the rhetoric of outrage. On 28 October, Blue petitioned Governor Thomas Brisbane, emphasising his age, his illustrious military record and his service to Macquarie, for which he claimed he was rewarded with land on either side of the cove and the ferry licence. His wealthy neighbour, Mr Wollstonecraft, had tried to buy his ferry, Blue asserted, and because the persistent offer was refused, 'Mr Wollstonecraft, and such Gentlemen as correspond with him, wish to take said premises from poor petitioner by arbitrary power'. Worse yet, they had 'seduced the Petitioners son, who is a young foolish boy away', so that Blue had no one to help him run his farm and provide for the family. Blue entreated Brisbane to make 'the greatest act of humanity and charity' and allow him, in his old age, the peaceable enjoyment of his ferry. In a second petition sent on 17 November 1823, Blue upped the ante by slyly hinting at malice on the part of Magistrate Edward Riley. When Blue was a water constable, the petitioner explained, he had seized a load of timber 'landed in a prohibited manner by Mr Reilly', and it was his zeal in preventing the evasion of duties 'agst the interest of such gentleman as Mr Reilly' that prompted the previous governor to reward him with the ferry that 'such gentleman' had taken from him.[16]

Brisbane was stung into action. On 6 November, the colonial secretary sent a stern letter to Wollstonecraft demanding explanation. In his high-handed reply, the magistrate denied Blue's allegations. The governor should be aware, Wollstonecraft wrote, that the area of Hunter's Hill and Lane Cove was a magnet for escaped convicts, ships' deserters and stolen goods, with Blue as 'the principal agent in carrying into effect this system of plunder, smuggling and escape'. He invited the governor to consult the superintendent of police, D'Arcy Wentworth, to verify these allegations. Blue's son was living with the local constable, Wollstonecraft admitted, but the implication was that this was all for the boy's good. The colonial secretary found Wollstonecraft's explanations to be 'perfectly satisfactory', and Blue continued to be denied the use of his ferry service.[17]

Just at the time when Blue was deprived of his main source of income (clandestine or otherwise), his nemesis William Gore was overwhelmed by spectacular disgrace. Gore's determination to protect his property rights was such that on 21 November 1823 he shot a soldier who had come on to his land to cut grass for the regiment's horses. When the man died from his wounds, Gore was charged with murder. On

19 January 1824, the very same magistrates to whom Gore appealed for the resumption of Blue's ferry licence, sentenced him to transportation to the coalmines at Newcastle 'for the term of his natural life'. Gore had quarrelled with almost everyone in Sydney; there was not much sympathy for him. A year later, in answer to the concern about Gore expressed by Lord Palmerston, Governor Brisbane provided this curt response that 'Mr Gore is so totally abandoned to drinking that I fear he is for ever lost to society'.[18]

Six months later, Blue himself was touched with disgrace. At the time of his petition, his 16-year-old son was living with the local constable, but it is unknown what William Jr's circumstances were on 30 June 1824, when he appeared in court charged with manslaughter. He had thrown a stone at a group of boys who were taunting him, hitting one of the boys, who later died. He was found guilty with a recommendation for mercy and given a six months' sentence. Imprisoned on remand from May, he had been free only a short while when his mother, Blue's wife of 20 years, Elizabeth, died on 29 November 1824, leaving the ageing Blue with the care of four children under 15. Blue never fully recovered from her death and his behaviour became increasingly eccentric. He may have been too preoccupied with his wife's death, his son's incarceration and the problem of feeding his motherless children to notice that the businessman and magistrate Edward Riley had killed himself on 21 February 1825. Blue, however, could not have failed to be aware of the announcement in the *Sydney Gazette* on 25 January 1825 that he was 'to have the use and occupation of his ferry ... which he formerly occupied'.[19]

Emboldened by his belated success in regaining his ferry, Blue again petitioned the governor on 12 August 1825. This time he asked for title to the small lot between his farm and the water in order to make a road to the ferry. He had always had the use of land, he said, and Macquarie had actually granted the land to him, but an oversight had prevented the undertaking of a formal survey. The colonial secretary was not impressed; he shrewdly suggested Blue tender documents to support his claim. Nothing more was heard of the matter. With or without the land, Blue managed to retain his ferry service, although his monopoly had long since ceased. To support his children he sold oysters and his farm's produce as a pedlar, in addition to the ferry fees. In March 1827, Blue claimed he was scarcely able to put food in his children's mouths. This time he petitioned Governor Ralph Darling to take his sons into an apprenticeship at the shipyard: Robert as carpenter and John as ship-wright. This too was refused. It was the wealthy merchant Simeon Lord who stepped into the breach, taking both boys as apprentice weavers, even though Blue was too poor to purchase their indentures. Perhaps Lord recalled with gratitude Blue's stubborn silence in the smuggling case nine years before.[20]

The 1828 census, the first in New South Wales's history, revealed that Robert and John Blue were residents in Simeon Lord's house, along with several other apprentices. It also showed that Mary Blue had married and was living with her husband at Broken Bay, while Blue's youngest daughter, Elizabeth, had died. William Blue had an elaborate and extended household: the eldest daughter Susannah remained at Northampton farm, with her husband, the prodigal son William Jr, two assigned convict men and one free by servitude, all of whom aided the running of the farm and ferry business. The census also provided a glimpse into the fortunes of the surviving black founders of New South Wales. John Moseley, who for many years was employed as a labourer on the wharves, had achieved some modest prosperity and was now a dealer in Essex Lane in the Rocks, with his own house where he employed two female servants. John Martin, with his wife and nine children, lived on his original grant and continued to work as a constable and pound keeper. Samuel Chinery had lost his land and now worked as labourer for another emancipated convict at Windsor.[21]

It was around the time of the census that it began to be noticed that Blue was fashioning a curious public persona. He had taken to walking about Sydney wearing a travesty of a naval uniform with a top hat, twirling the carved stick he always carried and calling out in a pre-emptory fashion to all and sundry that they must acknowledge him as 'the commodore'. Such behaviour drew comment from a correspondent to the *Sydney Gazette* in 1827 who was startled to find himself so addressed and fascinated by 'the old man's grotesque appearance'. Blue was far from senile however, as he showed that same year when he won a writ for £12 against a feckless Sydney gentleman for unpaid ferry fees. Nor did the magistrate's bench think he had lost his wits when they issued a summons against him for harbouring a runaway convict in early

July 1829. By then he was something of a Sydney celebrity, as was clear from the newspaper report: '[t]he old commodore, Billy Blue is about to be had up for harbouring a prisoner of the crown', the *Gazette* told its readers. 'Billy considers himself a privileged person, for this is not the first time he has been caught tripping.'[22]

As the newspaper suggested, Blue had long been suspected as a conduit for runaways to the North Shore who would then follow known tracks through the bush to lose themselves in a community of renegades around Pittwater and beyond. Actually, harbouring runaways and assisting with the distribution of smuggled goods was an activity shared among most of the small settlers on the North Shore; it was fundamental to the informal economy of those in the emancipist class who were being squeezed by the wealthy free settlers who despised them. That William Blue Jr was arrested and jailed for the same offence – harbouring an escapee – a month prior suggests Blue's household was under surveillance, initiated, perhaps, by Magistrate Wollstonecraft, who would have been delighted to see the last of his disreputable neighbour. Blue received a fine or gaol in lieu of payment. That a man of 90 or so was facing months in gaol because he was unable to pay the fine was hardly a source of concern for the free-settler class, so the intervention of one of their number to pay Blue's fine was regarded by some as a betrayal of class interest. For Timothy Goodwin Pitman the maintenance of exclusive class barriers was of no consequence. He was from Boston in the United States, and he came to New South Wales with £7000 to invest in the China trade and had become naturalised to take advantage of land grants available to free-born Britons. He lived on a very large property close to Blue at Hunter's Hill, which may have influenced him to rescue the old man from prison.[23]

From that point onward, Blue kept clear of the law, while at the same time he became much more ostentatious in his displays of eccentricity. Perhaps he understood that notoriety was his best defence. On 15 December 1829 the *Sydney Gazette* noted that 'Billy Blue, the Commodore of Port Jackson, has of late grown uncommonly eloquent; scarcely a morning passes without a loud oration from his loyal lips, descanting on the glories of the standard'. According to the lawyer James Dowling, who arrived in the colony in 1828 and became Chief Justice in 1834, this 'eccentric loquacious character' adopted the habit of boarding ships that arrived in the harbour wearing his tattered uniform and top hat, to welcome the captain 'in his official capacity as Commodore'. Blue expected to 'receive suitable homage from all of His Majesty's subjects, as befitted a man of his position', so the *Sydney Gazette* explained. Walking about, twirling his stick and declaiming 'True Blue forever', the old man demanded that men salute him, children doff their hats and women curtsy. Woe betide any who failed to respond; they suffered a cascade of abuse: 'You brute – you long legged brute – [you] forget the commodore!' On Sunday he would never speak above a whisper as he admonished everyone to 'remember the worship of God'. His perform-ance, calculated or not, had the effect of endearing Blue to all levels of Sydney society.[24]

The author Alexander Harris was curious to see the character he had heard so much about. Harris encountered Blue in the early 1830s when he must have been in his mid-90s. He described a wily, likeable fellow who had his wits about him, much like the character who gave the loquacious, but still coherent and effective, evidence in the 1832 court case. Judging from his appearance, Harris presumed the old ferryman was called Billy Blue because 'he was a very black black'. Blue told Harris, with 'a fatherly sort of authority', that he had rowed across a good many times that day and so Harris must row over to Sydney and Blue would row himself back. Noting that 'the Old Commodore' was consid-ered 'to possess a sort of universal freedom of speech', Harris agreed to this odd bargain, paying the fare to row the boat across to Sydney so that Blue could pull himself back again.[25]

Not everyone was enchanted by the licence granted Blue. An anony-mous correspondent to the *Sydney Gazette* on 31 October 1833 was outraged at 'the *black* guardism of Billy Blue', having seen 'two very respectable ladies bellowed after by this sweep [who] made use of such language as must have shocked every modest person'. Surely it was high time a stop was put to 'this *crying* nuisance', so that respectable people could walk the streets without being 'grossly insulted'. The editor sprang to the defence of Blue, chiding his correspondent that the commodore was a 'privileged person' who was nearly a hundred years old, and whose harmless muttering was pitiful rather than insulting: '[s]till alive; never die – never die'.

This image of a harmless dotard put forward by the *Gazette* was not that presented to the European aristocrat Baron von Hügel in February 1834. On coming ashore in Sydney, von Hügel was shocked to be confronted by an old black man standing in the middle of the street with a sack over his shoulder, 'saying something crazy in a loud voice at every passer by'. What von Hügel overheard was far from pitiful. Addressing one passing gentleman, Blue called out: '[w]ho is that long legged beauty, Your Honour? I wont say anything to your lady.' To another pedestrian he was slyly conspiratorial: '[n]ot a word about the pig'. On enquiring about this disreputable apparition, von Hügel could scare believe his ears to be told that this was 'the old commodore whom Governor Macquarie appointed port captain'. Blue must have been delighted to have so thoroughly fashioned his own legend.[26]

When William Blue died three months later at Northhampton farm no one was quite sure of his age. The *Sydney Herald* reported him to be 95, the *Australian* 99, and the *Sydney Gazette* 97. Each of the three Sydney newspapers dedicated prime space to an affectionate obituary, with the editor of *Sydney Gazette* producing two columns of high-flown praise where he extolled 'the gallant old commodore' as a privileged person whose memory would be 'treasured in the minds of the present generation, when the minions of ambition are forgotten in the dust'. Within days the *Australian* announced that a painting of Blue could be viewed at Cummings Hotel; in the opinion of this paper the likeness, executed in oils, 'ought to be preserved in Government House or some other institution'. The artist was J.B. East, a painter of some note who exhibited at the Royal Academy. East arrived in the colony a few years before Blue's death, seeking commissions, and undoubtedly he had produced the portrait as a speculative venture. He would have seen Blue often enough to have produced the painting from memory. It was very much a commemorative portrait: Blue was presented as a tall, almost graceful black man with a beatific smile, dressed in his rag-tag clothes and his signature top hat, carrying the well-known accoutrements of a bag slung over his shoulder and the carved stick. In acknowledgement of his supposed patron, the setting was Lady Macquarie's Chair in the governor's domain, while behind him the harbour provided glimpses of the shipping activity mistakenly thought to provide his *raison d'être* as 'the old commodore'.[27]

That a disreputable black man and serial offender should be the subject of a commemorative portrait must have enraged the exclusionist settlers, who wanted to excise the convict stain from respectable colonial life. Blue would surely have relished the irony that the *Sydney Gazette* had published such an extravagant obituary, since that very paper, thirty years earlier, had pronounced that Blue's heart was blacker than his extremities and had berated his uncommon criminality. Blue's past misdemeanours were swept aside by the second-generation *Gazette*, which chose to see 'the gallant old commodore' as a foundation father of New South Wales, telling the readers that 'the reign of Billy is coeval with the foundation of the colony'.[28]

Of course it was not true that Blue's life was coeval with that of the colony; New South Wales was into its thirteenth year at his arrival. It was, however, true of John Moseley, the Sydney dealer whose lonely death had not only gone unnoticed but had also been incorrectly recorded the year before. As it was true of John Martin, who lived quietly on his original grant with his wife Mary, daughter of John Randall, and 11 children, only five of whom he acknowledged as his own. Martin died on 21 December 1837, aged 88, leaving Samuel Chinery, working as a servant at Windsor, as the last of the black founders. He died on 13 April 1841 at the age of 74.[29]

AFTERWORD

In 1912, a young man named Thomas Conquit was shot by police in a remote mining hamlet in the Snowy Mountains. In view of Conquit's description as part Aboriginal, this was unremarkable. What took the case out of the ordinary was the police explanation that they were arresting Conquit for lunacy because he had declared that he was on a mission to kill the police who were part of a worldwide conspiracy to murder all black people. Putting aside the issue of whether or not this perception was dangerously paranoid, I find it astonishing that in 1912 an Aboriginal person might regard himself as part of a worldwide black community.[1]

The man's distinctive name of Conquit makes his ancestry easy to trace in the colonial records. His grandfather was Thomas Conquade, a white convict transported from England to Australia in 1819, whose common-law wife, Frances Martin, was described on his death certificate as Aboriginal. However, Frances was not Aboriginal; she was the third child of John Martin and Mary Randall. Both her father and grandfather were African-American. Her grandson correctly understood himself to belong to the African diaspora, even if the authorities did not.

In the year before Conquit was shot John Randall's youngest child, Ann, died at Windsor, aged 96. She was the last survivor of the foundation generation of African-Australians. Ann Randall had only the faintest memory of her father, who must have died or disappeared when she was six, and she explained her origins as being an 'islander', from 'the French Islands', presumably exotic Tahiti. A descendant who remembered the old lady from her childhood said that she was as 'black as the ace of spades'.[2]

In the early years of the new Federation of Australia there was intense racial anxiety among a majority settler population aggressively determined to define their society as inherently white. With their racial purity felt to be under threat, it was decided that 'Kanakas' and Chinese

*

workers were to be expelled, while in future non-European immigrants would be denied entry. The concept of 'white Australia' fashioned at the turn of the twentieth century had no capacity to encompass currency lads and lasses who were black, and no comprehension that there might exist Australians of African descent. Between 1788 and the middle of the nineteenth century, almost every convict ship carried people of the African diaspora to New South Wales and Van Diemen's Land. Settlers and soldiers brought African servants, while some settlers were themselves of the African diaspora. Each of the port communities of the colonies included plenty of African-American and Afro-Caribbean sailors. Yet the foundation narrative of the new nation promulgated an uncomplicated racial divide: white settlers (civilisation) displacing black Aborigines (stone-age savagery).[3]

In this narrative, any black individual in early colonial Australia could only be understood as the despised and excluded other. Therefore, early twentieth-century accounts of Billy Blue entirely overlooked the fact of his African heritage and black complexion, in order that a foundation legend, who lent his name to several Sydney landmarks, could be read as a white man. In the 1970s his first biographer found it impossible to ignore the evidence that Blue was not European, but still she insisted he wasn't really *black*. Despite the evidence of three portraits that show Blue to be unmistakably African, she argued that he was 'not predominantly Negro' and was perhaps part Carib. For sure, his children must have been white because none of them 'ever seem to be referred to as coloured'. The daughters, 'named as among the finest young women in Sydney Town and again as two of the most attractive colonial born young women of their time' were by implication white. In twentieth-century Australia, it was unthinkable that such complimentary remarks could be made about a colonial woman unless she had a European complexion. Even the historian who fully understands Blue as an African-American man persists in reading Blue in early colonial Sydney as 'the member of a despised and oppressed race', albeit one who was supremely adept at destabilising his status as the excluded 'other'.[4]

The tendency to read late nineteenth- and twentieth-century racial assumptions into early colonial Australia is almost universal among historians and social commentators, regardless of on what side of the history wars they fight. In any discussion of the foundation of Australia

✱

it is a given that racialisation was at work from the beginning, with white settlers confronting black Aborigines. A recent, finely nuanced study of early settlement by Inga Clendinnen continues to read early colonial history in terms of the black/white binary. She takes an incident at Port Jackson on 29 January 1788, where a crew of marines and sailors were dancing with Aborigines, to illustrate the book's theme that the white British invaders and black Aborigines 'began their relationship by dancing together'. As the watching officer, William Bradley, observed 'these people mixed with ours and all hands danced together'.[5]

The notions of 'these' and 'ours' in Bradley's statement has automatically been read as black and white, yet a week before this incident, the same William Bradley described 'these' attempting to engage with 'ours' in the interchange between the Aborigines and a black convict who was cutting grass at Botany Bay. I would have thought this was at least as telling an interracial exchange as the dancing, although the earlier incident has never commanded attention from Australian historians. Equally, the persistent rejection of Black Caesar by Aborigines, and the almost fatal confrontation between him and the warrior Pemulwuy at the same time that several European convicts were living with the Aborigines, has been passed over without notice. A white game shooter was deliberately speared, but a black game shooter went about his business in Aboriginal territory for many years without incident. The black convicts, John Randall and William Blue, enjoyed a level of patronage and special privilege far beyond the expectation of convicts in general. There is no fixed racial binary to be discerned in any of this.

As the stories of our black founders reveal, the settlement of Australia was a multi-racial process that took place at a time when the notion of 'race' was a highly malleable construct, understood in ways very different from the modern sense of innate nature, and the binary of black or white was not a reliable way of conceptualising difference. Among historians of empire, there is a common view about the elasticity of the concept of race and the prevailing uncertainty about the signifiers of difference. There is a general understanding that the decades between 1780 and 1830 – the formative decades for the colony of New South Wales – witnessed a sea change in attitudes toward race and identity that would solidify into fixed racial categories in the second half of the nineteenth century. Surely it is time that we jettisoned assumptions about the fixed racial boundaries and the naturalness of racialised identities in early Australian history. Such simplification would never be tolerated, let alone go unremarked, if it were applied to class. To paraphrase Edward Thompson: race is a relationship and not a thing.[6]

APPENDIX
Biographies of the black founders

Blue, William (c. 1738–1834)

William Blue was probably from a free black family in New York. Most likely he was recruited into the British Navy and served as an infantryman at the battle of Quebec in 1759 and then went to England where he enlisted as a Marine. He was involved in the invasion of Belle Isle in 1762 and with a Pioneer corps in Portugal and Minorca. He must have returned to America with the British army in 1776 and was evacuated in 1783, to be discharged in England around 1784 or 1785. Later he worked for the receiving ship HMS *Enterprise* at Tower Hill, which earned him the title of 'the Commodore'. In 1796 he was sentenced at Kent Assizes for stealing sugar and he was transported to New South Wales on the *Minorca* in 1801. He was free by servitude in 1803 and the following year was living in the Rocks with Elizabeth Williams, aged 26, who arrived as a convict on the *Experiment* in 1804. They married in 1805 and had six children: Susannah (1805), William (1807), Elizabeth (1809), Mary (1812), Robert (1814) and John (1815). He ran the first ferry service between the Cove and the North Shore and had a grant on what is today known as Blues Point. He died in 1834 said to be close to 100 years old.

His son William Blue Jr ran the ferry business till he died in 1841 and he had one son. Susannah married another ferryman, George Lavender, of Lavender's Bay, and they had seven children. Robert Blue had two children; John Blue had ten children; Mary married Robert Tiffin and had one child and Elizabeth died childless at aged 19.

Caesar (1764–96)

Caesar's origins are unknown. He was probably a Creole slave from America bought to England in the final British evacuation of 1783. He

*

was living in Deptford when he was sentenced to transportation for seven years at Maidstone, Kent, in March 1786. He was on the *Ceres* hulk and transported by the *Alexander* to New South Wales, where he became a serial absconder. He was sent to Norfolk Island in March 1790 where he formed a liaison with the convict Ann Poore from the *Lady Juliana*. Their daughter Mary-Ann Poore was born on Norfolk Island in March 1792. A second child, John, was born in September 1793. Caesar returned to Sydney in March 1793 and was killed by bounty hunters in February 1796. Ann Poore died soon after.

John Poore must have died before Norfolk Island was evacuated, but in 1813 Mary-Ann Poore and her children, Rebecca and Sarah (father unknown), travelled with Mary Randall and her common-law husband William Fisher (*aka* Blatherhorn) to Port Dalrymple in Van Diemen's Land. In 1821 the Poore family went to Port Macquarie with Mary Randall and her next husband, Thomas Cresswell, where Mary-Ann Poore married the convict George Greenaway After his death in 1825 she married Joseph Conner, not long before she herself died in October 1826.

Chinery, Samuel (1767–1841)

Sentenced at Exeter, Devon to transportation for seven years on 7 August 1786 for theft of a linen shirt and other goods, Chinery, aged 19, was put aboard the *Dunkirk* hulk and discharged into the *Charlotte* for transportation to New South Wales. At Sydney Cove he was servant to assistant surgeon Thomas Arndell until about 1803, after which he worked for several farmers in the Hawkesbury region. He died on 13 April 1841 at Windsor Hospital, described as a servant, and was buried at St Matthew's parish.

Coffin, John (1762– ?)

Sentenced at the Guildhall, Exeter, on 9 January 1786 to be transported beyond the seas for seven years for stealing some 'plates and other things' from the house in which he was a servant. Ordered to the *Dunkirk*, he was discharged into the *Charlotte* for transportation to New South Wales. He was transferred from Sydney Cove to Norfolk Island in March 1790, and he left Norfolk on a ship on 30 March 1795 after his time expired.

Francisco, George (1765–89)

Sentenced to seven years for stealing in 1784 following a three-year stint as a prisoner of war in France, Francisco was sent to the *Ceres* in April 1785 and transported to New South Wales on the *Scarborough*. He died in August 1789.

Gordon, Daniel/Janel/Jack (1738–1818)

Jack Gordon appears to have been abandoned or freed by Benjamin Gordon during the siege of Charleston in 1779. He came to New York and was listed as embarked to go to Nova Scotia in April 1783, but apparently he went to Portsmouth, England, instead. In April 1785, Janel Gordon was sentenced to transportation beyond the seas for seven years at Winchester, England, for theft and was sent to the *Ceres* hulk and transported on the *Alexander* to New South Wales, where he was sentenced to death in February 1788 (with John Williams), but was pardoned on the gallows. He was subsequently sent to Norfolk Island where he was listed as a free man in 1790. He was still on Norfolk Island working as a tailor in 1805, and he returned to Sydney in 1806. He died in October 1818 aged 80.

Martin, John (1747–1837)

A seaman from the American colonies who probably came to England during the American Revolution, Martin was sentenced at the Old Bailey in July 1782 for stealing clothing and sentenced to transportation for seven years. He was on the *Ceres* hulk before being transported on the *Alexander* to New South Wales. At the time of landing at Sydney Cove, Martin had technically one year left to serve. He married Ann Toy in August 1792. In November 1792 he was free and received a grant of 50 acres, and by 1806 he was a successful farmer, also employed as a constable. He had no children with his first wife, who died in 1806. In 1812 he married Mary Randall, the daughter of his fellow black First Fleeter, John Randall. Mary had eleven children registered with Martin as father but he only acknowledged the first five. When he died in December 1837, his age was given as 88. Nearly all the Martin children had large families, giving Martin and Randall over 60 grandchildren.

＊

Moseley, John (1757–1835)

As a youth enslaved to Edward Hack Moseley, Princess Ann County, Virginia, Jack ran away with two other youths in August 1775. In New York he got a berth aboard HMS *Loyalist* bound for England in October 1783. He was indicted under the name John Shore at the Old Bailey on 21 April 1784 for impersonating a fellow seaman on the *Loyalist* in order to receive his wages. As John Moseley he was sentenced to death, and in March 1785 he was reprieved to transportation for life to Africa. A daughter was born in 1785, mother unknown. He was on the *Ceres* hulk and then transported to New South Wales on the *Scarborough*. In April 1800 Moseley received a conditional pardon and in 1828 he was recorded as a dealer in Essex Lane, in the Rocks in Sydney, by which time he was 68. He died in 1835, said to be aged 77.

Orford, Thomas (c. 1761– ?)

Thomas Orford was a seaman when he was sentenced to seven years' transportation at the Old Bailey on 7 July 1784. On 5 April 1785 Orford was sent from Newgate to the *Ceres* hulk, and later embarked on the *Alexander* for New South Wales where he married Elizabeth Jones [Osborne] on 24 March 1788. His sentence expired in 1791 and in April 1794 he was granted 30 acres at Bulanaming. He applied to leave the colony in 1806.

Randall, John (1763–1822)

Probably the slave of Captain John Randall of Stonington, Connecticut, Randall could have been recruited as a musician for a British regiment and then evacuated with the regiment to England in 1783. He was sentenced to transportation for seven years at Manchester Quarter Sessions in April 1785. He was sent to the *Ceres* hulk and was transported to New South Wales on the *Alexander*. At Sydney Cove, Randall married Esther Howard in February 1788, who died in October 1789. A daughter Frances was born in 1790, mother unknown. In September 1790 he married again to Mary Butler, who died on 29 July 1802. They had two children that survived, Mary and John Jr. In November 1792, Randall received a grant of 60 acres, north of Sydney, which he sold in 1801 when he joined the New South Wales Corps. After his discharge in

April 1810 he briefly possessed a small holding at Kissing Point with his common-law wife, Fanny, by whom he had four children. In 1815 he moved this family to Pittwater, where his two young sons were killed in an accident in 1816. He himself appears to have died, unrecorded, in 1822 when Fanny Randall petitioned to have her two daughters taken into the Orphan Institution.

The eldest of his surviving children, Frances, married the black carpenter John Aiken, who arrived on the *Marquis Cornwallis* in 1796, in 1811 and had six children. Mary married John Martin in 1812 (as above). John Randall Jr worked as a seaman on coastal ships and may have died in 1830. Eliza Randall has not been traced. Ann Randall died in 1911.

Williams, James *aka* 'Black Jemmy' (1769– ?)

At the age of 16 James Williams was sentenced at the Old Bailey in May 1785 to seven years' transportation for the theft of clothing and shoes whilst on an errand for the captain of a West India ship. He was on the *Justinia* hulk and transported on the *Scarborough* to New South Wales in May 1787, where he was known as 'Black Jemmy'. Having twice tried to escape, he was allowed to leave Sydney when his sentence expired in 1792.

Williams, John *aka* 'Black Jack' (c. 1769–1830)

When he was 15 and resident in St Nicholas's parish, Deptford, in London, John Williams was sentenced to death, later reprieved to transportation for seven years. He was on the *Censor* hulk and transported on the *Scarborough* to New South Wales, where he was known as 'Black Jack'. In February 1788, he was again sentenced to death (with Daniel Gordon), with the sentence commuted to life. He was given a conditional pardon in 1804 and left Sydney on a sealing ship in 1805. He subsequently became a sealer on Kangaroo Island and the Bass Strait, living with several Aboriginal women, whom he kept as his slaves, but he seems to have fathered no children. He was drowned in 1830.

✳

NOTES

Prologue

1   For Winbow's biography and an account of the terrible Second Fleet, see Flynn. For the official report of the death of Black Caesar, promising a coroners inquest, see Hunter to Portland, 3 March 1796, *HRA*, vol. 1, 1788–96, 554–55. The reward notice is reproduced in *HRNSW*, vol. 3, 11. For land grant to Thomas Rose see *HRA*, vol. 1, 768. For Caesar's obituary, Collins, 381.

2   For the Madagascar Trade see Platt. Morgan, 65, cites the presence of Malagasy slaves in Virginia as evidence of the atypical nature of the eighteenth-century Virginian slave community. See also Chambers, 3–28, and Walsh, 162. The quotes are from runaway notices in the *Virginia Gazette*, cited by Gomes.

3   For the information on Randall being accepted into the New South Wales Corps, see Holt, 66–67.

4   'The Humble Petition of William Blue…', SRNSW CS R6052, 4/1764, 17 Nov. 1823, 215. Swords gives a brief account of the life of William Blue which systematically disputes the validity of these claims. His later claims are made in evidence given in the case Martin v. Munn, reported in *Sydney Gazette*, 25 Oct. 1832.

5   For detail on New York regiments, Anderson, 227, 318–21, 473, 529, 795. For the information on sailors recruited in New York I am indebted to Matthew Ward of the University of Dundee.

6   For information on Belle Isle, marines recruitment for Belle Isle and Portugal campaign see NA WO1/16; ADM 2/1157; WO1/165; SP 89/56 and SP 89/58.

7   For the Pioneers at Boston and later in New York, see Orderly Book of General Howe NA PRO 30/55/106 and 107;General Orders of General William Howe at Halifax and Staten Island, NA WO 36/5. The story about Benedict Arnold and John André is discussed in most accounts of the American Revolution. The immediate detail of Arnold's defection can be found in the log of HMS *Vulture*, NA ADM 52/2037.

8   The *Book of Negroes* can be found in the Carleton Papers, NA PRO 30/55/100. It is also reproduced as a searchable database at <http://www.gov.ns.ca>. For an analysis of the alliance between fugitive slaves and the British see Pybus, *Epic Journeys of Freedom* and 'Thomas Jefferson's Faulty Math'.

9   I am indebted to Fiona Pollack for this detail. Todd Braisted and Nan Cole have done some terrific detective work in the archives for their site <http://www.royalprovincial.com>.

10   Thompson, *Whigs and Hunters*, 115.

Chapter 1

1   Patrick Henry's speech was never written or recorded verbatim. For a fulsome account of Henry's performance at the Second Virginia Convention see Meade, 15–25; Washington to Fairfax, 24 August 1774, *Papers of George Washington: Colonial Series*, vol. 10, 155. Washington had been elected delegate for Fairfax County on 20 February 1775. Washington to John A. Washington, 25 March 1775, Washington, *Papers of George Washington: Colonial Series*, vol. 10, 308.

2   For Tidewater plantation life: Kulikoff, *Tobacco and Slaves*, and Isaac, *Transformation of Virginia*. Quote from 'John Adams's Diary', 24 Sept. 1775, *Diary and Autobiography of John Adams*, vol. 2, 183.

3   Madison to Bradford, Nov. 26, 1775, *Papers of James Madison*, vol. 1, 130.

✱

4   See Orderly Book of General Howe, vol. 1, NA PRO 30/55/106. The costly British victory is now known as the battle of Bunker Hill. Burgoyne quoted in Hibbert, 53–54.

5   Dunmore to Dartmouth, 1 May 1775, NA CO5/1353; a patroller quoted in Holton, 147. Dunmore to Dartmouth, 25 June 1775, NA CO5 /1353. For the attack on Hampton see Scribner (ed.), vol. 4, 69–70, 416. Jefferson to John Randolph, 29 Nov. 1775, *Papers of Thomas Jefferson*, vol. 1, 268–70.

6   For Moseley, see 'Virginia Runaways' project': <http://teacherlink.org/content/social/ instructional/runawayintro/home.html>. For John Cunningham, see Scribner (ed.), vol. 5, 360. In the *Book of Negroes* John Moseley said that before he joined the British in 1776 he 'Lived with John Cunningham, Portsmouth, Virginia as a freeman'.

7   Madison to Bradford, 19 June 1775, *Papers of James Madison*, vol. 1, 153; for Dunmore's 'Proclamation', Scribner (ed.), vol. 4, 334.

8   Washington to Reed, 15 December 1775, *Papers of George Washington: Revolutionary War Series*, vol. 2, 553. Purdie's *Virginia Gazette*, 24 Nov. 1774. Edmund Pendleton, 14 Dec. 1775, Fourth Virginia Convention, Scribner (ed.), vol. 5, 139. Pendleton to Lee, 27 Nov. 1775, *Letters and Papers of Edmund Pendleton*, vol.1, 133.

9   For Creole slave life: Kulikoff, *Tobacco and Slaves*; Stanton, *Slavery at Monticello.*

10 Dunmore to Germain, 20 Feb. 1776, NA CO5/1353.

11 Lund Washington to Washington, 3 Dec. 1775, *Papers of George Washington: Revolutionary War Series*, vol. 2, 571, 481–82.

12 For Edward Hack Moseley's arrest and forced removal, see Scribner (ed.), vol. 5, 141–42; for John Cunningham, ibid., 361, 408, and Purdie's *Virginia Gazette*, 19 Jan. 1776. The information on John Moseley was obtained from the *Book of Negroes.*

13 The Willoughby petition for his runaways can be found in VSL, Virginia Assembly House of Delegates: Petitions, 1776, 55. For sale of captured slaves to the West Indies, Scribner (ed.), vol. 6, 425.

14 An analysis of fugitive slaves in Virginia prior to 1775 can be found in Windley, 162–64. For a glimpse of the number of women with Dunmore: 'List of women embarked at Mill Point, May 21 1776', published in Purdie's *Virginia Gazette*, 31 Aug. 1776.

15 Quotes from Meade, 107–108. Information on Ralph Henry, *Book of Negroes.*

16 Lund Washington to Washington, Jan. 1776, *Papers of George Washington: Revolutionary War Series*, vol. 3, 129. Isaac, *Landon Carter*, 3–15.

17 For background on the smallpox epidemic see Fenn; also Ranlet, 218.

18 See Orderly Book of General Howe, vol. 2, NA PRO 30/55/107.

19 Purdie's *Virginia Gazette*, 8 March 1776. Narrative of Andrew Snape Hamond, William B. Clark et al. (eds), vol. 5, 321–22; and Dunmore to Germain, 30 March 1776, NA CO 5/1373. For evidence of the 300 graves, see Fenn, 58.

20 See William Howe's General Order Book, NA WO 36/5. For runaways from Boston see Frederick and Pompey in the *Book of Negroes*, Carleton Papers, NA PRO 30/55/100, as well as Newton Prince in the Loyalist Claims Commission, NA AO12/99/ 289.

21 7 June 1779, Daniel Jones, 'Orders Relative to Refugee Negroes', in Van Buskirk, 135; Rivington's *Royal Gazette*, 4 Nov. 1780.

22 In New Jersey there were four times as many fugitives in the seven-year period of the war as in the previous seventy years, see Hodges, *Root and Branch.*

23 See *1790 Census for New Haven and New London*, Conn., CD-ROM. Randall might have been recruited in September 1781 during the attack on New London, which was led by Benedict Arnold, who was always on the lookout for young black musicians.

24 Quote from Jones, *A History of New York*, 76. For housing and employment in New York see Ellen Wilson, 64 and Wray Papers, vol. 7, CL.

25 For Colonel Tye, see Hodges, *Slavery and Freedom*, 96–104. A contemporary account of his raids from *Pennsylvania Gazette and Weekly Advertiser*, 21 June 1780.

Chapter 2

1   Proclamation, 30 June 1779, NA PRO 30/55/17 also printed in Rivington's *Royal Gazette*, 3 July 1779; John André, 'Suggestions for gaining dominion over the 'American Colonies', undated [1780], Clinton Papers, CL.

2   Memorial of Walter Harris, NA AO12/99/334. See also Mary Willing Byrd to Jefferson, *Papers*

of *Thomas Jefferson*, vol. 4, 690–92; and Morgan, 284–85.

3   Quote from Isaac Jefferson in 'Memoir of a Monticello Slave', reprinted in Bear (ed.), 7. Other quotes: Madison to Madison, 18 Jan. 1781 and Jones to Madison, 17 Jan. 1781, *Papers of James Madison*, vol. 2, 293, 289. Jefferson's slaves from Richmond were taken to Portsmouth but subsequently returned to him.

4   For Washington's 1771 inventory of New Kent slaves, see *Papers of George Washington: Colonial Series*, vol. 8, 591. The evidence of slave defections in New Kent is complicated by the fact the detailed records of titheable property have been destroyed. For Dismal Swamp Company see Royster, 271–72. Log of HMS *Savage*, commanded by Captain Thomas Graves, NA ADM 51/862. Washington's runaways were: the overseer, Frederick; Sambo, a carpenter; Gunner, a brick-maker; Stephen, a cooper; and Watty, a weaver. Lucy, Deborah, Esther, Peter, Lewis, Peter (2), Thomas and Frank were house servants, while James, Tom and Daniel worked as labourers at one of the farms. They are named in an undated list probably drawn up for a claim against the British in 1782 or 1783. I do not believe they included Harry, as claimed on the list. See the undated list of Lund Washington, Henry Willard Papers, LC.

5   For the correspondence on Washington's slave losses see, Washington to Lund Washington, 30 April 1781, Fitzpatrick (ed.), 14–15; Lafayette to Washington, 23 April 1781, and Washington to Lafayette, 4 May 1781, in Idzerda (ed.), 60, 85; Lund Washington to Washington, 3 Dec. 1775, *Papers of George Washington: Revolutionary War Series*, vol. 2, 480.

6   Jefferson's losses in Betts (ed.), 503–505; Jefferson's 'Statements of his Losses to the British at his Cumberland Plantations in 1781', 27 Jan. 1783, *Papers of Thomas Jefferson*, vol. 6, 224–25.

7   Quote from Ewald, 305; For logistics of feeding the army see Bowler, 72–73; Lafayette to Washington, 20 July 1781, in Idzerda (ed.), 258.

8   Cornwallis to Clinton, 22 Aug. 1781, NA PRO 30/11/74; Cornwallis to Clinton, 16 Sept. 1781, NA CO5/103/182; Cornwallis to Clinton, 17 Sept. 1781, NA CO5/103/182.

9   For an account of the last days of Yorktown see James. Quote from Tucker, 'Journal of the Siege of Yorktown and Surrender of Cornwallis', 17 Oct. 1781, CWM.

10   Ewald, 335–36. Cornwallis to Clinton, 15 Oct.1781, *Cornwallis, Correspondence*, vol 1, 125.

11   Tucker, 'Journal', 17–19 Oct. 1781, CWM.

12   'Cornwallis Orderly Book', Boston Public Library; Ebenezer Denny quoted in Fenn, 130; Ewald, 342.

13   Nelson to Cornwallis, 26 Oct. 1781, NA PRO 30/11/90. For Washington's suspicions see Fitzpatrick (ed.), vol. 23, 252, 364, 315, 336.

14   Uhlendorf (ed.), *Revolution in America*, 480; Ewald, 343.

15   That clause was inserted at the last minute at the insistence of the South Carolina slave agent, Henry Laurens. See Richard Oswald's private letter to the judge advocate on his deliberations in Paris, 16 Nov. 1782, Richard Oswald Papers, CL; Laurens to Gervais, 4 March 1784, *Papers of Henry Laurens*, vol. 16, 403. For the original draft treaty with amendments, Oswald to Melbourne, 30 Nov. 1782, NA CO 5/110, 377. Laurens was exchanged for Lord Cornwallis after the fall of Yorktown. As he was mourning for the death of his son, he had delayed going to Paris till the last day, Wharton (ed.), vol. 6, 90–91.

16   Baurmeister, 19 April 1783, in Uhlendorf (ed.), *Revolution in America*, 556. Thomas Willis, an employee of the police, was paid a piece of gold coin to kidnap a runaway called Caesar, whom he bound and beat with a stick through the streets of Manhattan and on to a ship. Luckily, Willis was caught in the act. He was given a court-martial and Caesar was set at liberty once more, Wilson, 65.

17   Baurmeister, 17 June 1783, Uhlendorf (ed.), *Revolution in America*, 569; Boston King, 157.

18   Carelton to North, 14 April 1783, NA CO 5/8, and enclosures, NA CO 5/109. Carleton's orders, 15 April 1783, NA PRO 30/55/103.

19   For Willoughby, 'Petition of Sundry Inhabitants of Norfolk and Princess Anne Counties', 28 April 1783, NA PRO 30/55/92. Washington to Harrison, 30 April 1783 and Washington to Parker, 28 April 1783, Fitzpatrick (ed.), vol. 26, 364–65, 369–70.

20   British pass for Cato Ramsay, dated 21 April 1783, PANS.

21   'Substance of a Conference between General Washington and Sir Guy Carleton', 6 May 1783, Fitzpatrick (ed.), vol. 26, 402–406.

22. Washington quote, Fitzpatrick (ed.), vol. 28, 283.

23   Details found in *Book of Negroes*.

24   For an account of the victory parade and fireworks, Van Buskirk, 183.

✱

Chapter 3

1 Smollett, 151–52.
2 For HMS *Loyalist*, see NA ADM36/8202.
3 See Porter, 185–86, and Ackroyd, 294–96. The first hangings outside Newgate occurred on 9 Dec. 1783, and utilised the 'New Drop' system.
4 For joint petition, Loyalist Claims Commission, NA AO 13/79/744.
5 Opinion on memorial of John Baptist, NA AO 12/99/ 359.
6 Memorials of: John Twine, NA AO 12/54/142; Richard Weaver, AO 12/100/94; and John Provey, AO 13/27/ 230, AO 12/101/15.
7 Memorials of: Peter Anderson NA AO 12/99/354; Walter Harris, AO 12/99/334; Shadrack Furman, AO 13/29/658.
8 West Indian writer William Beckford quoted in Braidwood, 32. It is possible that the operation of the Poor Laws explains why some of the black refugees got baptised, which, in effect, attached them to a parish.
9 One man with paid employment was Newton Prince, the pastry cook who had witnessed the Boston Massacre; brought to London by a British officer in 1781, he subsequently made his living running a cook shop. Despite having an income, Prince was granted a quarterly pension by the commission, memorial of Newton Prince, NA AO 12/99/289.
10 Long, *Candid Reflections*, 75. Norton, 402–26, misjudges the demographics when she suggests a population in London of at least 1200 in the period immediately after the American Revolution. Braidwood puts the number at 7500, while Rudé estimates 10 000 or more. Myers analysed parish records to arrive at a number in excess of 10 000.
11 My analysis of records of black baptisms, 1770–1800, for the parishes of Greater London, using data supplied by the GLRO, indicates that about 1 per cent of baptised Londoners were black, but they underestimate the black population, many of whom were not Christian. Analysis of trial records from the Old Bailey, the Middlesex and Kent Assizes in the period immediately after the American Revolution, reveal about 0.9 per cent of indictments were identified as black, but racial identity was not always specified in the court documents. In the more detailed records for the prison hulks and transportation ships the percentage of black felons was 2 per cent. An average of all three indicators, suggests a population of about 1.3 per cent of a population of 750 000, that is, just under 10 000.
12 For slave-servants, Lorimer, 'Black Slaves and English Liberty', 121–31.
13 In June 1780, violent riots broke out in London as Lord George Gordon, the eccentric leader of the Protestant Association, marched on Parliament to present an anti-Catholic petition. For an account of the Gordon Riots, see Linebaugh, 341–51. For the subsequent trials of Benjamin Bowsey and John Glover, OBSP, 28 June 1780.
14 Trial of Caesar, NA ASSI 94/1271, ASSI 31/14.
15 To identify one particular Caesar in the Revolutionary records would be impossible; every second slaveholder had chattel named Caesar.
16 For further discussion of black seaman see Christopher. For James Williams, see OBSP, 1784–85, 745.
17 Equiano, 28. Blue 1823 petitions: 28 October 1823, SRNSW CS R6017, 4/5783, 438-40; 17 November 1823, SRNSW CS R6053, 4/1764, 215.
18 Bolster, 32; Equiano; Duffield, '"I Asked How the Vessel Could Go?"', 121–54. The majority of the black claimants to the Loyalist Claims Commission were seamen from the Royal Navy. Sadly, surviving musters for British warships in the American theatre rarely distinguish seamen by race, though common slave names can be readily identified in crew lists.
19 Trial record of John Williams, OBSP, 1783–84, 150; NA ASSI, 13/13; NA ASSI, 35/225. Williams's first partner in crime was also transported on the First Fleet.
20 Trial records of: John Martin, OBSP, 1781–82, 454; Thomas Orford, OBSP, 1783–84, 1016–17; George Francisco, OBSP, 1784–85, 164; James Williams, OBSP, 1784–85, 745.
21 Quotes from memorial of David King, NA AO12/99/356 and 'Memorial of Black London', NA AO 12/19/343, AO12/99/86.
22 Trial of John Moseley, OBSP, 1783–84, 557.
23. Long, *History of Jamaica*, 4. Johnson's friend is quoted by Lorimer, *Colour*, 30.
24 See Braidwood, 32.
25 *Public Advertiser*, 5 and 10 Jan. 1786; 17 Feb. 1786; 28 Jan. 1786.

26   Adams to Jay 15 Aug. 1785 and 25 May 1786 in Adams (ed.), 248–50, 394–96. See also
     Miller, 112. £5 million was approximately 2 per cent of the entire national debt of c. £245
     million in 1783, see Brewer, 114.
27   For a closer examination of currents in British opinion see Brown, *Moral Capital.*
28   See *Morning Chronicle,* 13 Feb. and 10 March 1786; *Morning Herald,* 14 Feb. 1786. See also
     Braidwood, 63–70. CRBP Minutes, NA T1/631.
29   Quote from *Morning Post,* 15 March 1786.
30   Before the 1834 Poor Law reforms, guardians were able to grant payments to able-bodied
     individuals who were, as they say today, job seekers. It was rare, but it did happen. Quote
     from *Morning Post,* 15 March 1786.

Chapter 4

1   For a discussion of the draconian Hanoverian repression, see Thompson, *Whigs and Hunters,*
     21–24, and Linebaugh, 16–18.
2   For John Martin, OBSP, 1781–82, 454.
3   See Foley.
4   For a discussion of the convict trade to America see Ekirch. For hulks see communication
     with Duncan Campbell, NA T29/56; Hulk Act 16 Geo III c. 43.
5   For a discussion of eighteenth-century prisons see: Linebaugh; Gatrell; and Hay et al. (eds).
6   Howard, 72.
7   Roberts to Ross, Dec. 1784, NA HO42/5/465–6; Miles to Germain, 8 July 1782, NA
     CO267/20; Miles to the African Committee, 1 Feb. 1783, NA T70/33.
8   For accounts of various men on the *Den Keyser* see Gillen; quote from Miles to African
     Committee, 1 Feb. 1783, NA HO70/33.
9   Roberts to Ross, Dec. 1784, NA HO42/5.
10   Sydney to Africa Company, 21 Dec. 1784, NA HO 43/1/355; Calvert to Treasury, 15 Jan.
     1785; see also NA HO 42/6/36, HO 42/6/ 4370, T 70/69, T/70/145.
11   For Richard Bradley's mission see *CJ,* vol. 43, 411, re. £457 10s 6d to Bradley per Thomas
     Cotton. For Camden, Calvert and King see NA T1/614; for draft order see NA T1/624. For
     Orford see OBSP, 1784–85, 532.
12   Duncan Campbell Letterbooks, 2 April 1785, ML A3229.
13   Quote from 'Minutes of the House of Commons respecting a plan for transporting felons to
     the island of Lemaine in the River Gambia', NA HO7/1.
14   The 63rd, originally raised in Manchester and later reconstituted as the West Suffolk
     Regiment, still had black drummers on its establishment a decade after 1785. There was a
     tradition of British regiments using black drummers dating from the seventeenth century and
     in regimental bands in the eighteenth century, see Paine, 22–23 and Fryer, 81–86. Randall's
     trial was reported in the *Manchester Mercury,* 19 April 1785.
15   For Moseley, OBSP, 1784–85, 532. Baptism record of Jane Moseley, Marylebone Parish
     Registers, GLRO.
16   Quote from 'Minutes of the House of Commons', HO7/1, NA. For Gordon see Hampshire
     Record Office, 5 April 1785. For the *Ceres* convicts, NA T1/637.
17   Duncan Campbell Letterbooks, ML A3327; *Ceres* lists, NA T1/637.
18   Burke, *CJ,* vol. 40, 954–59.
19   'Minutes of the House of Commons', NA HO7/1.
20   Lord Beauchamp's Report from the Committee Enquiring into the Transportation Act of
     1784, *CJ,* vol. 11, 1161–64; NA T1/624.
21   Matra, 'A Proposal for Establishing a Settlement in New South Wales', 23 Aug. 1783, NA CO
     201/5.
22   Smeathman, 'Substance of a Plan of a Settlement, to be made near Sierra Leone, …', in
     Wadström, 197–209.
23   Payment lists, 14 Aug.– 4 Sept. 1786, NA T1/635. Another Deptford resident was Benjamin
     Whitecuff from New York.
24   'Alphabetical list of black people who have received the bounty', CRBP Minutes, 28 June
     1786, NA T1/638; CRBP Minutes, 7 June, 6 Oct. 1786, T1/632, NA.
25   Sydney to the Admiralty Lords, 7 Dec. 1786, *HCSP,* vol. 67, 251.

*

26 Sydney to Lords of Treasury, 18 Aug. 1786, NA T1/369. Banks's evidence to the committee, 10 May 1786, NA HO 7/1.
27 Sydney to the Admiralty Lords, 7 Dec. 1786, *HCSP*, vol. 67, 251. NA T1/635; T1/638–9.
28 CRBP Minutes, 6 Oct. 1786, NA T1/636.
29 Navy Board Minutes, 29 Nov. 1786, NA ADM 106/2622. Lord George Gordon in *Public Advertiser*, 18 Dec. 1786. For a discussion of this controversy, see Braidwood, 132–43.
30 For the *Alexander* refit, see Navy Board Minutes, 10 Dec., 19 Dec. 1786, NA T1/369.
31 Gordon's prisoners' petition, 8 Jan. 1797, was printed by Thos. Wilkins at No. 23 Aldermanbury.
32 *Evening Post*, 19 Dec. 1786; Phillip to Nepean, 11 Jan. 1787, *HRNSW*, vol. 1, part 2, 46.
33 Navy Board to Vassa, 29 Jan. 1787, NA ADM 106/2347.
34 The letter in the *Public Advertiser*, 6 April, has been attributed to Ottobah Cugoano since the argument and language are nearly identical to those in his subsequent book, *Thoughts and Sentiments*.
35 'List of the Black Poor embarked for Sierra Leone', NA T1/643. Weaver to Sharp, 23 April 1788, and Elliot to Sharp, 20 July 1787, in Hoare, 320–22. Three years later a relief expedition organised by Sharp found only 46 survivors.

Chapter 5

1 John Rugluss, Thomas Lipmus and Samuel Woodham were on board the *Den Keyser* to Goree in 1782 but escaped back to England and were rearrested and transported to New South Wales in 1787. See chapter 4 above for a detailed description of this story.
2 Phillip's 'View on the Conduct of the Expedition and the Treatment of Convicts', *HRNSW*, vol. 1, part 2, 53.
3 John White, 47–51.
4 Coffin trial, *Exeter Flying Post*, 9 Jan. 1786. Chinery trial, NA ASSI 23/8.
5 Tench, 17.
6 Easty, 5. For flogging Royal Navy see Dening, 116–22, 383–86.
7 Easty, 5; Marines' petition, 7 May 1787, *HRNSW*, vol. 1, part 2, 100–101.
8 Tench, 18.
9 Phillip to Nepean, *HRNSW*, vol. 1, part 2, 108.
10 'Return of the Sick', 4 June 1787, *HRNSW*, vol. 1, part 2, 107. Clark, 12.
11 John White, 67; 'Return of Sick', 30 Aug. 1787, *HRNSW*, vol. 1, part 2, 111.
12 For a discussion of the ravages of scurvy and its final elimination see Stephen Brown.
13 Easty, 37; Clark, 52–53.
14 Bowes Smyth, 40; Easty, 57.
15 Collins, 82; Bradley translation given in note 5, 533.
16 Collins, 79.
17 Clark, 65.
18 Collins, 86; Hunter, 21; Bowes Smyth, 43; John White.
19 Easty, 66–67.
20 Clark, 82–85.
21 Easty, 87, 89; Clark, 90.

Chapter 6

1 Tench, 37.
2 The Eora were divided into various clan groups with demarcated territory. These men were Bediagal or Gweagal from Botany Bay. King, Journal, 34–35. Translation in Southwell Papers, *HRNSW*, vol. 2, 700.
3 On more than one occasion, the Eora showed intense interest that the newcomers had different coloured skin. Bradley, 62.
4 Bowes Smyth, 57; Clark, 92.
5 John White, 113.
6 Bowes Smyth, 67.
7 Bowes Smyth, 68.

✱

8   Phillip to Nepean, 9 July 1788, *HRNSW*, vol. 1, part 2, 156.
9   Ralph Clark, 97. Clark fathered a daughter, whom he named after his wife, with a convict woman who had been on the *Friendship* and was cohabiting with a sailor during the voyage, much to his disgust.
10 Collins, 14; Cobley (ed.), vol. 1, 82, 110. For the information on the women, see Gillen and <http://www.oldbaileyonline.org>.
11 Tench, 50; John White, 116–17.
12 Collins, 26, 65.
13 Evidence of Moseley and Randall sharing a hut comes from trial of John Thomas, SRNSW Court of Criminal Jurisdiction, 7 Nov. 1788, R655. Other circumstantial evidence is the death of a woman named Elizabeth Moseley 10 August 1791, Cobley (ed.), vol. 3, 101. The only woman that this could have been was Elizabeth Osborne, who married Thomas Orford, and must therefore have been confused as the wife of John Moseley. Interestingly Mary Hill also disappears from the records at this time.
14 Collins, 58.
15 Ibid.
16 Evidence of armed convicts Burn and McIntyre employed as game shooters from testimony given to the Magistrate's Court, 13 June 1788. Reference to the shooter for Ross from 'Journal of Daniel Southwell', 13 May 1788, *HRNSW*, vol. 2, 666. Collins, 108, names the three official game shooters as McIntyre, Burn and Randall.
17 John White, 156, 159; Phillip to Sydney, *HRNSW*, vol. 1, part 2, 191.
18 Records of the Judge Advocate's Bench, SRNSW 1/296. Worgan quoted in Cobley (ed.), vol. 1, 132.
19 Tench, 66. For an account of this gruesome punishment ritual see journal entry for 2 May 1788, Bradley, 104–105.
20 Collins, 44.
21 Collins, 28. For Bentham's reaction, see Currey, 140.
22 John White, 142.
23 Tench, 72; Ross to Nepean, 10 July 1788, *HRNSW*, vol.1, part 2, 176, 213.
24 Bradley, 117.
25 The origins of the smallpox epidemic is politically and historiographically controversial. For my account I have relied on Campbell, *Invisible Invaders*, which appears to make the most sense of a complex and highly charged issue. Michael Bennett has recently added to the controversy with his speculation that the smallpox could have been spread by convicts from the First Fleet.
26 Easty, 127.
27 Scott, 48.
28 Collins, 58–59; Caesar's response rendered in the convict argot can be found in Rickard's edition of *Barrington's Voyage*, a work that purported to be authored by the flash pickpocket George Barrington, who was transported to New South Wales in 1790.
29 Trial of John Calleghan, 31 July 1789, Minutes of the Court of Criminal Jurisdiction, SRNSW 1147A; Phillip to Ross, 17 August 1789, *HRNSW*, vol. 1, part 2, 265.
30 Trial of Daniel Gordon, 20 Aug. 1789, Minutes of the Court of Criminal Jurisdiction, SRNSW 1147A; Collins, 65.
31 For Coffin see Cobley, vol. 2,111; Collins. 73; Bradley, vol. 2, 124, 90.
32 Collins, 73, 76.
33 Tench, 116; Bradley, 186 (journal entry for 31 Jan. 1790).
34 Clark, 111; Collins, 58, 91.
35 Tench, 120.

Chapter 7

1   Collins, 80; Ralph Clark, 117.
2   Ralph Clark, 122.
3   Ralph Clark, 118–47, 293.
4   Tench, 120–22; Collins, 83; the letter, written in Tench's style, is published in Cobley (ed.), vol. 2, 184–85.

✱

5   Tench, 124–25.
6   Tench, 125; for Dawes see Phillip to Grenville, 7 Nov. 1791, *HRA*, vol. 1, 290–94; see Campbell to Ross, 13 Oct. 1788, enclosing 'Officer's Objections', *HRA*, vol. 1, 92–94.
7   Orford is called Halford in this case, see trial of Thomas Halford, 12 April 1790, Minutes of the Court of Criminal Jurisdiction, SRNSW 1147A. For identity of Elizabeth see note 13, chapter 6 above.
8   Tench, 125; trial of Williams and Lane, Minutes of the Court of Criminal Jurisdiction, SRNSW 1147A.
9   Collins, 87.
10   Tench, 127.
11   Collins, 97; Tench,127.
12   Collins, 99.
13   Johnson to Thornton in Mackaness (ed.), 30. The best account of this infamous episode is Flynn.
14   Mackaness (ed.), 33.
15   *HRNSW*, vol. 2, 768.
16   Evidence of John Beale, Quartermaster from the *Neptune*, given before the magistrate at Bow Street, London, in November 1791. His and other evidence implicates Captain Traill and his first mate in systematic brutality towards male and female convicts, as well as the crew and the soldiers, and finally of providing them with short rations. See NA TS11/341. Traill was finally tried for murder of the cook on the voyage, but was acquitted.
17   Captain William Hill quoted in Cobley (ed.), vol. 3, 251. Quote from Camden, Calvert and King in Flynn, 51. Dr Emma Christopher at Monash University has a detailed examination of the correspondences between the slave trade and the Second Fleet for her forthcoming book, *The Colour of the Cargo*.
18   Elizabeth Macarthur's Journal, 25 Jan. 1790, *HRNSW*, vol. 2, 490–92.
19   Tench, 132; Phillip to Grenville, 13 July 1790, *HRNSW*, vol. 1, part 2, 354–55.
20   Collins, 107; Phillip to Nepean, 23 Aug. 1790, *HRA*, vol. 1, 207.
21   Details of Ann Toy and Mary Butler in Flynn, 576, 187.
22   'Remarks and Observations on Norfolk Island', Ross to Phillip, Dec. 1790, *HRNSW*, vol. 1, part 2, 419.
23   *HRNSW*, 435–36, 443.
24   Ross to Phillip, 11 Feb. 1791, *HRNSW*, vol. 1, part 2, 447. 'Account of Sows and Supplies Delivered to the Convicts on Norfolk Island for their own support … commencing 5 February 1791', dated July 1791, NA CO201/9. Curiously, Anne Poore is not mentioned in this list. Gillen is the source for the relationship with Caesar which is confirmed by Flynn. There are very few marriage records from Johnson's time on Norfolk Island.
25   Tench, 165–67.
26   Tench, 164–76; Easty, 122–23.
27   The quote is a description of 1791 Parramatta from Tench, 156.
28   Ten per cent of the 2000 convicts on the Third Fleet died en route. The worst abuses, including systematic starvation, were on the ships *Active* and *Queen* carrying Irish prisoners from Cork. The contractor for the Third Fleet was again Camden, Calvert and King, but after the outcry over the condition of the convicts on the Second and Third Fleets they were awarded no more contracts.

Chapter 8

1   Ralph Clark, 307, 288–89.
2   Entry for Feb. 1792, Phillip Gidley King Journal 1792–94, NA CO 20/10. King to Nepean, 23 Nov. 1791, *HRNSW*, vol. 1, part 2, 562–63;. See also King to Phillip, 17 Nov. 1791, ML C 187.
3   For punishment of Coffin see Gillen. The birth of Mary-Ann Poore was registered subsequently when she was baptised by Rev. Henry Fulton, see Register of Henry Fulton, SRNSW BDM, vol. 4, R5005.
4   Collins, 184.
5   Marriage Register of St Johns Parramatta, SRNSW BDM, vol. 1, R5002.
6   Atkins Journal, 18 April, 26 June 1792, ML MSS 737. Convict Henry Hale quoted in Hughes, 107.
7   Atkins Journal, 21 May 1792.

✱

8   Ryan, *Land Grants*, Book 1a, 12.
9   Tench, 220
10   Atkins Journal, 7 Dec. 1792. Chinery was acquitted of robbing the assistant surgeon in 1795, see Records of Court of Criminal Jurisdiction, 7 Nov. 1795, SRNSW 5/1147. Burial notice, St Johns Parramatta, 13 Feb. 1793, SRNSW BDM, vol. 1, R5001. For the daily weather reading see Atkins Journal, 1792–93.
11   Easty, 139; King to Phillip, 19 Sept. 1792; Phillip to Dundas, 4 Oct.1792, *HRNSW*, vol. 1, part 2, 653–60.
12   King to Grose, 3 March 1793, King Letterbook, ML C187. Collins, 57, 232.
13   King to Sydney, 31 March 1783, King papers, ML C188. King to Dundas, 10 March 1794, *HRNSW*, vol. 2, 136–37. For problem over women and account of the mutiny, *HRNSW*, vol. 2, 103–10.
14   Grose to Dundas 16 Feb. 1793, *HRNSW*, vol. 2, 14–15.
15   Grose to Dundas 9 Jan. 1793, *HRNSW*, vol. 2, 2.
16   Collins, 220, 219.
17   The disgusted naval officer was Robert Murray quoted in Cobley (ed.), vol. 3, 68–70.
18   Account of the home invasion, Collins. Both Hunter and King railed against Grose's expropriation of convicts, but had little success in returning them to the public works. Quote from Governor Hunter's complaint to Under-Secretary King, 1 June 1797, *HRNSW*, vol. 3, 210–11. Birth of Mary Randall, Baptism Register of St Phillips Sydney, 13 Jan. 1794, SRNSW BDM, vol. 4, R5005.
19   Alexandro Malaspina, 'A Secret Report of the Convict Colony', in Flannery (ed.), 123.
20   Atkins Journal, 21 & 22 Dec. 1793. White to King, 12 December 1793, King Papers, ML C188, vol 1.
21   Collins, 295.
22   Collins, 319–20.
23   Atkins Journal, 17 June 1794.
24   Atkins Journal, 21 April 1794.
25   Bench of the Magistrates Court Parramatta, 17 Oct. 1794, SRNSW SZ 765. Collins to Laing, 11 June 1795, quoted in Currey, 106.
26   Collins, 354.
27   Collins, 364; Atkins Journal, 20 Nov. 1795.
28   Collins, 371. Pemulwuy was shot and captured during the confrontation in Parramatta and said to be dying, but made a miraculous escape, fostering the idea that Pemulwuy could not be killed by firearms.
29   Collins, 377.
30   Collins, 377, 378; *HRNSW*, vol. 3, 11.
31   *HRNSW*, vol. 3, 31; Collins, 381.

Chapter 9

1   For information on the *Reliance* and the *Experiment*, see Collins, 376, 379. John Poore's birth was 10 Sept. 1793, recorded subsequently when he was baptised by the Rev. Fulton, who arrived on Norfolk in 1801. It was common on Norfolk Island for the children to be listed with their mother's surname. Mary Anne Poore was adopted by Mary Randall from the *Lady Juliana*, who was living with John Blatherhorn *aka* Fisher. See Fulton's BDM Records, vol. 4, SRNSW R5005, and passengers aboard the *Lady Nelson* 20 Jan. 1813 in Wright. Mary Randall was an Irish woman who was arrested with John Randall's second wife Mary Butler.
2   Hunter to King, 1 June 1797, *HRA*, vol. 2, 13; Hunter to Portland, 3 March 1796, *HRNSW*, vol. 3, 30; Portland to Hunter, 2 March 1797, *HRA*, vol. 2, 9.
3   Hunter to Portland, 10 Jan. 1798, *HRNSW*, vol. 3, 346–47; 'Petition of Settlers from the Field of Mars', 19 Feb. 1798, *HRNSW*, vol. 3, 367–69; 'Report of Rev. Samuel Marsden and Assistant Surgeon Arndell', 2 March 1798, *HRNSW*, vol. 3, 346, 367–69, 370–75.
4   Hunter to Portland, 20 Aug. 1796, *HRNSW*, vol. 3, 79; see also Hunter to Portland, 10 June 1797, and Portland to Hunter, 31 Aug. 1797, *HRA*, vol. 2, 14–19, 108.
5   George Johnston took his first commission when only 12. The most famous of the black recruits of Lord Percy was the bare-knuckle boxer Bill Richmond.

6   Court of Criminal Jurisdiction 7 June 1799, SRNSW R655, 83.
7   Ibid. Hunter was forced to defend himself to the Duke of Portland in Nov. 1799 against anonymous charges of impropriety, including criminal activity involving the trafficking in spirits within Government House, see Portland to Hunter, 26 Feb. 1799, Hunter to Portland, 15 Nov. 1799, *HRNSW*, vol. 3, 637, 743.
8   Brownrigg to Paterson, 6 March 1799, *HRNSW,* vol. 3, 639–40. For King's harassment of Hunter see *HRA*, vol. 2, 502, 513, 516. For the arrest of Johnston, and King's sustained attack upon his character, see *HRNSW*, vol. 4, 82–83.
9   Murphy trial in Hall, 193.
10   1800 Muster book, *Musters and Lists*.
11   For the policy on recruitment of ex-convicts see Collins, 254. King to Bowering, 24 March 1799, *HRNSW*, vol. 3, 651, and recruitment notice, 24 Nov. 1799, *HRA*, vol. 3, 593.
12   Holt, 66–67.
13   For black drummers in British regiments see note 14, chapter 4 above. For regimental details see NA WO12/9900.
14   King to Portland, 9 Sept. 1800, *HRA*, vol. 2, 534. Regimental schools for soldiers and their children were established in the British army after 1800. A schoolmaster was appointed formally to the regiment in New South Wales in 1811, but before then the duty fell to William Cox, and maybe the chaplain, see NA WO 12/9901.
15   For the transaction on musical instruments see the Cox and Greenwood Ledger reproduced in Statham (ed.), 106, 140; French visitor was Peron, quoted in Flannery (ed.), 177.
16   Johnston benefited from the support of his powerful patron, the Duke of Northumberland who, as Lord Percy, had been his commanding officer when Johnston was a boy in the American Revolution.
17   King to Patterson, 1 Jan. 1802, *HRA*, vol. 3, 459.
18   King to Hobart, 7 June 1803, *HRA*, vol. 4, 303; *Sydney Gazette*, 1 April 1804, had a notice calling for anyone with claims on John Williams to represent them to the colonial secretary. Over the next few years 'Black Jack' came and went out of Sydney on various of Campbell's ships, before joining the semi-permanent sealing camps on Kangaroo Island. He was certainly part of the crew of the *Sophia* on 15 Feb. 1806. The *Sydney Gazette*, 18 May 1806, notes Thomas Alford was permitted to leave the colony.

Chapter 10

1   Blue's age is guesswork. He did not know his exact age and gave various accounts of it; at his death in 1834, his family and others who knew him believed him to be between 95 and 97. The quote from an early newspaper report is given without a source in Swords, 10.
2   My understanding of lumping and customary pillage owes much to Linebaugh, 416–25. He suggests that in the mid-1790s there was a crackdown on informal wages with customary rights becoming criminalised. My reading of the Old Bailey records supports his thesis. There are very few prosecutions for lumpers in this period – less than ten over the decade. Most of the cases occurred in 1796. Nearly all the trials for plundering and pillage come from the East India warehouses. Quote from *The Report of the Committee Appointed to Enquire into…Trade and Shipping in the Port of London* (1795–96), in Linebaugh, 419. Indictment of William Blue, KCA Q/SIW 422.
3   Deposition of William Blue, 29 Sept. 1786, KCA Q/SB 225. The information on chocolate comes from Coe & Coe.
4   Quotes from *The Report of the Committee to Enquire into Trade and Shipping*, in Linebaugh, 419. In 1796, the Old Bailey Sessions sentenced two lumpers to seven years' transportation: John Maharney for stealing logwood and sugar jointly worth 16 shillings; John Thiel for taking beaver skins worth 22 shillings. Two other lumpers, charged with smaller amounts of sugar (each under 10 pounds), received a year in a house of correction; and two more, both charged with large amounts, were acquitted, see <http://www.oldbaileyonline.org>; Deposition of William Blue, 29 Sept. 1796, KCA Q/SB 225.
5   Quote from Martin v. Munn, Supreme Court of New South Wales, 22 Oct. 1832, reported in the *Sydney Gazette,* 25 Oct. 1832. The records of Old Bailey trials also suggest that the press-gangs in London were less aggressive in 1796–97. Reprieved criminals did not make up

anything like the shortfall of men, especially since they were largely put into the West Indian regiments where they died like flies, so the press-gangs continued to be active taking huge numbers of men off the streets. For the records of the *Enterprise* see NA ADM 102.208, ADM 36/15418 to ADM 36/15428.

6   That only two died on the *Minorca* was all the more remarkable considering that the convicts had spent years in the unhealthy hulks. King to the Transport Commissioners, 2 Feb. 1802, *HRA*, vol. 3, 381.

7   For shipping in Sydney Oct.–Nov. 1803, see *HRNSW*, vol. 5, 288.

8   Holt, 89. Atkinson, 267, gives credence to this story, citing King's behaviour as evidence of his 'low jokes'. Blue gave evidence in two court cases in 1804, reported in the *Sydney Gazette*.

9   *Sydney Gazette*, 18 Aug. 1805.

10   Trial of Daniel McKay, Judge Advocate's Bench, 17 Aug. 1805, SRNSW R 656, 601. The exact meaning of term 'second wooden Jo' is unknown, McKay was a Scot and 'Jo' is a Scottish term for lover. 'Wooden' most likely derives from Scots word 'wuid', which means, among other things, an inferior form of coal; yet another meaning was to be crazy or beside oneself with rage.

11   Daniel McKay arrived on the *Royal Admiral* in 1792. In 1810 he petitioned the colonial secretary for amelioration of sentence for his common-law wife, Judith Quinlan, from the *Experiment*.

12   The earliest established ferry appears to have been the passage boat to Parramatta, and this was the first to be regulated, often on account of the boorish behaviour of the boatmen, see *Sydney Gazette*, 10 July 1803. In relation to the Harbour/Port district, Blue's ferry was the first of its kind, *Sydney Gazette*, 2 Aug. 1807.

13   Harris to King, 25 October 1807, *HRNSW*, vol. 6, 343; Bligh to Castlereagh, 30 June 1808, *HRA*, vol. 6, 533. Jamison and McKay were both implicated in an attempt to frame Bligh's close ally, Provost Marshall Gore. All three men were immediately reinstated by George Johnston after Bligh's arrest.

14   For the details of Randall's army career in New South Wales: NA WO12/9900, WO12/9901, WO12/9902, WO12/9903, WO12/9904, WO12/9905, WO12/8000, WO 25/642, WO25/1342. Cox and Greenwood ledger in Statham (ed.).

15   Quote on Bligh's temper from George Tobin in Dening, 59. Dening's superb study of Bligh's incendiary language provides the best insight into the manner in which Bligh's invective disturbed the equilibrium of an eighteenth-century ship. In the barely tamed world of New South Wales the issue was more complicated but, as Duffy argues, a significant element was the exaggerated code of honour by which officers of the New South Wales Corps were bound.

16   Harris to King, 25 Oct. 1807, Bligh to Grenville, 5 Nov. 1807, quoted in Duffy, 267. Evidence of Minchin and Whittle in Ritchie (ed.), 246, 368.

17   Evidence of Cox, Whittle and Atkins in Ritchie (ed.), 376, 368, 175.

18   Evidence of Macarthur and Whittle in Ritchie (ed.), 168–69, 371. Quote from Pvt Finnegan in Atkinson, 287.

19   The account of the trial of Macarthur, the mess dinner and the subsequent mutiny is drawn from a range of evidence in Ritchie (ed.). Quote re Kemp is William Bremlow's evidence, 115.

20   Members of Johnston's subsequent court martial were totally bemused about this trial from whence the mutiny had sprung: no one appeared to remember what it was all about. Quotes on Macarthur's protest and Kemp in Ritchie (ed.), 465–69, 432–33.

21   Ritchie (ed.), xv.

22   *HRNSW*, vol. 6, 549; Tench to Edward Macarthur, 2 Sept. 1808, *HRNSW*, vol. 6, 728; Bligh to Castlereagh, 30 June 1808, *HRA*, vol. 6, 533.

23   For McKay's contribution see Atkinson, 320; for bonfire Ritchie (ed.), 114; for signatures see evidence of Grimes and Devine, Ritchie (ed.), 287, 135. Two other men dining with Bligh that night suffered months of hard labour in the coalmines, Bligh to Castlereagh, 30 June 1808, *HRA*, vol. 6, 533.

24   For Veterans Company see Macquarie to Dundas, *HRNSW*, vol. 7, 458–59.

25   According to the *Gazette* index, John Randall was listed as intending to sail on several ships between 1810 when John Randall Jr would have been 12/13, and 1812, when he would have been 14/15. On the early voyages of the *Halcyon* (1810), the *Cyclops* (1812) and the *Governor Macquarie* (1814) he was listed as a 'boy'. For reorganisation of police see Police Regulations,

1 Jan. 1810, *HRNSW*, vol. 7, 479–86. For pilfering of government stores, 'Public Notice', 7 Sept. 1811, *HRNSW*, vol. 7, 585–86.

26 Auction notice, *Sydney Gazette*, 19 Feb. 1814; muster held on 17 Oct. – 16 Nov. 1814.

27 *Sydney Gazette*, 20 July 1816. Petition to colonial secretary, 8 May 1822, SRNSW CS R6040, 4/403, 85. Only Ann Randall was accepted and she, curiously, was taken into the Parramatta Native Institution where she was described as 'African half caste', said to be born at Broken Bay around 1816. She was later released 'into her mother's care', communication with the author from Dr Jim Kohen.

Chapter 11

1 Notice, 17 Aug. 1811, SRNSW CS Reel 6038, SZ758, 226.

2 Blue's petition, 17 Nov. 1823, SRNSW CS R6045, 4/1735,151; court case, Bench of Magistrates: Co. of Cumberland, Minutes of Proceedings Bench Book 1815–21, SRNSW R659, SZ775.

3 Atkinson, 323–45, describes effectively the impact of the Macquarie partnership and how their 'nuptial sweetness' inflected government and social order of the colony. Description of Blue as a 'sable veteran' from his obituary, *Sydney Gazette*, 8 May 1834.

4 This wasn't a racial reference, but expressed the sense that Macquarie shared some of the qualities of poor folk. In the argot of late eighteenth-century 'a brown' was a copper half-penny.

5 Quotes from Martin v. Munn Supreme Court of New South Wales, 22 and 23 Oct. 1832, reported in *Sydney Gazette*, 25 Oct. 1832.

6 For Blue's various grants and appointments: 'Return of Horned cattle from the Government herd': SRNSW CS R6048, 4/1742, 42; and R6045 4/1735, 151. For the folklore about the name 'Commodore', see Swords, 26. For the *Enterprise* see chapter 10 above.

7 Case against Blue, 10 Oct. 1818, Court of Criminal Jurisdiction, Informations, Depositions & Related Papers, SRNSW COD 445, SZ795, 421–35.

8 *Sydney Gazette*, 17 Oct. 1818.

9 Wylde to Macquarie, 16 Oct. 1818, SRNSW CS R6047, 4/1741, 47–50; Magistrates Court, 24 Oct. 1818, SRNSW R 659, SZ775, 147.

10 For increase in excise see 'Public Notice', *Sydney Gazette*, 31 Dec. 1814, and again 31 March 1818; Macquarie to Bathurst, 15 May 1818, *HRA*, vol. 9, 772–73.

11 For the *Portsea*, see Campbell to Sorrell, 27 Oct. 1818, SRNSW CS R6006, 4/3499, 118.

12 For the previous trouble with Captain Nicholls see SRNSW: CS R6002, 4/3490C, 103; R6042, 4/1725, 190; and R6002, 4/3490D, 132–33. For a discussion of the *Portsea*, as well as the inter-related business dealings of the three magistrates, and the depression of 1812–18, see Hainsworth, 75–76, 91–101.

13 Wylde to Macquarie, 16 Oct. 1818, SRNSW CS R6047, 4/1741, 47–50; Bench of Magistrates: Co. of Cumberland, Minutes of Proceedings Bench Book 1815–21, SRNSW R659; SZ775; Wylde to Macquarie, 30 Oct. 1818, SRNSW CS R6047, 4/1741, 76–77.

14 In the index of the magistrate's bench books very few entries are found relating to smuggling. Perhaps the offender had to be caught red-handed, like Blue, to afford the opportunity of prosecution, and with Blue himself heavily implicated in smuggling, the likelihood of such arrests were minimal. Blue was, after all, poacher and gamekeeper rolled into one. See SRNSW: Government Order, 24 Oct. 1818, CS R6047, 4/1741, no. 74; Campbell to Macquarie, 26 Oct. 1818, CS R6047, 4/1741, no. 77.

15 Gore to Wollstonecraft, 23 Sept. 1824, SRNSW CS R6056, 4/1765.

16 Blue's Petitions in 1823, SRNSW: 28 Oct., CS R6017; 4/5783, 438–40; 17 Nov., CS R6056 4/1764, 215.

17 Wollstonecraft to Goulbourn, 18 Nov. 1823, SRNSW CS R2173, 4/1765, 216; Goulbourn to Wollstonecraft, 6 Dec. 1824, SRNSW CS R6011, 4/3509, 665. William Jr was living with George Dowling, the local constable.

18 'Report of prisoners tried at Criminal Jurisdiction, NSW, 19 January 1824'; Brisbane to Horton, 6 Nov. 1824, *HRA*, vol. 11, 415. Gore was pardoned, probably due to Lord Palmerston's concern, in April 1825, SRNSW CS R6014, 4/3513, 667.

19 Report of R. v. Blue, Supreme Court of NSW, *Sydney Gazette*, 8 July 1824.

*

20 Petition of Blue to Brisbane, 12 Aug. 1825, SRNSW CS R6062, 4/1782, 86; Petition of Blue to Darling, 12 March 1827, SRNSW Box 4/1926, item 27/2898.
21 1828 census and householders returns SRNSW 4/1238.1-2, 4/1239.1-2, 4/1240, 4/1241.
22 Quote from the *Sydney Gazette* in Swords, 45. For Blue v. Mathew, see petition of Daniel Deering Mathew protesting this decision, *HRNSW*, vol. 13, 313–15; *Sydney Gazette*, 9 July 1829.
23 The Blue cases, son and father, are in SRNSW R852, 4/6431, 23 and 25. Pittman's career in NSW was short but luminous. No hint of scandal or corruption attached to his name and he was much admired by both the *Sydney Gazette* and the *Australian*. He contracted consumption in 1830 and left for Tahiti where shortly after he died.
24 Dowling quoted in Swords, 39; other descriptions from Blue's obituary in the *Sydney Gazette*, 8 May 1834.
25 Harris, 90.
26 Extract from Baron von Hügel, *New Holland Journal*, in Flannery (ed.), 251.
27 *Sydney Gazette*, 8 May 1834. The *Australian*, 8 May 1834, quoted by Swords, 55. The gamble with the painting did not pay off for East; it was not acquired for the public and was sold at a public raffle the following year with tickets at £1 each. There were also two caricatures produced for the mass market. Duffield's 'Billy Blue' has an excellent discussion of these representations.
28 *Sydney Gazette*, 8 May 1834.
29 John Moseley's death record has his name as Moses. Apparently Martin believed he too was a 'second wooden Jo', since his will left his property to be divided between his five children and 1 shilling to his wife Mary. There is no mention of the other seven children. In 1847 Mary Martin, the daughter of 'Black' Randall, a widow with twelve children, was recorded as living on an encroachment on the common at the Field of Mars.

Afterword

1 I am indebted to Dr Michael Powell of the University of Tasmania for this story. In 2003, *The Tracker*, starring David Gulpilil, was the headline film in the African Diaspora Film Festival in New York, but this was an aberration. As a rule, Aboriginal people in Australia have not perceived any commonality with people of the African diaspora.
2 Information on Ann Randall comes from a Randall-Martin descendant, Ray Fairall, communication with author.
3 For a discussion of the Immigration Restriction Bill and the Pacific Island Laborers Bill introduced in 1901 and racial ideas at the time of Federation, see Reynolds, 85–96.
4 Swords, 19–20; Duffield, 'Billy Blue', 6.
5 Clendinnen, 8.
6 Recently, Wheeler argued forcefully that earlier scholars have placed too much emphasis on skin colour as encoding difference in the eighteenth century, while, as Hudson, Bayly, Drescher and Kathleen Wilson all argue, the idea of inherent racial difference was not fixed in public discourse and social behaviour until well into the second half of the nineteenth century. Thompson's famous formulation that class is a relationship comes from the 'Preface' (written in 1963) to *The Making of the English Working Class*, 9.

BIBLIOGRAPHY

Archival and manuscript sources

Boston Public Library
Cornwallis Orderly Book, 28 June–19 October 1781

British Library, London
Boulden-Thompson Papers
Clarkson Papers
DuBois Journal
Melville Papers
Peel Papers
Proceedings of the Committee for the Abolition of the Slave Trade

Clements Library, University of Michigan
Henry Clinton Papers
Howe Orderly Books
Frederick Mackenzie Papers
Miscellaneous Revolutionary Papers
Richard Oswald Papers
George Wray Papers

College of William and Mary
Journal of St George Tucker

Greater London Records Office
Anglican Parish Records for Greater London
Court Records of the Middlesex and Westminster Sessions
Records of the Boards of Guardians of the Poor

The Guidhall, London
Parish Records for Inner London

Library of Congress, Manuscript Division
British Army Regimental Order Book, 2 July–2 October 1779
Peter Force Collection
Force Historical Manuscripts
Benjamin Harrison Papers
Diary of Robert Honyman
Papers of the Members of Congress
George Washington Papers
Henry Willard Papers

Mitchell Library, State Library of New South Wales
Richard Atkins Journal
Duncan Campbell Letterbooks

Henry Fulton Papers
Phillip Gidley King, Letterbook, 1788–1799
Phillip Gidley King, Norfolk Island Journal, 1791–1794
Phillip Gidley King Papers
Register St John's Church, Parramatta
Register St Phillip's Church, Sydney

National Archives, UK
Records of Admiralty 1758–1810
Records of the Auditor 1783–86
Records of Colonial Office, 1774–1840
Carleton Papers (PRO 30)
Chatham Papers (PRO 30)
Cornwallis Papers (PRO 30)
Records of Foreign Office 1774–85
Records of Home Office 1787–1801
Records of the Justices of Assizes 1785–87
Records of the Secretary of State 1758–1780
Records of Treasury 1776–87
Records of War Office, 1758–1810

The Public Archives of Nova Scotia
Annapolis Muster, 1784
Army Muster Books
Birchtown Muster, 1784
British Military and Naval Records
Ward Chipman Papers
Commissary General's Department Receipts for Provisions, 1784
Diary of Alex Huston, 1778–1788
Letters of Bishop Charles Inglis
Judicial Records of Court of General Sessions, Shelburne County
Land Grants, 1783–1786
List of Black Loyalist Settlers at Digby, Annapolis and Granville, 1784
List of Loyalist Refugees to Halifax
Poll Tax Records
Marion Robertson Papers
Tax Assessor's Statements and Accounts
White Collection

State Records of New South Wales
Proceedings of the Bench of Magistrates, 1788–1820
Colonial Secretary's Papers
Proceedings of the Court of Civil Jurisdiction
Proceedings of the Court of Criminal Jurisdiction
Register of Pardons

University of Virginia
Lee Family Papers
Ralph Wormeley Papers

Virginian State Library
Virginia Assembly House of Delegates: Losses in Norfolk, 1777–1836
Virginia Assembly House of Delegates: Petitions
Papers of the House of Delegates, May 1782
Virginia Assembly House of Delegates: Report of Losses Sustained From the British, 1782–83

Contemporary newspapers
Morning Chronicle (London)
Morning Post (London)

Morning Herald (London)
Mercury (Manchester)
Public Advertiser (London)
Rivington's Royal Gazette (New York)
Sydney Gazette
Sydney Morning Herald
Dixon and Hunter Virginia Gazette
Purdie and Dixon Virginia Gazette
Purdie's Virginia Gazette

Printed primary sources

1790 Census for New Haven and New London, Connecticut, CD-ROM, Conn.: Blue Roses Publishing Company, n.d.

Adams, Charles Francis (ed.), *The Works of John Adams*, 8 vol., Boston: Little, Brown and Company, 1850–56

Adams, John, *Diary and Autobiography of John Adams*, 2 vol., ed. L. H. Butterfield, Cambridge, Mass.: Belknap Press, 1961

Ballagh, James Curtis (ed.), *The Letters of Richard Henry Lee*, 2 vol., New York: Macmillan, 1911

Betts, Edwin Morris (ed.), *Thomas Jefferson's Farm Book: with Commentary and Relevant Extracts From Other Writing*, Charlottesville: University Press of Virginia, 1953

Bowes Smyth, Arthur, *The Journal of Arthur Bowes Smyth: Surgeon, Lady Penrhyn 1787–1789*, eds Paul Fidlon and R.J. Ryan, Sydney: Australian Documents Library, 1979

Bradley, William, *A Voyage to New South Wales: the Journal of Lieutenant, William Bradley RN of HMS Sirius, 1786–1792*, Sydney: Ure Smith, 1969

Campbell, Archibald, *Journal of an Expedition against the Rebels of Georgia in North America under the Orders of Archibald Campbell Esquire Lieut. Colol. of His Majesty's 71st Regimt. 1778*, ed. Colin Campbell, Darien: Ashantilly Press, 1981

Cappon, Lester J (ed.), *The Adams–Jefferson Letters: The Complete Correspondence Between Thomas Jefferson and Abigail and John Adams*, Chapel Hill: University of North Carolina Press, 1959

Carter, Landon, *The Diary of Colonel Landon Carter of Sabine Hall, 1752–1778*, ed. Jack P. Greene, Charlottesville: University Press of Virginia, 1965

Clark, William Bell, Morgan, William James and Crawford, Michael J (eds), *Naval Documents of the American Revolution*, vols 3–10, Washington: Naval History Division, 1968–96

Clark, Ralph, *The Journal and Letters of Ralph Clark, 1787–1792*, eds Paul Fidlon and R.J. Ryan, Sydney: Australian Documents Library, 1981

Clinton, Henry, *The American Rebellion: Sir Henry Clinton's Narrative of his Campaigns, 1775–1782, with an Appendix of Original Documents*, ed. William B. Willcox, New Haven: Yale University Press, 1954

Cobbett's Parliamentary History of England from the earliest period to the year 1803, London: Hansard, 1806–1820

Cobley, John (ed.), *Sydney Cove: 1788–1800*, 5 vols, Sydney: Angus & Robertson, 1962–86

Collins, David, *An Account of the English Colony of New South Wales: With remarks on the Dispositions, Customs, Manners, etc, of the Native Inhabitants of that Country*, vol. 1, ed. Brian Fletcher, Sydney: Reed, 1975

Cornwallis, Charles, *An Answer to that Part of the Narrative of Lieutenant-General Sir Henry Clinton, K.B. which Relates to the Conduct of Lieutenant-General Earl Cornwallis, during the Campaign in North-America, in the year 1781*, London: J. Debrett, 1783

——, *Correspondence of Charles, First Marquis of Cornwallis*, 3 vols, ed. Charles Ross, London: John Murray, 1859

Cugoano, Ottobah, *Thoughts and Sentiments on the Evil of Slavery*, ed. Vincent Carretta, London: Penguin, 1999

Davies, K.G. (ed.), *Documents of the American Revolution, 1770–1783*, vols 11–12, Calendar 1781–1783 and Addenda 1770–1780, Shannon: Irish University Press, 1978–82

Easty, John, *Memorandum of a Voyage from England to Botany Bay, 1787–1793: A First Fleet Journal*, Sydney: Angus & Robertson, 1965

Equiano, Olaudah, *The Interesting Narrative and Other Writings*, ed. Vincent Carretta, London: Penguin, 2003

*

Ewald, Johann, *Diary of the American War: A Hessian Journal*, trans. & ed. Joseph P. Tustin, New Haven: Yale University Press, 1979

Fitzpatrick, John C. (ed.), *The Writings of George Washington*, vols 23–28, Washington: United States Government Printing Office, 1937–38

Francklyn, Gilbert, *Observations, Occasioned by the Attempts Made in England to Effect the Abolition of the Slave Trade*, London: Logographic Press, 1789

Harris, Alexander, *Settlers and Convicts, or, Recollections of Sixteen Years' Labour in the Australian Backwoods*, foreword by Manning Clark, Melbourne: Melbourne University Press, 1964

Historical Records of Australia, series 1, Canberra: Commonwealth Parliament, 1914

Historical Records of New South Wales, vols 1–10, Sydney: Government Printer, 1892–

Hoare, Prince, *Memoirs of Granville Sharp*, London: Henry Colburn, 1820

House of Commons Journal, New York: Readex Microprint, n.d.

House of Common Sessional Papers for the Eighteenth Century, Wilmington, NC: Scholarly Resources, 1975

Holt, Joseph, *A Rum Story: The Adventures of Joseph Holt Thirteen Years in New South Wales, 1800–1812*, ed. Peter O'Shaughnessy, Sydney: Kangaroo Press, 1988

Howard, John, *An Account of the Present State of the Prisons, Houses of Correction, and Hospitals in London and Westminster*, London: The Society … Against Vice and Immorality, 1789

Hunter, John, *An Historical Journal of Events at Sydney and at Sea, 1787–1792*, Sydney: Angus & Robertson, 1968

Idzera, Stanley J. (ed.), *Lafayette in the Age of the American Revolution: Selected Letters and Papers, 1776–1790*, vol. 4, Ithaca: Cornell University Press, 1981

James, Bartholomew, *Journal of Rear Admiral Bartholomew James, 1752–1828*, London: Navy Records Society, 1896

Jefferson, Thomas, *The Papers of Thomas Jefferson*, vols 1–24, ed. Julian P. Boyd, Princeton: Princeton University Press, 1950–90

Jones, Thomas, *History of New York During the Revolutionary War, and of the Leading Events in the Other Colonies at that Period*, New York: New York Historical Society, 1879

Journal of the House of Delegates of the Commonwealth of Virginia, Richmond, VA: Thomas White, 1827

King, Boston, 'Memoirs of the Life of Boston King, a Black Preacher Written By Himself During his Residence at Kingswood School', *The Methodist Magazine*, 1789

Laurens, Henry, *The Papers of Henry Laurens*, vols 10–16, ed. David R. Chesnutt, Columbia: University of South Carolina Press, 1985–2003

Lists and Returns of Connecticut Men in the Revolution, Bowie: Heritage Books, 1995

Long, Edward, *A History of Jamaica*, vol. 1, New York: Arno Press, 1972

——, *Candid Reflections on the Judgment Lately Awarded by the Court of the King's Bench in Westminster Hall on what Is Commonly Called the Negroe-Cause*, London: T. Lowndes, 1772

Mackaness, George (ed.), *Some Letters of the Rev. Richard A. Johnson BA: First Chaplain of New South Wales*, Sydney: Australian Historical Monographs, 1954

McIlwaine, H.R. (ed.), *Official Letters of the Governors of the State of Virginia: The Letters of Patrick Henry*, Richmond: Virginia State Library, 1926

Madison, James, *The Papers of James Madison*, vols 1–7, eds William T. Hutchinson and William M.E. Rachal, Chicago: University of Chicago Press, 1962–71

Musters and Lists, New South Wales and Norfolk Island, 1800–1802, Sydney: Australian Biographical and Genealogical Record, Sydney, 1988

Newsome, A.R., 'A British Orderly Book, 1780–1781', *The North Carolina Historical Review*, vol. 9, January–October 1932

Old Bailey Session Papers: The Proceedings of the King's Commission of the Peace for the City of London, 1780–1789, London: E. Hodgson, 1780–89

Palmer, William P. (ed.), *Calendar of Virginia State Papers and Other Manuscripts*, Richmond: n.p., 1881

Pendleton, Edmund, *The Letters and Papers of Edmund Pendleton*, vols 1–2, ed. David John Mays, Charlottesville: University Press of Virginia, 1967

Rippon, J., *The Baptist Annual Register 1790–1802, Including Sketches of the State of Religion among Denominations of Good Men at Home and Abroad*, 4 vols, London: n.p., 1803

Ritchie, John (ed.), *A Charge of Mutiny: the Court Marshall of Colonel George Johnston for Deposing Governor William Bligh in the Rebellion of 26 January 1808*, Canberra: National Library of Australia, 1988

Scribner, Robert L. (ed.), *Revolutionary Virginia: The Road to Independence*, vols 2–7, Charlottesville: University Press of Virginia, 1976–83

Scott, James, *Remarks on a Passage to Botany Bay: A First Fleet Journal, 1787–1792*, Sydney: Angus & Robertson, 1963

Simcoe, J.G., *Simcoe's Military Journal: A History of the Operations of a Partisan Corps called the Queen's Rangers, Commanded by Lieut. Col. J.G. Simcoe During the War of the American Revolution*, New York: Bartlett and Welford, 1844

Smeathman, Henry, *A Short Sketch of the Temporary Regulations for Intended Settlement of the Grain Coast near Sierra Leone*, London: H. Baldwin, 1788

Smith, James Morton (ed.), *The Republic of Letters: The Correspondence Between Thomas Jefferson and James Madison 1776–1826*, New York: Norton, 1995

Smith, Paul H. (ed.), *Letters of Delegates to Congress, 1774 to 1789*, vols 19 & 20, Washington: Library of Congress, 1992–93

Smith, William, *Historical Memoirs of William Smith, 1778–1783*, ed. William H.W. Sabine, New York: New York Public Library, 1971

Statham, Pamela (ed.), *A Colonial Regiment: New Sources Relating to the New South Wales Corps, 1789–1810*, Canberra: n.p., 1992

Tarleton, Banastre, *A History of the Campaigns of 1780 and 1781*, London: Cadell, 1787

Tench, Watkin, *1788: Comprising a Narrative of the expedition to Botany Bay and A Complete Account of the Settlement at Port Jackson*, ed. Tim Flannery, Melbourne: Text Publishing, 1996

Uhlendorf, Bernhard A. (ed. & trans.), *Revolution in America: Confidential Letters and Journals 1776–1784 of Adjutant General Major Baurmeister of the Hessian Forces*, New Brunswick: Rutgers University Press, 1957

——, ed. & trans., *The Siege of Charleston: With an Account of the Province of South Carolina: Diaries and Letters of Hessian Officers*, Ann Arbor: University of Michigan Press, 1938

Wadström, C.B., *An Essay on Colonisation, particularly applied to the Western Coast of Africa*, London: Edgerton, 1792

Washington, George, *The Diaries of George Washington*, vols 2–3, ed. Donald Jackson, Charlottesville: University Press of Virginia, 1976–78

——, *The Papers of George Washington: Revolutionary War Series*, vols 2–3, eds W.W. Abbott and Dorothy Twohig, Charlottesville: University Press of Virginia, 1987–88

——, *The Papers of George Washington: Confederation Series*, vol. 1, eds W.W. Abbott and Dorothy Twohig, Charlottesville: University Press of Virginia, 1992

——, *The Papers of George Washington: Colonial Series*, vols 7–10, eds W.W. Abbott and Dorothy Twohig, Charlottesville: University Press of Virginia, 1990–95

Wharton, Francis (ed.), *The Revolutionary Diplomatic Correspondence of the United States*, vol. 6, Washington: Government Printing Office, 1889

White, John, *Journal of a Voyage to New South Wales*, Sydney: Angus & Robertson, 1962

Worgan, George, *Journal of a First Fleet Surgeon*, Sydney: Library of Australian History, 1978

Select secondary sources

Ackroyd, Peter, *London. The Biography*, London: Vintage, 2001

Anderson, Fred, *Crucible of War: the Seven Years' War and the Fate of Empire in British North America, 1754–1766*, London: Faber, 2000

Alpin, Graeme (ed.), *A Difficult Infant: Sydney before Macquarie*, Sydney: UNSW Press: Sydney 1988

Andrews, William L, *To Tell a Free Story: The First Century of African American Autobiography*, Urbana: University of Illinois Press, 1986

Anstey, Roger, *The Atlantic Slave Trade and British Abolition, 1760–1810*, London: Macmillan 1975

Atkinson, Alan, *The Europeans in Australia: A History*, vol. 1, Melbourne: Oxford University Press, 1997

Atkinson, Alan, and Aveling, Marian, *Australians 1838*, Sydney: Fairfax, Syme and Weldon, 1987

Barker, Anthony J., *The African Link: British Attitudes to the Negro in the Era of the Atlantic Slave Trade, 1550–1807*, London: Frank Cass, 1978

Barnwell, Joseph W., 'The Evacuation of Charleston By the British in 1782', *South Carolina Historical and Genealogical Magazine* vol. 11, 1910

✱

Bateson, Charles, *The Convict Ships 1787–1868*, Glasgow: Brown, Son & Ferguson, 1969

Bayly, C.A., 'The British and Indigenous people 1760–1860: Power, Perception and Identity', in *Empire and Others*, eds Halpern and Daunton, Philadelphia: University of Pennsylvania Press, 1999

Bear, James A. (ed.), *Jefferson at Monticello*, Charlottesville: University of Virginia Press, 1967

Berlin, Ira, 'The Revolution in Black Life', in *The American Revolution*, ed. Alfred F. Young, DeKalb: Northern Illinois University Press, 1976

——, *Many Thousands Gone: The First Two Centuries of Slavery in North America*, Cambridge, Mass.: Belknap Press, 1998

Blackburn, Robin, *The Overthrow of Colonial Slavery, 1776–1848*, London: Verso, 1988

——, *The Making of New World Slavery: From the Baroque to the Modern, 1492–1800*, London: Verso, 1997

Benthien, Claudia, *Skin: the Cultural Border Between the Self and the World*, trans. Thomas Dunlap, New York: Columbia University Press, 2004

Bolster, W. Jeffrey, *Black Jacks: African American Seamen in the Age of Sail*, Cambridge: Harvard University Press, 1997

Bowler, R. Arthur, *Logistics and the Failure of the British Army in America 1775–1783*, Princeton: Princeton University Press, 1975

Braidwood, Stephen, *Black Poor and White Philanthropists: London's Blacks and the Foundations of the Sierra Leone Settlement 1786–1791*, Liverpool: Liverpool University Press, 1994

Brewer, John, *The Sinews of Power: War, Money and the English State, 1688–1783*, London: Unwin Hyman, 1989

Brown, Christopher L., 'Empire Without Slaves: British Concepts of Emancipation in the Age of the American Revolution', *William and Mary Quarterly* 3rd series, 56, April, 1999.

——, *Moral Capital: Foundations of British Abolitionism*, Chapel Hill, University of North Carolina Press, 2006

Brown, Stephen, *Scurvy*, Toronto: Thomas Allen, 2003

Byrnes, Dan, 'Emptying the Hulks: Duncan Campbell and the First Three Fleets to Australia', *The Push from the Bush* 24, 1987

Byrnes, Paula, *Criminal Law and Colonial Subject: New South Wales 1810–1830*, Cambridge: Cambridge University Press, 1993

Campbell, Judy, *Invisible Invaders: Smallpox and Other Diseases in Aboriginal Australia 1780–1880*, Melbourne: Melbourne University Press, 2002

Carretta, Vincent (ed.), *Unchained Voices: An Anthology of Black Authors in the English-Speaking World of the Eighteenth Century*, Lexington: University Press of Kentucky, 1996

——, 'Olaudah Equiano or Gustavus Vassa: New Light on an Eighteenth Century Question of Identity', *Slavery and Abolition* 20, no. 3, 1999

Carter, Paul, *The Road to Botany Bay: An Essay in Spatial History*, London: Faber & Faber, 1987

Chambers, Douglas B., 'The Transatlantic Slave Trade to Virginia', in *Afro-Virginian History and Culture*, ed. John Saillant, New York: Garland Publishing 1999

Christopher, Emma, *Slave Trade Sailors and Their Captive Cargoes 1730–1808*, New York: Cambridge University Press, 2006

Clendinnen, Inga, *Dancing With Strangers*, Melbourne: Text Publishing, 2003

Cobley, John, *The Crimes of the First Fleet Convicts*, Sydney: Angus & Robertson, 1970

Coe, Sophie E. and Coe, Michael D., *The True History of Chocolate*, London: Thames & Hudson, 1996

Coleman, Deirdre, *Romantic Colonization and British Anti-Slavery*, Cambridge, Cambridge University Press, 2005

Connor, John, *The Australian Frontier Wars 1788–1838*, Sydney: UNSW Press, 2002

Coquery-Vidrovitch, Catherine and Lovejoy, Paul E. (eds), *The Workers of African Trade*, Beverly Hills, CA: Sage Publications, 1985.

Cumpston, J.S., *Shipping Arrivals and Departures, Sydney 1788–1825*, Canberra: Roebuck, 1964

Currey, John, *David Collins: A Life*, Melbourne: Melbourne University Press, 2000

Curtin, Phillip, *The Image of Africa: British Ideas and Action, 1780–1850*, Madison: University of Wisconsin Press, 1964

Dabydeen, David (ed.), *The Black Presence in English Literature*, Manchester: Manchester University Press, 1985

——, *Hogarth's Blacks: Images of Blacks in Eighteenth Century English Art*, Athens: University of Georgia Press, 1987

Dalzell, Robert E. and Dalzell, Lee Baldwin, *George Washington's Mt Vernon: At Home in Revolutionary America*, New York: Oxford University Press, 1998

Dening, Greg, *Mr Bligh's Bad Language: Passion Power and Theatre on the Bounty*, Cambridge: Cambridge University Press, 1992

Drescher, Seymour, 'The Complexion of Race', *Journal of Social History* 35, no. 2, 2001

Drescher, Seymour and Bolt, Christine (eds), *Anti-Slavery, Religion and Reform: Essays in Memory of Roger Anstey*, Hamden: Archon Books, 1980

Duffield, Ian, 'Martin Beck and Afro-Blacks in Colonial Australia', *Journal of Australian Studies* 16, May 1985

——, 'The Life and Death of "Black" John Goff: Aspects of the Black Convict Contribution to Resistance Patterns during the Transportation Era in Eastern Australia', *Australian Journal of Politics and History* 33, 1987

——, 'Billy Blue: Power, Popular Culture and Mimicry in Early Sydney', *Journal of Popular Culture* 33, no. 1, Summer 1999

——, 'Constructing and Reconstructing "Black' Caesar"', in *Romanticism and Wild Places*, ed. Paul Hullah, Edinburgh: Edinburgh University Press, 1999

——, '"I Asked How the Vessel Could Go?"', in *Language, Labour and Migration*, ed. Anne Kershen, Aldershot: Ashgate, 2000

Duffy, Michael, *Man of Honour: John Macarthur – Duellist, Rebel Founding Father*, Sydney: Pan Macmillan, 2003

Ekirch, Roger, *Bound for America: Transportation of British Convicts to the Colonies, 1716–1775*, Oxford: Clarendon, 1987

Fenn, Elizabeth, *Pox Americana: The Great Smallpox Epidemic of 1775–82*, New York: Hill and Wang, 2001

Flannery, Tim (ed.), *The Birth of Sydney*, Melbourne: Text Publishing, 1999

Flynn, Michael, *The Second Fleet: Britain's Grim Convict Armada of 1790*, Sydney: Library of Australian History, 1993

Foley, Daniel J., 'The Botany Bay Decision: Another Look', *Australian Studies* 17, no. 2, Winter 2002

Foucault, Michel, *Discipline and Punish; the Birth of the Prison*, New York: Vintage, 1979

Francis, A.D., 'The Fantasy War of 1762–63', *Journal of the Society for Army Historical Research* LIX, no. 237, Spring 1981

Frey, Sylvia, *Water From the Rock: Black Resistance in a Revolutionary Age,* Princeton: Princeton University Press, 1991

Frost, Alan, *Convicts and Empire: A Naval Question, 1776–1811*, Melbourne: Oxford University Press, 1980

——, *Botany Bay Mirages: Illusions of Australia's Convict Beginnings*, Melbourne: Melbourne University Press, 1994

Fryer, Peter, *Staying Power: The History of Black People in Britain*, London: Pluto Press, 1984

Gattrell, V.A.C., *The Hanging Tree: Execution and the English People, 1770–1868*, Oxford: Oxford University Press, 1994

Gillen, Mollie, *Founders of Australia: A Biographical Dictionary of the First Fleet*, Sydney: Library of Australian History, 1989

——, 'The Botany Bay Decision 1786: Convicts not Empire', *English Historical Review* 97, 1982

Gomes, Michael A., *Exchanging Our Country Marks: The Transformation of African Identity in the Colonial and Antebellum South*, Chapel Hill: University of North Carolina Press, 1998.

Gould, Eliga H., *The Persistence of Empire: British Political Culture in the Age of the American Revolution*, Chapel Hill: University of North Carolina Press, 2000

Hainsworth, R.D., *The Sydney Traders: Simeon Lord and His Contemporaries, 1788–1821*, Melbourne: Cassell, 1972

Hall, Barbara, *A Desperate Set of Villains*, Sydney: Barbara Hall, 2000

Hall, Stuart, 'Cultural Identity and Diaspora', in *Identity: Community, Culture, Difference*, ed. Jonathon Rutherford, London: Lawrence and Wishart, 1990

Halpern, Rick and Daunton, Martin (eds), *Empire and Others*, Philadelphia: University of Pennsylvania Press, 1999

Hay, Douglas et al., *Albion's Fatal Tree: Crime and Society in Eighteenth-century England*, New York: Pantheon Books, 1975

Hibbert, Christopher, *Redcoats and Rebels: The American Revolution through British Eyes*, New York: W.W. Norton, 1990

✱

Hirschfeld, Fritz, '"Burn All Their Houses": The Log of HMS *Savage* during a Raid up the Potomac River, Spring 1781', *Virginia Magazine of History and Biography* 99, 1991

Hirst, J.B., *Convict Society and its Enemies: A History of Early New South Wales*, Sydney: Allen & Unwin, 1983

Hodges, Graham Russell, *Slavery and Freedom in the Rural North: African Americans in the Monmouth County, New Jersey 1665–1865*, Madison: Madison House, 1997

——, *Root and Branch: African Americans in New York and East Jersey 1613–1863*, Chapel Hill: University of North Carolina Press, 1999

Hoffman, Ronald, 'The "Disaffected" in the Revolutionary South', in *The American Revolution: Explorations in the History of American Radicalism*, ed. Alfred E. Young, DeKalb: Northern Illinois University Press, 1976

Holden, Robert, *Orphans of the First Fleet*, Melbourne: Text Publishing, 1999

Holton, Woody, *Forced Founders: Indians, Debtors, Slaves, and the Making of the American Revolution in Virginia*, Chapel Hill: University of North Carolina Press, 1999

Hudson, Nicholas, 'From Nation to Race: The Origin of Racial Classification in Eighteenth Century Thought', *Eighteenth Century Studies* 29, no. 3, 1996

Hughes, Robert, *The Fatal Shore: A History of the Transportation of Convicts to Australia, 1787–1868*, London: Collins Harvill, 1987

Isaac, Rhys, *The Transformation of Virginia, 1740–1790*, Chapel Hill: University of North Carolina Press, 1982

——, *Landon Carter's Uneasy Kingdom*, New York: Oxford University Press, 2004

Jones, George Fenwick, 'The Black Hessians: Negroes Recruited by the Hessians in South Carolina and Other Colonies', *South Carolina Historical Magazine* 83, 1982

Kaplan, Sidney and Kaplan, Emma Nogrady, *The Black Presence in the Era of the American Revolution*, rev. ed., Amhurst: University of Massachusetts Press, 1989

Karskens, Grace, *The Rocks: Life in Early Sydney*, Melbourne: Melbourne University Press, 1997

Kulikoff, Allan, 'Uprooted Peoples: Black Migrants in the Age of the American Revolution, 1790–1820', in *Slavery and Freedom in the Age of the American Revolution*, eds Ira Berlin and Ronald Hoffman, Charlottesville: University Press of Virginia, 1983

——, *Tobacco and Slaves: The Development of Southern Cultures in the Chesapeake, 1680–1800*, Chapel Hill: University of North Carolina Press, 1986

Lindsay, Arnot G., 'Diplomatic Relations between the United States and Great Britain Bearing on the Return of Negro Slaves, 1783–1828', *Journal of Negro History* 5, 1920

Linebaugh, Peter, *The London Hanged: Crime and Civil Society in the Eighteenth Century*, Cambridge: Cambridge University Press, 1992

Linebaugh, Peter and Rediker, Marcus (eds), *The Many-Headed Hydra: Sailors, Slaves, Commoners and the Hidden History of the Revolutionary Atlantic*, Boston: Beacon Press, 2000

Lorimer, Douglas, *Colour Class and the Victorians; English Attitudes to the Negro in the Mid-nineteenth Century*, Leicester: University of Leicester Press, 1978

——, 'Black Slaves and English Liberty: A Re-examination of Racial Slavery in England', *Immigrants and Minorities* 3, no. 2, July 1984

Maxwell-Stewart, Hamish, 'The Bushrangers and the Convict System of Van Diemen's Land, 1803–1864', unpublished PhD thesis, University of Edinburgh, 1990

——, and Frost, Lucy (eds), *Chain Letters: Narrating Convict Lives*, Melbourne: Melbourne University Press, 2001

Meade, Robert Douhat, *Patrick Henry: Practical Revolutionary*, New York: J.B. Lippencott, 1969

Miller, John Chester, *Wolf by the Ears: Thomas Jefferson and Slavery*, Charlottesville: Charlottesville Free Press, 1991

Morgan, Philip D., *Slave Counterpoint: Black Culture in the Eighteenth Century Chesapeake and Low Country*, Chapel Hill: University of North Carolina Press, 1998

Myers, Norma, *Reconstructing the Black Past: Blacks in Britain 1780–1830*, London: Frank Cass, 1996

Nagle, J.F., *Collins, the Courts and the Colony: Law and Society in Colonial New South Wales*, Sydney: UNSW Press, 1996

Nash, Gary B., *Forging Freedom: The Formation of Philadelphia's Black Community, 1720–1840*, Cambridge: Harvard University Press, 1988

Norton, Mary Beth, 'The Fate of Some Black Loyalists of the American Revolution', *Journal of Negro History* 58, 1973

Olwell, Robert, *Masters, Slaves and Subject: Culture and Power in the South Carolina Low Country, 1740–1790*, Ithaca: Cornell University Press, 1998

Paine, J., 'The Negro Drummers of the British Army', *Royal Military College Magazine and Record* 33, 1928

Perry, T.M., *Australia's First Frontier: The Spread of Settlement in New South Wales 1788–1829*, Melbourne: Melbourne University Press, 1963

Platt, Virginia Beaver, 'The East India Company and the Madagascar Slave Trade', *William and Mary Quarterly* 3rd series, vol. 26, no. 4, Oct. 1969

Porter, Roy, *London: A Social History*, Penguin: Harmondsworth, 2000

Pulis, John W. (ed.), *Moving On: Black Loyalists in the Afro-American World*, New York: Garland Publishing, 1999

Pybus, Cassandra, 'A Touch of the Tar: African Settlers in Colonial Australia and the implications for issues of Aboriginality', *London Papers in Australian Studies* No. 3, London: Menzies Centre for Australian Studies, University of London, 2001

——, 'From "Black" Caesar to Mudrooroo: The African Diaspora in Australia', in *Mongrel Signatures: Reflections on the Work of Mudrooroo*, ed. A. Oboe, Amsterdam: New York: Rodopi, 2003

——, 'The World is all of One Piece: The African Diaspora and Transportation to Australia', in *Routes of Passage: Rethinking the African Diaspora*, ed. Ruth Hamilton, Lansing: Michigan State University Press, 2005

——, 'Thomas Jefferson's Faulty Math: The Question of Slave Defections in the American Revolution', *William and Mary Quarterly* 3rd series, 62, no. 2, 2005

——, 'The Many Escapes of John Moseley', *Journal of Australian Colonial Studies* 7, 2005

——, 'Harry Washington: A Founding Father's Slave', in *The Human Tradition in the Black Atlantic 1500–2000*, eds Beatriz Gallotti Mamigonian and Karen Racine, New York: Scholarly Resources, 2006

——, *Epic Journeys of Freedom: Runaway Slaves of the American Revolution and their Global Quest for Liberty*, Boston: Beacon Press, 2006

Quarles, Benjamin, *The Negro in the American Revolution*, rev. ed., Chapel Hill: University of North Carolina Press, 1996 [1961]

Ranlet, Phillip, 'The British, Slaves, and Smallpox in Revolutionary Virginia', *Journal of Negro History* 84, 1999

Rediker, Marcus, *Between the Devil and the Deep Blue Sea: Merchant Seamen, Pirates, and the Anglo-American Maritime World, 1700–1750*, Cambridge: Cambridge University Press 1987

Reece, Bob, *The Origins of Irish Convict Transportation to New South Wales*, Basingstoke: Houndmills, 2001

Rees, Sian, *The Floating Brothel*, London: Hodder, 2001

Reiss, Oscar, *Medicine and the American Revolution: How Diseases and their Treatments Affected the Colonial Army*, Jefferson: McFarland & Co., 1998

Reynolds, Henry, *Nowhere People*, Melbourne: Penguin, 2005

Rickard, Suzanne (ed.), *George Barrington's Voyage to New South Wales*, Leicester: Leicester University Press, 2001

Robinson, Portia, *The Women of Botany Bay: A Reinterpretation of the Role of Women in the Origins of Australian Society*, Sydney: Macquarie Library, 1988

Rodger, N.A.M., *The Wooden World: An Anatomy of the Georgian Navy*, Annapolis: Naval Institute, 1986

Royster, Charles, *The Fabulous History of the Dismal Swamp Company: A Story of George Washington's Times*, New York: Knopf, 1999

Rudé, George, *Hanoverian London, 1714–1808*, London: Secker & Warburg, 1971

Ryan, R. J., *Land Grants 1788–1809: A Record of the Registered Grants and Leases in New South Wales and Norfolk Island*, Sydney: Australian Document Library, 1981

Schwarz, Philip J. (ed.), *Slavery at the Home of George Washington*, Mount Vernon: Mount Vernon Ladies Association, 2001

Sheenan, W.J., 'Finding Solace in Eighteenth Century Newgate', in *Crime in England 1590–1800*, ed. J.S. Cockburn, London: Methuen, 1977

Shyllon, F.O., *Black People in Britain 1555–1833*, Oxford: Oxford University Press, 1977

Smollett, Tobias, *The Expedition of Humphry Clinker*, Harmondsworth: Penguin, 1985

Stanton, Lucia C., *Slavery at Monticello*, Charlottesville: Thomas Jefferson Memorial Foundation, 1996

*

——, *Free Some Day: The African-American Families of Monticello*, Charlottesville: Thomas Jefferson Memorial Foundation, 2000

Sweig, Donald M., 'The Importation of African Slaves to the Potomac River, 1732–1772', *William and Mary Quarterly* 3rd series, 42, Oct. 1985

Swords, Meg, *Billy Blue: The Old Commodore*, North Sydney Historical Society, Sydney, 1979

Thompson, E. P., *The Making of the English Working Class*, rev. ed., Harmondsworth: Penguin, 1968 [1963]

——, *Whigs and Hunters. The Origin of the Black Act*, Harmondsworth: Peregrine, 1977

Tyson, George, 'The Carolina Black Corps: Legacy of Revolution, 1783–1798', *Revista/Review Interamericana* 5, 1975–76

Van Buskirk, Judith L., *Generous Enemies: Patriots and Loyalists in Revolutionary New York*, Philadelphia: University of Pennsylvania Press, 2002

Walsh, Lorena S., 'The Chesapeake Slave Trade: Regional Patterns, African Origins and Some Implications', *William and Mary Quarterly* 3rd series, vol. 58, no. 1, Jan. 2001

Walvin, James (ed.), *Slavery and British Society, 1776–1846*, Baton Rouge: Louisiana State University Press, 1982

——, *Questioning Slavery*, London: Routledge, 1996

Wheeler, Roxann, *The Complexion of Race, Categories of Difference in Eighteenth Century British Culture*, Philadelphia: University of Pennsylvania Press, 2000

White, David O, *Connecticut's Black Soldiers*, Chester: Pequod Press, 1973

White, Shane, *Somewhat More Independent: The End of Slavery in New York City, 1770–1810*, Athens: University of Georgia Press, 1991

Wiencek, Henry, *An Imperfect God: George Washington, his Slaves and the Creation of America*, New York: Farrar, Straus, Giroux, 2003

Wilson, Ellen Gibson, *The Loyal Blacks*, New York: Capricorn Books, 1976

Wilson, Kathleen, *The Island Race: Englishness, Empire and Gender in the Eighteenth Century*, London: Routledge, 2003

Windley, Lathan A., *A Profile of Runaway Slaves in Virginia and South Carolina from 1730 through 1787*, New York: Garland Publishing, 1995

Wright, Reg, *The Forgotten Generation of Norfolk Island and Van Diemens Land*, Sydney: Library of Australian History, 1986

INDEX

A

Aborigines 1, 87–88, 95, 104–105, 132, 179, 180–81, 187
  attitudes to black convicts 88, 95, 181
  resistance to white occupation 116–17, 132–33, 134
  and smallpox 101
  white aggression against 117–18, 132–33, 134
Adams, John 12, 53
Addison, Joseph 87
Admiralty 80, 83
Aetna, HMS 48
Africa 4, 24, 46, 51, 59–62, 63, 64, 65, 66, 67, 68, 70, 88, 13, 186
Africa Company 59, 60, 61
African diaspora 3, 48, 51, 179, 180
Aikin, John 155, 187
Ajar, John 153–54
Albermarle County, USA 30
Alexander 3, 71, 72, 74, 75, 76, 77, 79, 81–82, 83, 85, 86, 87, 88, 89, 99, 184, 185, 186
America 4, 5, 6, 8, 14, 19, 25, 66, 101, 131, 165, 183
  see also America, United States of
America, colonies 4, 6, 9, 21, 34, 35, 53, 56, 185
America, United States of 9, 38, 53, 142, 175
American colonies, Declaration of Independence 18
American Continental Army 13, 20, 22, 30
American Revolution 5, 8, 11–39, 47, 49, 93, 101, 166, 185
  see also individual engagements
  black founders and 7–8
  British defeat 32–34
  militias and militiamen 11, 13–14, 27
  threat of 11–13
  Treaty of Paris (2nd) 34, 35, 37
Anderson, Amos 41, 42, 50–51
André, John 5–6, 7, 26–28
Annandale, NSW 145

Anson, George 80
Antigua 17
army, Britain 6–7, 63, 68, 77, 183, 186
  see also individual departments, Ethiopian regiment, New South Wales Corps, regiments
American Revolution 7, 8, 11, 13–14, 15, 16, 20, 21, 22 23, 24, 26, 32–34, 53, 101
  blacks and 5, 6, 8, 16, 18, 20, 21, 22, 23, 24, 26, 28–29, 30, 31, 33–39, 47, 52–53, 101
  drummers and musicians, black 5, 24, 28, 29, 63, 186
army, Portugal 7
army, Spain 7
Arndell, Thomas 93, 120, 124, 125
Arnold, Benedict 7, 26–27, 28, 29, 30, 43
Artarmon, NSW 171
Atkins, Richard 122–23, 124, 125, 130, 131, 132, 133–34, 153, 154, 158, 159
Atlantic 70, 120, 121, 122, 127
Australia 3, 9, 10, 87, 101, 181
  Federation 179
  White Australia 180

B

Baltimore, USA 60
Bank of England 52
Banks, Joseph 69, 89, 139
Barber, Francis 46
Barnes, John 61
Bass Strait 142, 146, 187
Batavia 99, 107, 110, 118
Beauchamp Committee 65–66
Belisarius 70, 71, 120, 121, 122, 127
Belle Isle, battle of 7, 48, 183
Bengal, India 169, 170
Bentham, Jeremy 97
Birch, Samuel 36
Black Brigade 25
black community

and the Committee for the Relief of the Black
    Poor 54–55
crime 46, 49–51
in England 45
in London 45–46
and the maritime community 47–50
and marriage 50–51
as servants 46–47
and the Sierra Leone scheme 67–71
and slavery 45–47
white attitudes to 51–52
black drummers and musicians see army, Britain
black founders 3–4, 5, 7–8, 10, 177, 181,
    183–87
black refugees
in London 41–42
and the Loyalist Claims Commission 42–44,
    50, 51
and the maritime community 47–50
as paupers and indigents 42, 44–45, 50, 52, 53
white attitudes to 52–55
black seamen and sailors 6, 37, 41, 47–51, 55,
    56, 62, 89, 122, 155
Blane, Gilbert 80
Blaxcell, Garnham 169, 170
Bligh, William 155, 156–58, 159, 160, 161
Blue, Elizabeth 152–54, 173
Blue, Elizabeth (daughter of William and
    Elizabeth) 174
Blue, John 174, 183
Blue, Mary 174, 183
Blue, Robert 174, 183
Blue, Susannah 152, 174, 183
Blue, William 70, 148, 151, 153–54, 162, 177,
    180, 181, 183
    as constable and watchman 164, 166–67
    character described 153, 165, 174, 175–76
    as 'the commodore' 150, 164, 166, 167, 174,
        175–77, 178
    ferry business 5, 152, 153, 154–55, 164,
        165, 166–67, 171–72, 173, 174, 176
    harbouring runaway convicts 174–75
    and land grants 166–67, 171, 173
    Macquaries, relations with 165–66, 170, 171
    marriage and family 152–54, 164, 172, 173–74
    occupations 5, 68, 148–52
    origins 5
    and patrons 155
    petitions 5–6, 150, 171–72, 173, 174
    physical appearance 148, 177
    prosecution and sentence 5, 149–50
    service in American Revolution 5, 7, 13, 20,
        21, 27, 28, 30, 32, 34, 165–66
    service in Seven Years' War 5, 48, 166
    and smuggling 167–71, 174
Blue, William (jnr) 173, 174, 175, 183
Blues Point, Sydney, NSW 5, 167, 183
Board of Longitude 100

Bonetta, HMS 33–34
Book of Negroes 8–9, 37, 41, 46, 64
Boston, USA 7, 11, 13, 14, 20, 21, 50, 175
Botany Bay, NSW 66, 70, 71, 72, 74, 77, 82,
    85–86, 87, 88–89, 95, 117, 181
Sierra Leone scheme, relationship with 69–70
Bounty, HMS 157
Bowes Smyth, Arthur 82, 83, 84
Bradley, James 61–62
Bradley, Richard 62
Bradley, William 4, 82–83, 88, 99, 104–105,
    181
Bramble, Squire Matt 40
brandy 59, 84, 104
Breeds Hill, battle of, USA 14
    see also Bunker Hill
Brickfields, NSW 102
Bridge Street, Sydney, NSW 160
Brisbane, Thomas 5, 171–72, 173
Britannia 128, 129, 130
British army see army, Britain
'The British Grenadiers' 160
Broken Bay, NSW 95, 101, 116, 163, 174
Brown Bess 94
Bryant, Mary 119
Bryant, William 119
Buckingham, Marchioness of (Mary Elizabeth
    Grenville) 54
Bulanaming, NSW 131, 186
Buller, Francis 56
Bunker Hill, battle of, USA 14
Burgoyne, John 7, 14
Burke, Edmund 65
Burn, Patrick 94–95
bushranging and banditry 3, 134–35, 136
Butler, Mary 115, 116, 186
    see also Randall, Mary
Byrd Plantation, Westover, USA 28
Byrd, Mary 28, 30
Byrd, Wat see Harris, Walter 28, 30

C

Caesar aka 'Black Caesar' 89, 127, 181
    on the Alexander 71, 74, 77, 79, 87
    American Revolution 38, 46–47
    as assigned servant 93
    as bushranger and absconder 2–3, 102,
        104–105, 119, 131, 134–35
    character described 88, 94, 104–105, 116,
        131
    death 1–3, 135, 136
    diarists, attention from 4
    imprisonment 64, 68
    marriage and family 116, 122, 126
    names and naming 3, 29, 68

on Norfolk Island 106, 116, 121–22
origins 4, 29, 46–47
physical appearance 2, 4, 47, 94
prosecution and sentence 3, 46, 64
secondary sentences in NSW 96, 101, 102,
    105, 121, 126, 131
Calcutta, India 120, 121, 122, 142, 152, 169
Calleghan, John 103
Calvert, Anthony 60, 61, 62
Camden, Calvert and King 60, 61, 62, 67, 71,
    113, 114
Campbell, Duncan 56, 57, 62, 64, 66–67, 71
Campbell, Robert 142–43, 146, 155, 161, 164,
    170, 171
Campbell, Robert (jnr) 163, 164
Cape Coast Castle, West Africa 59, 60, 61
Cape of Good Hope, South Africa 110
Cape Town, South Africa 82, 83, 84, 101
Caribbean 46, 48, 180
    see also West Indies
Carleton Papers 8
Carleton, Guy 8, 35–37, 53
Carter, Landon 18
Carter, Paul x
cat o'nine tails 76, 96
Cato 87
cattle see livestock
Censor 57, 71, 187
Ceres 62, 63, 64–65, 68, 71, 72, 74, 134, 184,
    185
Channel see English Channel
Charleston, USA 26, 36, 50, 92, 185
Charlotte 75, 78, 81, 83, 89, 184
Chesapeake Bay, USA 16, 18, 21
China 66, 67, 106, 107, 114, 142, 152
Chinery, Samuel 89, 90, 147, 174, 178, 184
    as assigned servant 93, 120
    on the Charlotte 75
    as free servant 120, 125, 178
    prosecution and sentence 3, 75
chocolate 149
Clark, Ralph 76, 78, 80, 81, 83, 84, 85, 86,
    89, 91, 106–107, 121, 126
Clendinnen, Inga 181
Clinton, Henry 7, 9, 21, 26, 27, 36
Coffin, John 89, 98, 184
    on the Charlotte 75
    departure from colony 136
    on Norfolk Island 106, 121
    occupation 75
    prosecution and sentence 3, 75
    secondary sentences in NSW 103–104, 121
Collins, David 2–3, 9, 82, 83, 84, 92, 93, 94,
    96–97, 101–102, 103–104, 105, 106,
    107, 108, 110, 111, 114–15, 120, 125,
    126, 130, 131, 133, 134, 135
Colonel Tye 25
Commissary store 92, 103, 109, 116, 124, 129,

130, 131, 133, 141, 142, 143,156, 163
Committee for the Relief of the Black Poor 9,
    52, 54–55, 67, 68, 70
Commons, House of 63, 64, 65, 66
Concord, HMS 39
Congress, American 13, 18, 35, 36, 38
Connecticut, USA 22, 23, 24, 49, 63, 186
Conner, Joseph 184
Conquade, Thomas 179
Conquit, Thomas 179
convicts 57, 77, 78, 87, 96, 97, 102, 106, 109,
    116, 126, 127, 129, 131, 165, 181
    and slaves compared 102, 113
    assigned 91, 93, 121, 127, 129–30, 137, 174
    escapes and absconding 1–3, 78, 82, 90,
        98–99, 102, 104–105, 110, 114,–15, 119,
        132, 134, 172, 174, 175, 184
    and labour 57, 60–61, 90–91, 94, 100, 101,
        105, 115, 116, 121, 123, 124, 127, 129,
        130, 133, 137, 138, 156
    and marriage 91–92, 115
    mortality of 75, 100, 108, 123
    as outlaws, bushrangers & banditti 3,
        134–35, 136
    rations 94, 100, 103, 105, 108, 110–11, 114,
        119, 122–23, 126, 127, 129, 130, 133, 136
    resistance 136
    and rum 1–2, 128
    sexual relations among 90, 91
    sickness among 72, 74, 75, 76, 78, 79–81,
        83, 84, 85, 86, 89, 99–100, 119, 123, 130
    transportation to Africa 66
    transportation to NSW 2, 10, 66–67, 71–72,
        74, 76, 93, 119, 151, 183–87
convicts, black 4, 72, 74, 82, 101, 109, 180
    relations with aborigines 88, 181
    as assigned servants 93
    described by diarists 88, 93
    as a distinct minority 93
    families 70
    as labourers 94
    physical advantages over white convicts 94
    white attitudes towards 92, 93
    relations with white convicts 92
convicts, emancipists 4, 115, 137, 140, 143,
    144, 146, 152, 154, 171, 174, 175
    as farmers 132
    and land grants 120, 123–24, 131
    on the store 120, 124, 131, 141
convicts, women 90–92, 115
    on the First Fleet 76, 77, 78–79, 81, 83
    and marriage 91–92, 115, 152
    on Second Fleet 110, 112–13, 115
    on Third Fleet 119
Cook, James 66, 88, 94
Coram's foundling hospital, England 63
Cornwallis, Charles 5–6, 8, 21, 28–34, 53,
    129, 165

cotton 60–61, 62
Cowes, England 48
cows *see* livestock
Cox, William 141, 144
Cresswell, Thomas 184
crime
    assault 129, 152
    bushranging and banditry 3, 134–35, 136,
        171, 172
    harbouring absconders 174–75
    highway robbery 135, 162
    manslaughter 173
    murder 152, 172
    mutiny 151, 160
    Norfolk Island, crime rate 126–27
    personation 3–4
    rape 153–54
    smuggling 167–70, 172, 174, 175
    theft 3, 5, 46, 49–50, 56–57, 63, 64, 90, 92,
        96, 98, 101, 102, 103, 104, 105, 108,
        109, 119, 123, 126, 127, 134, 138–39,
        140, 148–50, 183, 184, 185, 186, 187
    treason 159
criminal court, NSW 3, 90
Cumberland County, USA 30
Cummings Hotel 177
Cunningham, John 15, 17

D

Danger, HMS 38
Darling, George 153, 154
Darling, Ralph 174
Das Voltas Bay, West Africa 66, 67, 69
Dawes Point, NSW 142, 162
Dawes, William 93, 100, 108–109
Den Keyser, HMS 59
Deptford, London, England 45, 47, 48, 49, 51,
    68, 149, 150, 184, 187
Devon, England 3, 89, 184
Devon assizes 75
Devonshire, Duchess of (Georgiana Cavendish) 54
disease and diseases 19, 20, 30, 54, 57, 58, 65,
    75, 100, 112, 119
    dysentery 20, 83, 84, 89, 99, 112
    gaol fever 59
    scurvy 2, 20, 64, 76, 79–81, 83, 84, 86, 89,
        94, 99–100, 112
    smallpox 19–21, 30, 31–33, 92, 101
    typhus 20, 30, 31, 59, 83, 112
    variola 20
Domain, the Governor of NSW's 157, 164,
    166, 168
Dowling, James 175–76
drunkenness and alcoholism 41, 59, 81, 92,
    107, 122, 130–31, 137, 152, 173

Dunkirk 98, 104, 184
Dunmore, Earl of (John Murray) 11, 14–15,
    16, 17, 18, 19, 20, 21–22, 26, 29, 44, 101
Dutch East India Company 82
    see also VOC
dysentery *see* disease and diseases

E

East India Company 52, 66
East River, USA 24
Easty, John 76, 77, 82, 85–86, 102, 118, 126
Elijah 41
Elk Hill Plantation, USA 30
England 4, 8, 9, 21, 32, 35, 38, 40, 44, 45, 46,
    47, 48, 50, 51, 53, 56, 59, 60, 69, 74, 75,
    86, 93, 94, 98, 100, 103, 105, 106, 107,
    122, 123, 131, 138, 139, 140, 142, 145,
    155, 156, 157, 162, 179, 183, 185, 186
English Channel 78
Enterprise, HMS 150–51, 167, 187
Eora, the 87–88, 101, 116, 117, 118, 132, 134
Equiano, Olaudah 48–49
    see also Vassa, Gustavus
Essex Lane, Sydney, NSW 174
Essex, Countess of (Harriet Cappel) 54
Ethiopian regiment 16, 20, 21, 22, 101
Evening Post 71
Ewald, Johann 33, 34
Execution Dock, London, England 41
Exeter, England 3, 75, 184
Experiment 152, 154, 183

F

Fairfax County, USA 11
Fairfax, Bryan 12
Fanning, Edward 42
Fanny 17
farms, farming and agriculture 99–101, 102,
    106, 108, 116–17, 119, 121–22, 123–24,
    125, 127, 132, 137, 141
ferries and ferrymen 5, 152, 154–55, 164, 165,
    166, 167, 171–73, 174, 176, 183
Field of Mars, NSW 137, 155
First Fleet 80, 101, 113, 114, 115
    see also ships, convict transports
    black founders and 3–4
    costs 113
    diarists 3, 4, 9, 81, 88, 93
    livestock aboard 83, 85
    New South Wales, arrival 87–88
    preparations 72, 74–78
    supply of 79, 83

voyage of 74–86
Fisher, William *aka* Blatherhorn 184
flogging and whipping
see also cat o'nine tails
in Britain 49
on the First Fleet 76
in NSW 90, 96–97, 98, 101, 103, 105, 108, 109, 118, 119, 121, 131
food
see also farms, livestock
black market in 108–109
hunger, starvation and famine 95–96, 97, 98, 100–101, 105, 106–10, 118–19, 123, 125, 126, 129, 130–31, 132, 133, 134
hunting and fishing 93, 94–96, 105, 106–107, 108, 116–17, 123, 130
livestock 98–99, 104, 106, 121, 123, 124, 128, 129, 130, 138
rations 94, 96, 103, 105, 108–109, 110–11, 114, 119, 120, 122, 123, 125, 126, 127, 129, 130, 131, 133, 134
supply of 100–101, 106–108, 110–11, 114, 118–19, 120, 122–23, 127–28, 129, 131
theft of 96–99, 102, 104, 108–109, 119, 123, 126, 127
fowl *see* livestock
Fox, Charles 158
France 84, 150, 185
Francisco, George 64, 89, 185
American Revolution, service in 50, 84
on the *Ceres* 85
death 100
occupations 50
prosecution and sentence 3, 50
on the *Scarborough* 75, 84–85
Franklin, Benjamin 67
free settlers 123, 132, 171, 175
French Revolutionary War 150
Friendship 76, 83, 85, 86, 99
Furman, Shadrack 43–44, 45

G

Gambia 61, 62, 65
Ganges, river, India 122
gaol fever *see* disease and diseases
George II 6, 48
George III 7, 89, 97, 98
Germany 7
Gillen, Mollie 3
Gloucester Point, USA 32
Gold Coast, West Africa 48
Goochland County, USA 30
Goodman's Fields, London, England 42
Gordon riots 46, 58
Gordon, Benjamin 26, 185

Gordon, Daniel 89, 93, 147, 185
see also Gordon, Jack and Gordon, Janel
on the *Alexander* 71, 74, 77
American Revolution, service in 26, 36, 101
on the *Ceres* 64
as free settler 121
on Norfolk Island 106, 121, 136
occupations 26, 92, 121
prosecution and sentence 3, 64
secondary sentences in NSW 92–93, 98, 103
Gordon, George (Lord) 70–71, 74
Gordon, Jack 26, 36, 185
see also Gordon, Janel and Gordon, Daniel
Gordon, Janel 3, 63, 64, 71, 74, 89, 185
see also Gordon, Jack and Gordon, Daniel
Gore, William 171–73
Goree, island of, West Africa 59–60
Government House, Sydney, NSW 138–39, 141, 157, 159, 160, 161
Government Wharf, Sydney, NSW 161
Grain Coast, West Africa 67
Gravesend, England 61, 72
Great Dismal Swamp, USA 29
Greenaway, George 184
Greenwich, London, England 47, 115
Grose, Francis 125, 127, 128, 129, 130, 131, 136, 138, 142, 156
Gwynn Island, USA 20

H

habeas corpus 97
Halifax, Nova Scotia 8
Hampton, USA 15, 16
hanging 27, 41, 56–57, 60, 90, 92, 96, 99, 102, 103, 104, 119, 151, 160, 185
Hanway, Jonas 52
Harris, Alexander 176
Harris, John 153, 154, 155, 157, 159–60
Harris, Walter 28, 30, 32, 34
see also Byrd, Wat
Harrison, Benjamin 29, 35, 36, 37
Havannah, Germany 48
Hawkesbury River, NSW 132, 133, 134,147
Heaving Down Place, Sydney, NSW 164
Heights of Charlestown, USA 13–14
see also Bunker Hill, battle of
Henry, Patrick 11, 12, 18, 22, 23, 38
Henry, Ralph 18, 22, 23, 38–39
Hesse and Hessian Soldiers 21, 26, 30, 33, 34–35
Hill, Mary 92
Hill, William 113
Hobart, Tas. 152, 169
Holt, Joseph 141–42, 152
Home Office 60–63, 99, 113

Hope 2, 128
horses *see* livestock
Hospital Wharf, Sydney, NSW 143, 154, 158
Howard, Esther 92, 186
   see also Randall, Esther
Howard, John 57, 58,
Howe, William 6, 7, 21, 36, 166
Hudson River, USA 7, 22, 24, 27, 28, 36
Hügel, Charles von 177
Hulk Act (1776) 57
hulks, prison 4, 6, 57, 62, 64, 69, 71, 151
   see also individual hulk names
   living conditions 64
   sickness and health on 72, 75
Hunter, John 76, 84, 93, 131, 133, 134–35,
   136, 137, 138–40
Hunter's Hill, Sydney, NSW 172, 175

I

India 66, 128, 129, 131, 136, 142
India Board 62
Isle of Wight, England 48

J

'Jack Boddice' 157, 158
   see also Macarthur, John
Jamaica 5, 45, 149
James River, USA 14, 16, 28, 30, 31
Jamison, Thomas 153, 154, 155
Jefferson, Isaac 28–29
Jefferson, Martha Wayles 28
Jefferson, Thomas 14, 28, 39, 30, 33
Johnson, Charles 63, 64
Johnson, Richard 111–12, 116, 135
Johnson, Samuel 46, 52
Johnston, George 93, 95, 125, 138, 139–40,
   141, 145, 146, 148, 153, 155, 156, 158,
   159–60, 161, 162, 165
Jones, Elizabeth (or Osborne) 92, 186
   see also Moseley, Elizabeth and Orford,
    Elizabeth
Justinia 57, 71, 187
Justinian 110–11

K

Kable, Henry 146
Kanakas 179
Kangaroo Island, SA 187

kangaroos 94, 95, 104, 108, 117, 130, 132
Kemp, Anthony Fenn 159, 160
Kent, England 184
Kent Assizes, Maidstone, England 3, 46, 47,
   64, 150, 183
Keppel, Augustus 7, 48
King, Phillip Gidley 93, 106, 121–22, 126–27,
   139, 143, 145, 146, 151, 152, 156
Kings Wharf, Sydney, NSW 170–71
Kissing Point, Sydney, NSW 163, 186
Kitty 126
Kloster Kampen, battle of 7

L

Lady Jane Halliday 149
Lady Juliana 110, 112, 116, 136, 184
Lady Macquarie's Chair 177
Lady Penrhyn 76, 83, 92
Lafayette, Marquis de 29–31
Lancashire, England 63
land grants 128, 129, 142, 155, 166
   and emancipists 120, 123–24, 131
   and free settlers 123, 132
   and the New South Wales Corps 127
   retired marines 121
Lane Cove, Sydney, NSW 164, 172
Lane, William 109
Lascars 52
Lavender, George 183
Lavender's Bay, Sydney, NSW 183
Lemaine, island of, West Africa 61–62, 65, 67,
   69
Liberty Plains, NSW 1, 2
liquor *see* spirits
Little York, USA 6, 31
   see also Yorktown
livestock 31, 83, 84, 88, 107, 124, 128, 129,
   130
   cattle 29, 69, 83, 98–99, 104–105, 138, 166
   on First Fleet 83, 85
   fowl 83, 84
   horses 20, 23, 31, 83, 140, 172
   pigs 83, 121, 123, 124, 141, 155
   sheep 83, 85, 128, 155
London Abolition Society 54
London, England 8, 40, 41, 44–48, 49, 51,
   52–53, 54, 55, 56, 57, 58, 59, 62, 64, 69,
   71, 76, 90, 92, 95, 148, 150, 152, 187
   see also individual parishes and districts
   East End of 40, 41, 45, 47, 54
   West End of 40
Long Island, USA 21
Long, Edward 45, 51–52
Lord, Simeon 140, 143, 146, 154, 170, 174
Loyalist Claims Commission 8, 9, 42–44, 50, 51

Loyalist, HMS 40–41, 50–51, 186
Loyalists 17, 18, 20, 21, 22, 24, 34–38, 66

M

Macarthur, Elizabeth 114
Macarthur, John 114, 133, 137, 138, 141, 145, 157, 158–59, 160, 161
McIntyre, John 94–95
McKay, Daniel 153–54, 155, 158, 160–61, 162, 163
Macquarie, Elizabeth 165
Macquarie, Lachlan 161–62, 163, 164, 165–66, 168, 169, 170–71, 173, 177
Madagascar 4
Madison, James 12–13
Madras, India 152
Magna Carta 97
Maidstone, England 116, 184
'Major Andrews' 5, 7, 27, 28
 see also André, John
Manchester, England 3, 63, 64, 186
Manly Beach, NSW 163
Manly Cove, NSW 95
Mansfield, Lord Chief Justice (William Murray) 42, 45, 46, 53
marines 2, 6–7, 89, 90, 92, 100, 101, 102, 104, 111, 114, 117, 181, 183
 on First Fleet 75, 76–77, 78, 80, 81, 82, 83, 84, 85, 86
 on Norfolk Island 106, 115–16, 121, 125–27
 officers and trade 108–109
 relations with convicts 91
Marquis Cornwallis 155, 187
Marquis Wellington 164
Marsden, Samuel 155
Martin, Frances 179
Martin, John 89, 102–103, 114, 120, 122, 128, 130, 144, 179, 185, 187
 on the *Alexander* 71, 74, 77
 as a free farmer 123–24, 125, 131, 137, 141, 147, 155–56, 174
 character described 137
 marriage and family 115, 122, 155, 174, 178
 in Newgate Prison 58–59, 64
 occupations 49, 74, 77
 prosecution and sentence 3, 49, 56–57, 91
 secondary sentences in NSW 97
Martin, John (son of John Martin and Mary Randall) 156
Mary Ann 119
Maryland, USA 5, 56
Marylebone, London, England 45, 46, 52, 54, 63
Massachusetts, USA 13, 49

Matra, James 66
Meehan, James 166
Mercury 75
Middlesex, England 56
militias and militiamen *see* American Revolution
Millers Point, Sydney, NSW 166, 171
Minerva, HMS 38
Minorca 7, 183
Minorca 5, 145, 148, 151, 152, 183
Mona Vale, NSW 163
Monticello plantation, USA 30
Moseley, Daniel 14
Moseley, Edward Hack 14, 17, 18, 23, 186
Moseley, Elizabeth 120, 128, 129, 142, 155, 166
 see also Jones, Elizabeth and Orford, Elizabeth
Moseley, Jack *see* Moseley John 14–15, 17, 22, 23
Moseley, Jane 63
Moseley, John *aka* Shore, John 89, 93, 144, 147, 161, 174, 178, 186
 American Revolution, service in 17, 20, 21, 22, 24, 101
 as slave 5, 14, 17
 on the *Ceres* 64, 72, 75
 as fugitive 17, 20
 in London 40–42
 marriage and sexual relationships 63, 92, 109, 120
 name change 23
 in Newgate prison 63
 occupations 40–41
 prosecution and sentence 3, 50–51, 63, 65
 on the *Scarborough* 75
Moseley, Peter 14
Motherbank, England 74, 75, 76
Mount Pitt, Norfolk Island 107
Mount Vernon plantation, USA 11, 12, 13, 16, 18, 29, 33, 39
Murphy, Kit 140

N

Nautilus, HMS 66, 69, 72
Naval Office 50
Navy Board 69, 70, 76, 150
navy, France 31
Nepean, Evan 61–62, 65, 66–67, 113, 115, 121
Nepean, Nicholas 111, 113–14, 116, 129, 130, 135
Neptune 111, 112, 113–14, 115
New Haven, USA 5, 24, 92
New Jersey, USA 22, 25
New Kent, USA 29, 33
New London, USA 24

New South Wales 1, 4, 85, 122, 136, 139,
    157, 162, 174, 175, 181
  African diaspora and 180
  black founders in 142, 162, 174, 178,
    183–87
  Botany Bay decision 66–67, 69
  criminal court and the law in 3, 97, 108, 165
  emancipists and 165
  landscape 88
  natural resources of 99, 123
  penal system in 90–91, 98, 122, 146
  transportation and 3, 6, 74, 93, 119, 151,
    183–87
New South Wales Corps 111, 113, 116, 120,
    125, 130, 133, 134, 136, 137, 138, 141,
    142, 146, 155, 157, 161–62, 163, 186
  land and land grants to 127, 128–29, 136,
    157–58
  officers and trade 2, 127–29, 136–37, 138,
    139–40, 141, 142–43, 145, 154, 156, 157
  officers' mess 144–45, 156, 158–59
  recruitment to 4, 24, 125–26, 141
  regimental band 142, 144–45, 156, 158–59,
    160, 161, 162
New York 5, 7, 8, 17, 21, 22, 23, 24, 25, 26,
    27, 28, 30, 33, 34, 35, 36–39, 41, 46, 50,
    66, 138, 152, 183, 185, 186
New Zealand 142
Newcastle, NSW 146, 152, 173
Newgate Prison, London, England 41, 46, 49,
    58–59, 60, 63, 64, 71, 76, 92, 186
Nicholls, John 169–70
Nore Mutiny 151
Norfolk, USA 15, 16, 17
Norfolk Island 106–107, 115–16, 121–22,
    125–26, 136, 146, 147, 156, 184, 185
North Carolina, USA 30
North Head, NSW 142
North Shore, Sydney, NSW 171, 175, 183
Northampton farm, Sydney, NSW 167, 174, 177
  see also Blues Point
Northern Boundary, Parramatta, NSW 123–24,
    128, 132, 141, 155
Northumberland, 2nd Duke of (Hugh Percy)
    138, 145
Nova Scotia 7, 8–9, 20, 21, 35–37, 41, 64, 185

O

Office for Free Africans 67
Old Bailey, London, England 3, 50, 56, 62, 63,
    64, 92, 150, 185, 186
Orangetown, USA 36
Orford, Elizabeth 93, 109
  see also Jones, Elizabeth and Moseley,
    Elizabeth

Orford, Thomas 89, 134, 146, 186
  on the Alexander 71, 74, 77
  as emancipist on the store 120
  imprisoned 64
  land grant 131
  marriage 92, 93
  occupations 49–50, 74, 77, 92
  prosecution and sentence 3, 49–50, 62
  secondary sentences in NSW 109, 111, 119
Orphan Institution, NSW 163, 187

P

Palmerston, Lord (Henry John Temple, 3rd
    Viscount) 173
Parker, Daniel 36–37
Parliament, Houses of 42, 57, 65, 70
Parramatta 2, 115, 117, 118, 120, 123–24,
    125, 130, 131, 132, 133, 134, 137, 138,
    140, 147, 156
Parramatta Gaol 137
Paterson, William 133, 138, 139, 141, 142,
    145, 146
patriots 16, 18, 20, 22, 24, 29, 38
Pemulwuy 117, 118, 132–33, 134, 181
Philadelphia, USA 13
Phillip, Arthur 74, 75, 76, 77, 78, 80, 83, 85,
    87, 88–89, 90–91, 94, 95, 97, 98, 103,
    105, 106, 107, 108, 110, 111, 114, 115,
    116, 117, 118, 119, 126, 127, 129, 157
pigs see livestock
pioneers 6, 7, 13, 20, 21, 22, 24, 26, 183
Piper, Dulcibella 152, 153, 154
Piper, Edwin 152
Pitman, Timothy Goodwin 175
Pitt, William (the younger) 53, 54, 151
Pittwater, NSW 95, 175, 187
  see also Broken Bay
Plymouth, England 49, 75, 110
police 153, 162–63, 168, 169, 172, 179
Polly 36
Pool of London, England 40, 42, 150
Poor Law 44, 45–46, 52
Poore, Anne 116, 122, 126, 136, 184
Poore, John 136, 184
Poore, Mary-Ann 122, 126, 136, 184
Poore, Rebecca 184
Poore, Sarah 184
Port Dalrymple, Tas. 156, 184
Port Jackson, NSW 89, 95, 101, 106, 119,
    175, 181
Port Macquarie, NSW 184
Portland, 3rd Duke of (William Henry
    Cavendish Bentinck) 139
Portsea 169, 170
Portsmouth, England 59, 64, 74, 75, 76, 77, 185

Portsmouth, USA 14, 15, 16, 17, 20, 28, 29, 30, 31
Portugal 7, 166, 183
Potomac, river 11, 29
Powers, John 79, 82
press gangs 6, 41, 49, 150–51
Prince of Wales 99
Prince Regent 139
Princess Anne County, USA 14, 17, 186
prisons and imprisonment
  see also individual prisons
  administration of 58
  Bridewells 57
  conditions in 57, 58–59, 63, 69
  and hard labour 57
  reform and reformers 57, 58
Providence, USA 152
Provision Department 22
Public Advertiser 52, 70–71
punishment *see* individual punishments and convicts

Q

Quarter Master General's Department 22
Quebec, battle of, Canada 5, 6, 7, 148, 166, 183
Queenborough, Norfolk Island 136
Quota Acts (1795) 151

R

race and racism 43, 51–52, 179–82
Randall, Ann 163, 179, 187
Randall, Eliza 163, 187
Randall, Esther 93, 109
  see also Howard, Esther
Randall, Fanny 155, 162, 163, 187
Randall, Frances 109, 144, 146, 155, 186, 187
Randall, John 64, 89, 101, 130, 137, 140, 144, 160, 161, 178, 181, 185, 186–87
  on the *Alexander* 71, 74, 77
  American Revolution, service in 23–24, 63, 77
  as free farmer 123–24, 125, 137, 141, 163
  drummer, musician and bandsman 5, 24, 63, 142, 156, 158, 159
  as game shooter 93, 94–95, 100, 116–18, 120, 125, 129, 130, 138
  imprisoned 63
  marriage and family 92, 93, 109, 115, 118, 120, 125, 129, 138, 140–41, 144, 145–46, 155, 156, 162, 163
  in the New South Wales Corps 4, 24, 141–42, 144–45, 155, 156, 162

origins 5, 23–24, 63, 92
  and patrons 139, 156, 162
  physical appearance 94, 100, 141
  as police constable 162–63
  prosecution and sentence 3, 63
  relations with Aborigines 116–18
  secondary sentences in NSW 100, 138–39
Randall, John (Capt.) 24, 186
Randall, John (jnr) 138, 140, 144, 155, 162, 186, 187
Randall, Lydia 118, 125
Randall, Mary (daughter of John and Mary Randall) 144, 146, 155, 178, 179, 185, 186, 187
Randall, Mary *nee* Butler 118, 125, 129, 136, 140, 144, 146
  see also Butler, Mary
Rappahannock, river, USA 18, 19
Recovery 61, 113
Redfern, William 151
Redman, John 154, 158, 162, 167
regiments
  see also individual departments, regiments, Ethiopian regiment and New South Wales Corps
  4th 63
  47th 63
  63rd 63
  71st 165, 166
  73rd 161–62, 164
  84th 165
Reliance 136
Rhode Island, USA 50
Richmond, USA 11, 28–29, 30
Riley, Alexander 169
Riley, Edward 169, 171, 172, 173
Rio de Janeiro, Brazil 79, 80, 99
Roberts, John 60–61
Rocks, the, Sydney, NSW 143–44, 147, 151–52, 155, 161, 162, 162, 174, 183, 186
Rose, George 55
Rose, Thomas 2, 3
Ross, Robert 77, 93, 94, 95, 99, 103, 106, 107, 108, 115–16, 121
Royal Arsenal Woolwich, London, England 57
Royal Artillery Department 22, 24
Royal Military Asylum 146
Royal Naval Dockyard, Deptford 47
Royal Navy 6, 47, 48, 50, 71, 80, 97, 183
  and American Revolution 33, 37, 49, 101
  black seamen 6, 37, 41, 48–49
  impressment 6, 41, 49, 150–51
rum 1–2, 77, 108, 128–29, 131, 140, 169, 170
  see also spirits
  black market in 108
  smuggling of 167–70

S

Salisbury, Countess of (Emily Mary Cecil) 54
Sandy Neck, USA 21
Savage, HMS 29
Scarborough 75, 77, 78, 81, 83, 84, 85, 86, 88,
   89, 111, 185, 186, 187
scurvy *see* disease and diseases
Second Fleet 99, 110–11, 114, 115, 135
   costs 113
   living conditions on 112–14
   mortality on 111
   sickness on 2, 111–13
Senegal 65
Seven Years' War 5, 6–7, 21, 48, 165
Shadwell, London, England 40
Shairp, James Maitland 79, 93, 96
Sharp, Granville 45, 53, 54, 67, 73
sheep *see* livestock
ships, convict transports 2, 71, 142
   discipline on 76–77, 78, 82, 112–13
   livestock aboard 83, 85
   living conditions on 74, 75, 76, 81, 84,
      112–14
   mortality on 75, 79, 86, 111, 151
   mutiny on 81–82
   profiteering 114
   sexual relations on 78–79, 81, 112–13
   sickness and health on 72, 74, 75, 76, 78,
      79–81, 83, 84, 85, 86, 111–12, 119, 151
ships, West India 5, 50, 148, 149, 187
Shore, John 52, 70–71
   see also Moseley, John
Sierra Leone 48, 65, 68, 69, 70, 71, 72
Sierra Leone scheme 67–73
   Botany Bay scheme, relationship to 69–70
Sierra Leone, river 67, 72
'Silly Old Man' 161
Sirius, HMS 82, 100–101, 106, 115, 116
slavery 11, 34, 44, 51, 52, 55, 72, 74, 82, 92,
   122
   see also slaves
   abolition and anti–slave movement 45, 48,
      53–54
   American Revolution, impact upon 7–9,
      12–13
   in England 41–42, 45, 46, 53–54
   owners 9, 12–13, 14, 15, 16, 18, 34, 35
   slave ships 48, 60, 61, 66, 73, 74, 113
   trade in 4, 13, 17, 19, 41, 45, 47–48, 51–52,
      54, 59, 60, 62, 65, 67, 71, 113
   and transportation compared 74, 77, 92,
      113, 122
   West India lobby 45, 51–52
slaves
   see also slavery
   Britain, legal status of 41–42, 45, 46

British army, service with 5–8, 13, 14–19,
   20, 21, 22, 23, 24, 28, 30, 31, 52–53, 93
   and convicts, compared 102, 113
   culture of 12, 15–16, 24–25
   families 15–16, 25
   fugitives 4, 5, 6, 8–9, 10–12, 13, 14–19, 21,
      22, 23, 24, 26, 28, 29, 30, 32–38, 53, 93,
      138, 186
   and Middle Passage 74
   names and naming 4, 22–23, 29, 46–47
   Nova Scotia, evacuation to 8–9, 35–37,
      40–41
   runaways *see* fugitives
smallpox *see* disease and diseases
Smeathman, Henry 65, 76
Smollet, Tobias 40
smugglers and smuggling 167–70, 174, 175
Snowy Mountains, Eastern Australia 179
Society of Friends 54
Soho 45–46
Somerset Decision 42, 45, 46, 47, 53
Sophia 146
South Carolina, USA 21, 26, 49, 64, 101, 165
South East Cape, South Africa 92
South Head, NSW 99
Spain 7
spirits 2, 3, 58, 77, 81, 85, 107, 128, 131,
   135, 137, 139, 140, 143, 145, 154, 156,
   162, 167–70
   see also brandy, drunkenness, rum, wine
Spitalfields 40
Spithead 7, 47, 48, 72, 80
St Giles 45–46
Staten Island, USA 21, 38
Steele, Thomas 55
Stepney 40, 46, 51
Stonington, USA 24, 186
Stony Point, USA 7, 27, 165
Straits of Macassar 99
sugar 5, 85, 133, 137, 143, 149, 183
Supply 85, 106, 107, 110, 118
Surprize 111, 113
Surrey Lane, Sydney, NSW 162
Sydney, NSW 1, 5, 10, 102, 107, 109, 110, 115,
   117, 121, 125, 126, 127, 131, 136, 145,
   151, 154, 159, 163, 164, 168, 176, 177
   black founders in 122, 129, 130, 147, 156,
      162, 180–81, 184–87
   building and public works at 100, 137
   foundation of 88–89
   growth of settlement 131–32, 142–43
   land and leases 157–58
   living conditions in 89–90, 93–94, 99–100
   trade and commerce 120, 128, 142–43, 146,
      151–52, 169–70
Sydney Cove, NSW 1, 2, 3, 87, 89, 94, 95, 98,
   99–100, 106, 109, 116, 118, 119, 142, 143,
   152, 157, 161, 164, 166, 184, 185, 186

see also Sydney, Sydney harbour
  ferries, ferrymen and watermen 152,
    154–55, 165, 171–73, 183
  regulation of port and 164, 170–71
smuggling at 167–68
Sydney gaol 137, 154, 155, 158
Sydney Gazette 9, 153, 154, 163, 166, 168,
    170, 173, 174, 175, 176–77, 178
Sydney harbour, NSW 89, 93, 95, 100, 101,
    102, 111, 123, 143, 151, 165, 167, 169,
    176, 177
Sydney Herald 177
Sydney, 1st Viscount (Thomas Townshend) 61,
    62, 63, 66, 67, 68–69, 89, 90

T

Tahiti 179
Tank Stream, Sydney, USA 160
tea 85, 96, 137, 140, 143
Tench, Watkin 76, 77–78, 87, 93, 99, 105,
    107, 108, 109, 110, 116–18, 119, 124
Tenerife 77, 79, 82
Thames, River, England 40, 41, 47, 57, 61, 64,
    68, 70, 72, 148, 150
The Road to Botany Bay x
Third Fleet 99, 119, 123
Thompson, Edward (Capt.) 69, 72
Thompson, Edward (historian) 10, 182
Thornton, Henry 111, 112
Tiffin, Robert 183
Timor 118, 119
tobacco 5, 14, 56, 60, 137, 143
  black market in 108
Toongabbie, NSW 130
Tower Hill, London, England 41, 150, 167,
    183
Tower of London, England 42, 45
Toy, Ann 115, 120, 122, 185
trade 142–44, 146, 152, 162
  with China 66, 67, 142, 175
  with India 66, 142, 154
  and the New South Wales Corps 127–28,
    137, 138, 139–40, 141, 142, 156, 157
  rum and spirits 128, 139–40, 143, 145, 154,
    156, 168–70
  ships' masters, profiteering 114
Traill, Donald 112–13, 114, 115
transportation 63, 135, 179
  to Africa 59–62, 63, 64–66, 67, 68, 186
  to American Colonies 56, 60
  Beauchamp Committee 65–66
  black founders and 3–4, 10, 49–50, 64–65,
    183–87
  Botany Bay decision 67, 69–70
  costs 67, 99, 113

Das Voltas Bay scheme 66, 67, 69
First Fleet 3, 9, 72, 74–85
Goree scheme 59–60
and hard labour 90–91
and the hulks 57, 62
Lemaine scheme 61–62, 64–65, 67, 69
Second Fleet 2, 99, 110–15, 135
sentenced to 56–57, 115, 116
and slavery, compared 74, 77, 98, 102, 113
Third Fleet 99, 119
to New South Wales 3, 6, 74, 93, 119, 151,
    183–87
Transportation Act (1719) 56
Treasury 55, 61, 62, 66, 69, 72
Treaty of Paris (1783) 34, 53
typhus see disease and diseases

U

Underwood, Joseph 146

V

Van Diemen's Land 92, 146, 180, 184
variola see disease and diseases
Vassa, Gustavus 48
  see also Equiano, Olaudah
Veteran's Company 162
Virginia, USA 4, 5, 10, 11–13, 14, 16, 17, 18,
    20, 21, 27, 28–29, 30, 33, 35, 43, 49, 53,
    56, 137, 186
Virginia Convention 11, 15, 17, 18
Virginia Gazette 15, 20
vitamin C 79–80, 93, 109
VOC (Verenigde Oostindische Compagnie) 82,
    83
Vulture, HMS 27

W

Wagon Master General's Department 17, 22, 24
Wapping, London, England 40, 41, 46, 50, 51,
    52
Washington, Daniel 39
Washington, George 11–12, 13, 15, 18, 20, 21
    22, 23, 26, 27, 29, 31, 32–34, 35–39
Washington, Harry 22, 23
Washington, Lund 16, 18, 29, 36
watermen 152, 154
  see also ferries and ferrymen
Watkins, Thomas 42, 43
Watson, John 38, 47

Wentworth, D'Arcy 114, 140, 162, 168, 169–70, 171, 172
West Indies 13, 17, 19, 41, 51, 55, 60, 148
West Point, USA 27
Westminster, London, England 45, 46
Whigs, the 158
White Plains, USA 21
White Raven, London, England 54, 55
White, John 75, 76, 79, 80, 83, 84, 89, 95, 98, 99–100, 103, 113
Whitechapel, London, England 40, 42
Whittle, Thomas 158, 159, 160, 161
Wilberforce, William 54, 113
Wilkes, John 158
Williams, Elizabeth 152, 183
  see also Blue, Elizabeth
Williams, George 167–70
Williams, James *aka* 'Black Jemmy' 64, 89, 127, 187
  escape attempts 110, 118, 120, 122
  as free seaman 122
  occupation 50, 89
  prosecution and sentence 3, 50
  on the *Scarborough* 75
  secondary sentences in NSW 101, 109, 118
Williams, John (landlord) 42
Williams, John *aka* 'Black Jack' 64, 89, 93,
    120, 146, 185, 187
  prosecution and sentence 3, 49, 92, 119, 146
  on the *Scarborough* 75
  as seaman 89, 146
  secondary sentences in NSW 92, 119, 146
Williamsburg, USA 11, 14, 17, 18
Willis Creek Plantation, USA 30
Willoughby, John 18
Winbow, John 1–2, 135
Winchester, England 3, 64, 185
Windsor, NSW 174, 178, 179
wine 49, 92, 104, 158, 159
Wolfe, James 5, 6, 7, 148, 166
Wollstonecraft, Edward 171–72, 175
Woolwich, London, England 57, 71, 74

Y

Yorkshire Stingo, London, England 54, 55
Yorktown, USA
  see also Little York
  Articles of Capitulation 33–34
  British surrender 32, 34
  siege of 5, 6, 31, 34, 165, 166